More Praise

"Perhaps the finest book on Zionism written in recent memory. This slim, brilliant volume probes with rare equanimity every volatile corner of this topic with its focus squarely on why it generates such promiscuous, even universal heat. Derek Penslar is an outstanding historian who knows so well how to marshal knowledge of the past to illuminate the aching complexities of the present."

—Steven J. Zipperstein, author of *Pogrom: Kishinev and the Tilt of History*

"Derek Penslar has written a brave and thought-provoking book that seeks to understand the well-springs of hope and belief in Zionism. Yet he does not shy away from less attractive passions, especially hatred in the name of Zionism and hatred of Zionism itself. Anyone keen to understand the way such deep emotions animate and shape history must read this compelling book."

—Ruth Harris, author of *Dreyfus: Politics, Emotion, and the Scandal of the Century*

"Derek Penslar's masterfully written history of emotions adds a whole new dimension to our understanding of both Zionism and the State of Israel and is crucial reading for anyone interested in grasping the nature of modern nationalism."

—Michael Brenner, author of *In Search of Israel: The History of an Idea*

"Derek Penslar introduces a 'new key' to the history of Zionism with his examination of the emotions involved, helping us understand the passionate dynamics of both Zionist and anti-Zionist sensibilities as they have emerged and developed over time. This is a must read."

—Ute Frevert, author of *Emotions in History: Lost and Found*

"For a topic as contentious and complex as Zionism, Penslar's expertise, sober voice, and informed critique shine through as he provides a much-needed addition to ongoing debates that touch at the heart of Jewish identity today."

—Shaul Magid, author of *Meir Kahane: The Public Life and Political Thought of an American Jewish Radical*

"Why does Zionism evoke such intense passions? Because as much as it is a political and ideological movement, it is also an emotional movement. Penslar has outdone himself with this intriguing history of the emotions of Zionism's champions and its adversaries."

—Susannah Heschel, author of *The Aryan Jesus: Christian Theologians and the Bible in Nazi Germany*

"If you think you understand Zionism, read this book and think again. Carefully, elegantly, and with tremendous erudition, Derek Penslar takes an ideology many think they understand and illuminates it in a fascinating new way."

—Peter Beinart, author of *The Crisis of Zionism*

ZIONISM

Key Words in Jewish Studies

Series Editors
Deborah Dash Moore, University of Michigan
Jonathan Boyarin, Cornell University

ZIONISM

An Emotional State

DEREK J. PENSLAR

RUTGERS UNIVERSITY PRESS
New Brunswick, Camden, and Newark, New Jersey
London and Oxford

Rutgers University Press is a department of Rutgers, The State University of New Jersey, one of the leading public research universities in the nation. By publishing worldwide, it furthers the University's mission of dedication to excellence in teaching, scholarship, research, and clinical care.

Library of Congress Cataloging-in-Publication Data

Names: Penslar, Derek Jonathan, author.
Title: Zionism : an emotional state / Derek J. Penslar.
Description: 1. | New Brunswick, New Jersey : Rutgers University Press, [2023] | Series: Key words in jewish studies | Includes bibliographical references and index.
Identifiers: LCCN 2022045142 | ISBN 9780813576091 (paperback) | ISBN 9780813576107 (hardcover) | ISBN 9780813576114 (epub) | ISBN 9780813576121 (pdf)
Subjects: LCSH: Zionism—History. | Land settlement—Palestine.
Classification: LCC DS149 .P4238 2023 | DDC 320.54095694—dc23/eng/20220922
LC record available at https://lccn.loc.gov/2022045142

A British Cataloging-in-Publication record for this book is available from the British Library.

References to internet websites (URLs) were accurate at the time of writing. Neither the author nor Rutgers University Press is responsible for URLs that may have expired or changed since the manuscript was prepared.

rutgersuniversitypress.org

Contents

Foreword

The Rutgers book series Key Words in Jewish Studies seeks to introduce students and scholars alike to vigorous developments in the field by exploring its terms. These words and phrases reference important concepts, issues, practices, events, and circumstances. But terms also refer to standards, even to preconditions; they patrol the boundaries of the field of Jewish Studies. This series aims to transform outsiders into insiders and let insiders gain new perspectives on usages, some of which shift even as we apply them.

Key words mutate through repetition, suppression, amplification, and competitive sharing. Jewish Studies finds itself attending to such processes in the context of an academic milieu where terms are frequently repurposed. Diaspora offers an example of an ancient word, one with a specific Jewish resonance, which has traveled into new regions and usage. Such terms migrate from the religious milieu of Jewish learning to the secular environment of universities, from Jewish community discussion to arenas of academic discourse, from political debates to intellectual arguments and back again. As these key words travel, they acquire additional meanings even as they occasionally shed long-established connotations. On occasion, key words can become so politicized that they serve as accusations. The sociopolitical concept of assimilation, for example, when turned into a term—assimilationist—describing an advocate of the process among Jews, became an epithet hurled by political opponents struggling for the mantle of authority in Jewish communities.

When approached dispassionately, key words provide analytical leverage to expand debate in Jewish Studies. Some key words will be familiar from long use, and yet they may have gained new valences, attracting or repelling other terms in contemporary discussion. But there are prominent terms in Jewish culture whose key lies in a particular understanding of prior usage. Terms of the past may bolster claims to continuity in the present while newly minted language sometimes disguises deep connections reaching back into history. Attention must be paid as well to the transmigration of key words among Jewish languages—especially Hebrew, Yiddish, and Ladino—and among languages used by Jews, knitting connections even while highlighting distinctions.

An exploration of the current state of Jewish Studies through its key words highlights some interconnections often only glimpsed and holds out the prospect of a reorganization of Jewish knowledge. Key words act as magnets and attract a nexus of ideas and arguments as well as related terms into their orbits. This series plunges into several of these intersecting constellations, providing a path from past to present.

The volumes in the series share a common organization. They open with a first section, Terms of Debate, which defines the key word as it developed over the course of Jewish history. Allied concepts and traditional terms appear here as well. The second section, State of the Question, analyzes contemporary debates in scholarship and popular venues, especially for those key words that have crossed over into popular culture. The final section, In a New Key, explicitly addresses contemporary culture and future possibilities for understanding the key word.

To decipher key words is to learn the varied languages of Jewish Studies at points of intersection between academic disciplines and wider spheres of culture. The series, then, does not seek to consolidate and narrow a particular critical lexicon. Its purpose is to question, not to canonize, and to invite readers to sample the debate and ferment of an exciting field of study.

Jonathan Boyarin
Deborah Dash Moore
Series Coeditors

ZIONISM

Introduction

The word "Zionism" was coined in Central Europe more than 130 years ago. Over time it has undergone myriad changes and is used in the early twenty-first century in ways that late nineteenth-century Jews would have scarcely understood. The fact that the word retains currency, however, means that people find value in it and that they believe in its continuity with earlier usage, even when that continuity is, in fact, tenuous. This combination of malleability and continuity demonstrates Zionism's function as what the British cultural critic Raymond Williams called a keyword—a term with origins in a fixed time and place that remains current and accumulates new meanings.[1]

Zionism is a keyword inside another keyword: nationalism. Nationalism is the belief that human beings are divided into groups called nations, which share a territory, language, and culture and aspire to self-determination. Self-determination may take various forms ranging from autonomy to sovereign statehood. Zionism, in turn, is the belief that Jews constitute a nation that has a right and need to pursue collective self-determination within historic Palestine. Like other forms of nationalism, Zionism is both an ideology—a coherent, sustained interpretation of experience in terms of fundamental values—and a movement: a set of practices designed to realize ideological goals. When nationalist movements realize their goals, such as the attainment of autonomy or sovereignty, nationalist ideology does not disappear, because it serves to bolster the legitimacy of the state. Similarly, although the State of Israel was created in 1948, Zionism exists to this day. It signifies both diaspora Jews' attachments to the state and the nationalistic sentiments of Israeli Jews.

Zionism has not been the only form of Jewish nationalism. During the half-century before the establishment of the State of Israel, some

Jewish nationalists aspired to gain Jewish autonomy in Eastern Europe, which was home to the world's largest Jewish community before the Holocaust. In this region in the early twentieth century, a combination of diaspora nationalism and socialism fueled support for the General Jewish Labor Bund, which for some time was one of Zionism's chief rivals. Another form of Jewish nationalism, known as Territorialism, sought a place anywhere in the world where Jews could build a homeland and dwell in safety. These movements expressed solidarity with and compassion for the Jewish people, but ultimately Zionism proved to be the most enduring. Stalinist oppression and Nazi genocide wiped out the Bund, and Territorialism remained a fringe movement, incapable of fostering the feelings of love, pride, loyalty, and willingness to sacrifice that are associated with modern nationalism.

Until 1948 Zionism's goal was to create a Jewish homeland in a territory with which Jewish civilization was intimately linked: the ancient Land of Israel. *Zion* is a biblical word that refers to a hill in Jerusalem and, by extension, to the city of Jerusalem and thence to the entirety of the ancient Land of Israel. Because it was tied to a specific territory, Zionism had a common vocabulary with other nationalisms, which were all territorially based. Unlike other nationalisms, however, pre-1948 Zionism's claim on territory was aspirational, based in ancient memories and future hopes. Until well into the twentieth century, a negligible number of Jews lived in the Land of Israel. Even after the State of Israel was created, its population grew into the millions, and it became a regional military superpower, Zionism retained a sense of fragility, vulnerability, and incompleteness.

These feelings account for the ongoing salience of Zionism, a word that connotes more than an idea or movement. It is a belief that Jews have a moral right and historic need for self-determination within historic Palestine. It is a project to gather Jews from throughout the world, to ensure that they dwell in safety, and to nurture a homeland that is in turn a source of inspiration for Jews everywhere. To the extent that

Israeli Jews and Israel's supporters abroad see this project as incomplete, Zionism still has relevance.

This book relates the history of Zionism through the lens of emotion. It argues that the energy propelling the Zionist project comes from a series of emotional states: bundles of feeling whose elements vary in volume, intensity, and durability across space and time. Emotion lies at the heart of nationalism, whose narrative of eternal community offers, if not a cure, then at least a tonic to allay the fear of death. The idea that one belongs to a certain nation—and that others do not—draws social boundaries that provide people with a sense of ontological security, of having a rooted, stable identity, even while living in a condition of personal insecurity. Nationalism is an extension of modern concepts of romantic love that joins humans into long-lasting pair bonds and makes possible the continuation of the species. It is no coincidence that the first Zionist groups were organized under the term *hibat tsion* (love of Zion) and that Zionism often presents itself as epitomizing the rabbinic concept of *ahavat Yisra'el* (love of the Jewish people).

Understanding Zionism in terms of emotion explains why a word originally associated with territorial aspiration survives almost seventy-five years after Israel's creation. For Jews who choose to identify as Zionists, Zionism connotes liberation and redemption. The word perpetuates venerable Jewish self-conceptions of uniqueness and vulnerability while striving for collective security and integration into the community of nations. It is also a signifier of potent feelings that vary enormously depending on who employs the word and how it is used. An affirmation of Zionism and self-identification as a Zionist can be an expression of love of the Jewish homeland and hope for its future or of ethnic pride and collective Jewish solidarity. Feelings of fear for Israel's survival or hatred of Israel's enemies serve to intensify that solidarity. For some Jews, Zionism is a source of profound discomfort, and Jews who reject it are no less passionate than those who embrace it.

People the world over have strong feelings about Israel. Scores of millions of evangelical Christians profess love for Israel born of the belief that it is a fulfillment of biblical prophecy. Yet, Israel's dispossession of Palestinians from their land and oppression of those who remain have made it one of the most disliked countries on the planet.[2] Not wishing to recognize Israel by name, media in the Arab Middle East have long referred to Israel as a "Zionist entity." Doing so denies Israel's legitimacy as a state and links it with a word whose pejorative meanings are almost as old as its positive ones. Since the 1920s, Zionism has been associated with exercises of malign power, ranging from Western colonialism to alleged Jewish conspiracies to control humanity for the Jews' benefit. Calling the State of Israel the "Zionist entity" is an act of nonrecognition that expresses powerful negative emotions, ranging from frustration to hatred.

In some academic and intellectual circles in the Western world, the very mention of Zionism evokes similar feelings. Arguments rage at America's most prestigious colleges and universities about whether Zionism is racist, Israel is a settler-colonial state, and a boycott campaign against the country is antisemitic. Sympathizers with the Palestinian cause decry the dispossession of an Indigenous people from their land in a region that has long endured Western imperial intervention. Jewish anti-Zionists depict Israel as a violation of Jewish ethical norms. Divided into political camps, students and faculty produce public statements declaiming their solidarity, anger, and frustration with one side or the other. Colleges are often sites of strong emotional tides, but Zionism and Israel spawn emotional tsunamis.

True to its title, this book seeks to explain why Zionism induces such an emotional state. It explores the role emotion has played in the realization of the Zionist project to create and maintain a Jewish national home. The book seeks to accomplish its goals not by replicating passionate rhetoric but by understanding it. Throughout my career, I have been fascinated by Zionism—its position within modern Jewish life, its distinct qualities, and its shared history with other nationalisms over the past 150 years. A decade ago, I became interested in the history of emotions. The more I read about the subject, the more convinced I became that its insights, when applied to the history of Zionism, would be illuminating and even transformative.

The first comprehensive histories of Zionism, which were written by early Zionist activists such as Nahum Sokolow and Adolf Boehm, dealt with emotion head-on in their presentation of Zionism as a movement catalyzed by visceral sentiment, as well as by instrumental reasoning and moral values.[3] Unfortunately, academic scholarship on Zionism, which began to be written in the late 1950s, focused more narrowly on elite ideology and political institutions. For example, Arthur Hertzberg's influential anthology *The Zionist Idea* (1959) presented Zionism through the lens of some three dozen thinkers and leaders. In contrast, David Vital's pioneering trilogy *The Origins of Zionism*; *Zionism: The Formative Years*; and *Zionism: The Crucial Years* (1975, 1982, 1987) offered a detailed political history of the Zionist Organization, with emphases on its internal fissures and its leaders' diplomatic dealings with the Great Powers. In recent decades, scholars of Zionism turned increasingly to social and cultural history, analyzing grassroots Zionist politics and the construction of new forms of Jewish identity and self-perception.[4] This literature often refers to emotion, but it does so in passing, rather than treating it as a primary factor or organizing principle.[5] This lacuna is striking, given that emotion is one of the most important cohesive forces within social movements (such as Zionism) or states (such as Israel). Moreover, group dynamics cannot be understood without reference to the desires and feelings of the individual.

One of the founders of the discipline of social history, Lucien Febvre, noted as much in 1941, and during the 1970s two great historians of modern Europe, Theodore Zeldin and Peter Gay, explored the history of what they called "passion" in multivolume works.[6] Recent historical scholarship on the revolutions of the eighteenth century and on nineteenth-century abolitionism emphasizes the significance of emotions such as sentimentality, empathy, compassion, and humanitarianism.[7] In the social sciences, the vast literature on ethnicity, nationalism, and other forms of what the sociologist Rogers Brubaker calls "groupness"[8] is filled with references to emotion. That said, this literature tends to focus on negative emotions such as fear, anger, and hatred, failing to take sufficient account of the generative force of positive emotions such as love, hope, compassion, and pride.[9] As Benedict Anderson tartly observes, "Nations inspire love, and not merely a transitory lust."[10]

The study of groupness has much to gain from the work of pioneering scholars of the history of emotion such as William Reddy and Barbara Rosenwein. In his book *The Navigation of Feeling*, Reddy develops the concept of an "emotional regime," which he defines as "a set of normative emotions and the official rituals, practices, and emotives that express and inculcate them."[11] For Reddy, "politics is just a process of determining who must repress as illegitimate, who must foreground as valuable, the feelings that come up to them in different contexts and relationships."[12] Much of Reddy's work is set in territorially delimited states and empires, leaving us uncertain as to how nonstate actors without centralized authority, such as diaspora Jews or other members of ethnic minorities, form, express, and dispute emotions.[13] In contrast, Barbara Rosenwein's concept of an "emotional community" can accommodate ethnic minorities like modern Jews whose social cohesion is voluntarist and whose points of emotional discursive production are diffuse. For Rosenwein, an emotional community is a group of people sharing common norms and modes of emotional expression, as well as goals, interests, and values. Their utterances or texts express desire, bounded by communal norms of what may and must not be said.[14]

The Zionist project has combined aspects of both the statist emotional regime and the more decentralized emotional community. The former was present in pre-1948 Palestine, where its Jewish community established autonomous governmental and educational institutions, and then in the State of Israel itself. Diaspora Jewry has represented something of a hybrid between an emotional regime and an emotional community. On the one hand, it is diffuse, and throughout most of the Jewish world in the twentieth century, membership in Jewish institutional life was voluntary. On the other hand, over the course of the second half of the century, major diaspora Jewish communities became increasingly well organized, with strong ties to the State of Israel, which has sought to influence how Jewish communities talk and feel about Israel.

Engaging in the history of emotions not only brings exciting opportunities but also presents unusual challenges. In most historical subfields, there is widespread agreement on the meaning of the subject of study (e.g., states or regions; groups defined by gender, ethnic, or religious ascription; agriculture, commerce, and capital; labor and cities). But in the field of the history of emotions, the fundamental objects of inquiry lack any objective or even consistent definition. Across and even within fields, writers have conceived of emotion in profoundly different ways. At the turn of the twentieth century, the philosopher William James located emotion in the body, whereas the physician Sigmund Freud placed it in the unconscious. Both approaches continue to have adherents, especially the former, considering the scholarly interest in the neurological bases of human behavior. But in recent decades neuroscientists have formed a consensus with social scientists and humanists that emotion is a cultural construction. This coalition has called into question simplistic associations between the external manifestation of an emotion and ever-present psychological processes.[15] Other scholars do not even attempt to penetrate the black box of the individual psyche but are content to study emotional codes, what Peter and Carol Stearns call "emotionology."[16]

Despite this emerging consensus, there is no uniform definition of emotion, nor are there consistent distinctions between words such as emotion, affect, feeling, and passion. I find particularly clear and useful political scientist Roger Petersen's definition of emotions as psychological mechanisms that "change the level of saliency of desires."[17] Emotions as varied and opposed as love and hate, resentment and admiration, yearning and hostility all suppose an object of desire, which can be external or interior to the self. This definition recalls ancient and medieval divisions of emotion into "motions" of approach and engagement, and withdrawal and disconnection.[18] Translated into a contemporary idiom, we can distinguish emotions that express anticipated or attained fulfillment of desire from those produced by a state of disequilibrium and frustration. We can thereby distinguish positive emotions such as pride, contentment, and magnanimity as expressions of equilibrium, of having achieved certain wants and needs, from negative emotions—such as fear, resentment, hatred, rage, and jealousy—that derive from thwarted desire.

Another useful perspective comes from the sociologist Theodore Kemper, who defined emotion as "a relatively short-term evaluative response, essentially positive or negative in nature, involving distinct somatic (and often cognitive) components."[19] In other words, emotions originate in bodily sensations—the flutter of the heart, the quickening of breath—but it is only when they are cognitively processed and articulated that the individual subject or others can perceive the emotion as such.

Affect, in contrast, according to sociologists Paul Hoggett and Simon Thompson, "concerns the more embodied, unformed and less conscious dimension of human feeling." Emotion is "anchored in language and meaning," but "affect is experienced in a bodily way." It is a "disposition without a particular targeted object, such as anxiety; it becomes an emotion such as jealousy, when it is directed at a specific object."[20] Affect is to emotion what a computer's operating system is to its applications; the latter are dependent on the former, which is always running. The late Lauren Berlant described all forms of attachment, whether to abstract causes, objects, or people, as products of an affective state she called "optimism," which she used not in the conventional sense of the word but in the sense that an object of desire fulfills a perceived need. This "optimistic" affective foundation sustains multiple and contradictory forms of emotional expression.[21]

This book is about emotion, rather than affect or disposition. Unlike affect, which envelops our being but of which we are not usually aware, emotion is articulated through language, either our mind's internal monologue or speech. Emotion is a component of cognition, and there is no contradiction or even divide between emotions and ideas. Ideas are sustained interpretations of experience in terms of beliefs and values. They function via both deductive and inductive logic, first principles, and empirical observation. They lay claim to rationality, although they need not be rational. They can have unconscious sources and are therefore not sealed off from feeling. Moreover, although emotion is often considered to be irrational or nonrational, we often justify our emotions in terms of both reality and logic. People may base logical argumentation on preposterous assumptions or draw conclusions from biased observations.

Emotions are subject to manipulation, but that manipulation is only successful when the recipient of the message is receptive to an emotional appeal. The ability of elites to inspire or incite the public depends not only on their skill in crafting an emotionally powerful message but also on their reading of what the public desires and fears. People who warm to a politician's emotional message are expressing a form of agency, just as those who resist it may respond positively to a different set of messages coming from other types of leaders, such as revolutionaries or rebels. Moreover, emotional messaging need not be transmitted only from elites downward: it can have multiple and simultaneously functioning vectors of transmission or spread rapidly via a process of contagion. As this book will show, there is much more to the diffusion of emotion than manipulation of the masses.

Feelings associated with the fate of the collective are known as political emotions, and they lie at this book's heart.[22] Nationalism is another word for a political emotional affinity, a passionate attachment that leads, or is expected to lead, to significant action such as financial or physical sacrifice for the collective.[23] For most scholars who write on political emotion, fear is the base of all collective feeling. Political fear is the apprehension that something horrid will happen to us as a collective, not as individuals. Fear can, of course, be expressed by an individual or any sort of collective, but it underlies the formation of society. As Corey Robin has observed, collective fear of aggression by another group does not necessarily induce solidarity. People may respond to the same threat with pacifism or aggression, with a willingness to sacrifice for the greater good or efforts to minimize personal risk and maximize personal bene-fit.[24] According to Joanna Bourke, fear should be differentiated from anx-iety, which falls into the substrate of affect. Fear is amorphous and lacks a specific, immediate object. State regimes foster fear among populations so that they will come together, rather than fall victim to anxieties that dull the spirit and lead to social withdrawal. Fear can encourage volun-tarism, watchfulness, self-denial, and denunciation of perceived shirkers or traitors.[25]

Zionism has been frequently steeped in fear, and it is sustained by chronic anxiety felt by Jews in even relatively comfortable and secure environments. As in other forms of nationalism, fear and resentment of others can escalate into outright hatred. Nationalisms, however— Zionism included—are not sustained by such negative emotions alone but also by the intertwining of love and hope, whose presence depends on the possibility of an alternative to an undesired, even unbearable, pre-sent situation.[26] Moreover, like many forms of nationalism, Zionism evokes pride and expresses a desire for honor that, as Ute Frevert argues, was one of the most prominent political emotions in nineteenth- and early twentieth-century Europe.[27]

Emotions come in bundles. They bond together and break apart, and their varying admixtures produce disparate outcomes. Barbara Rosen-wein has made this argument primarily for individuals, in that people

can have numerous feelings simultaneously and one emotion can stimulate another.[28] This observation can also be fruitfully applied to groups.
For this reason, I organize the chapters that deal with emotion around
clusters of emotions, rather than isolated feelings.

Before applying the emotional turn to Zionism, the book discusses
current understandings and debates about the meaning of Zionism. The
first part, "Terms of Debate," unpacks meanings and performances of
Zionism within the context of both nationalist movements and Jewish
civilization over the past 130 years. I explore Zionism's historic self-
presentation as both an idea and a set of practices. I problematize existing taxonomies of Zionism, arguing that they were created by engaged
historical actors and should not be used as analytical categories. I propose a new, transhistorical, and transnational set of categories that take
account of the changing needs and desires of those who have identified
as Zionists. Of particular importance here is parsing Zionism's relationship with Judaism. Nationalist movements draw on and legitimize themselves in terms of religious tradition, yet they also reject and recast much
of that tradition. Zionism is no exception.

The second part, "State of the Question," explores the most prominent controversy in contemporary scholarly literature on Zionism: the
relationship between Zionism and colonialism. This section forms a
bookend to the first part in that the relationship between Judaism and
nationalism within Zionism is very much an internal debate among
Zionists, whereas the discourse on Zionism and colonialism comes
largely from without, from Zionism's critics. If the first section was about
the different ways in which Zionism has been seen to benefit Jews, part II
deals with Zionism's victims and those scholars who theorize this victimization as the product of colonialist attitudes and practices.

The final and longest part, "In a New Key," consists of four chapters
that place emotion at the center of Zionism's numerous meanings.
Chapter 3 covers the mid-nineteenth through the mid-twentieth centuries. It presents a gradual coalescence of an abstract, romantic attachment

to Eretz Israel (the biblical Land of Israel) in the 1800s into a more material, bodily, and erotic love of the blossoming Jewish national home during the period of the British Mandate. This passionate form of Zionism
was most prominent in Central and Eastern Europe and in Palestine
itself. In the United States, in contrast, pre-1948 Zionism was more
philanthropic and couched in the language of pride and solidarity. The
fourth chapter focuses on emotional responses elicited by Jewish sovereignty and perceived threats to the Jewish state from its creation in 1948
to the present day. Both within the State of Israel and abroad, Zionism
assumed the form of a romance in the literary sense of the word; that is,
it was a story of a great quest, filled with miraculous events and both
tragic and joyful elements. Feelings ranging from pride to fear, exhilara-
tion to disappointment, and connection to estrangement have formed
the axes of a three-dimensional Cartesian grid onto which individuals'
Zionist sensibilities may be mapped.

Chapters 5 and 6 consider the entirety of the history of Zionism from
two different perspectives. Chapter 5 focuses on the affective dimensions
of Zionism's relationship with the Great Powers and with the international community as a whole. The operative emotions here, which were
present from the Zionist movement's beginnings and continue until the
present, are gratitude and feelings of betrayal—both of which are signs
of dependency and limited agency, even long after Israel became a
regional superpower. The sixth and final chapter treats Zionism as both
an object and generator of hatred. As Brian Porter has argued, nationalism is rooted in perceptions of collective difference, but it becomes
hateful only under specific historic circumstances.[29] Understanding why,
how, and when Zionism encourages hatred throws new light on the
Israeli-Palestinian conflict, particularly over the past twenty years, when
violent acts by Israeli Jews toward Palestinians became more common
and socially acceptable. Whereas chapters 3 and 4 depict emotion as a
constructive force in the forging of a national project, the final two

chapters demonstrate how emotion can poison that project, generating destructive and self-destructive ways of thinking and acting.

This is a small book that sets out to accomplish several big things. First and foremost, it seeks to demonstrate the salience of emotion for the history of not only Zionism but also nationalism as such. It also offers a new vocabulary to understand Zionism that is more flexible, capacious, and accurate than current usage. It addresses ongoing controversies about the relationship between Zionism and colonialism. It traces continuities and ruptures within Zionist sensibilities across critical points in the history of the movement and of the state of Israel. The book's scope is global, presenting Zionism as a form of Jewish nationalism throughout the world and as a nation-building movement within historic Palestine. In sum, this book conceives of Zionism as a single, albeit complex, equation of which emotion is an ever-present variable.

A Note on Place Names

Emotion saturates every aspect of Zionism's history, including the names used to describe the object of Zionist territorial desire. The land is only about 28,000 square kilometers or 11,000 square miles—a bit smaller than Belgium—but it is deeply contested. It is venerated by Christians and Muslims, as well as Jews, and is claimed by both Palestinian Arabs and Zionists. Its names have changed across time, and at any given moment what it is called depends on the observer's political and religious position.

In the Jewish tradition, the land's names include *Eretz Israel*, *Eretz ha-Kodesh* (the Holy Land), and *Tsion* (Zion). Christians also often call it the Holy Land (*terra sancta* in Latin), and for Muslims the Arabic equivalent is *al-Ard al-Muqaddasah*. Since late antiquity, the territory associated with these names has been widely referred to as Palestine (*Palaestina* in Latin, *Filastin* in Arabic). In the Ottoman Empire, Palestine was not an administrative district, but the word was commonly used.[30] Early Zionists used

"Palestine" and "the Land of Israel" interchangeably. Under British rule (first under a military occupation and then as a mandate authorized by the League of Nations) between 1917 and 1948, the territory was called Palestine or "Palestine-E.I." (for Palestine-Eretz Israel). In Hebrew, Palestine's Jewish community was also known as the *Yishuv*.

In 1947, the United Nations determined that Palestine should be divided into Jewish and Arab states. In the warfare that accompanied Israel's establishment in 1948, almost two-thirds of Palestine's Arabs went into exile, and some of the territory that under the UN plan would have comprised the Palestinian Arab state was taken by Israel; the rest was taken by Jordan and Egypt. Those territories became known as the West Bank (including eastern Jerusalem) and the Gaza Strip, respectively.

During the 1967 Middle East war, Israel captured these territories. In 1988, the Palestine Liberation Organization declared a state of Palestine with unspecified borders. Its powers are limited, however, to self-rule in portions of the Israeli-occupied territories via the Palestinian National Authority, which was established in the Israeli-Palestinian Oslo Accords of 1993. Nonetheless, the United Nations accords Palestine the status of a "non-member observer state," and Palestine is recognized by three-quarters of the countries in the world.

In this book, when I am reconstructing the thoughts and feelings of individual actors, I use the place names that they would have employed. When analyzing matters from a distance, for the period before 1948 I use the then-neutral term "Palestine." For the historical narrative of events after 1948, I refer to Israel, the West Bank, and the Gaza Strip; for events after 1967, the latter two are also referred to as the Occupied Palestinian Territories. When discussing current political debates, I use the term "Israel/Palestine," which has gained currency among scholars, educators, and activists to acknowledge the presence and justice of claims on historic Palestine by both Israeli Jews and Palestinian Arabs.

PART I

TERMS OF DEBATE

1   *Staging Zionism*

Nationalism is both immensely popular and in bad odor. In the current U.S. political culture, the term "white nationalism" is a euphemism for white supremacy. Former president Donald Trump proudly called himself a nationalist, a term his supporters see in a positive light as an expression of American patriotism but which his detractors see as proof of racism.[1] Hungary, India, and Poland are illiberal democracies headed by populists who appeal to nationalist sentiments via language laced with fear of ethnic and religious minorities, rival states, proponents of universal human rights, and advocates of global economic integration. Russia's invasion of Ukraine in February 2022 was motivated by, among other things, a fierce and intolerant nationalism that refuses to accept Ukraine as an independent state and Ukrainians as a people entitled to self-determination.

Critics of Israel see it as another chauvinist, illiberal democracy. They invoke the Israeli government's longstanding oppression of Palestinians living in the territories occupied in 1967 and institutionalized discrimination against the state's Palestinian citizens as well as more recent efforts to manipulate the media, limit judicial autonomy, demonize non-Jewish asylum seekers, and tar those who disagree with government policy as leftist, anti-Zionist, or antisemitic. The 2022 Israeli elections, which produced a solid right-wing majority and made the extremist Jewish Power party the third largest in the Israeli parliament, promised a considerable intensification of these actions. For many academics, public intellectuals, and activists in North America and Europe, not to mention legions of people in the Global South, contemporary Israel's dominant political ideologies are the essence of Zionism, which in turn epitomizes toxic nationalism.

Zionism is, however, heterogeneous. As the writer Amos Oz famously remarked, Zionism is a family name, claimed by a vast number of people whose relations may be intimate or distant but who do bear a certain family resemblance.[2] This chapter explores those areas of difference and resemblance between varieties of Zionism in the nineteenth through twenty-first centuries. Most scholars who draw a Zionist family tree are content to call the family's members by their given names and to accept at face value claims by one family member of propinquity or distance from another. During the Zionist movement's formative decades, activists defined themselves via categories such as "Political," "Practical," "Cultural," "Labor," "Revisionist," and "Religious." These terms had meaning for the people who used them, but they obscure similarities between allegedly opposed Zionist camps, as well as difference within each camp. This chapter therefore critiques old taxonomies of Zionism and offers a new one.

Before it tackles Zionist self-understanding, however, the chapter critiques Zionist perceptions of its relationship with the Jewish past. Like other nationalisms, Zionism justifies itself through appeals to history, but it does so anachronistically. It transforms rabbinic Judaism's concepts of the sacred—the Jews' common devotion to the God of Israel, veneration of the biblical Land of Israel, and the concept of an eventual Jewish return to that land in the messianic era—into a modern nationalist idiom. Following a long line of theorists, I argue for the sustained existence of a Jewish *ethnos* in whose religious-textual tradition the Land of Israel played an important mythic role. Nonetheless, the origins of Zionism, as both theory and praxis, affect and action, lie squarely in the post-Enlightenment era of secular ideologies. If Zionism is analogous to a nuclear family whose members clash as much as they bond, it is but one unit of the extended family of modern Jewish nationalism, which was itself part of a clan of modern Jewish political movements. These movements all asserted coherence and clear divisions from their rivals but were in fact deeply interconnected.

Modern Jewish politics forms a three-dimensional curve, whose axes span the range between Orthodoxy and secularism, assimilation and nationalism, and conservatism and radicalism. In the late 1800s, Zionism emerged from the same set of challenges and crises that gave birth to modern Jewish politics as a whole. Poverty and persecution in Eastern Europe were the most severe problems, but Jews also faced deeply unsettling and occasionally violent forms of antisemitism in Central and Western Europe, as well as North Africa. Even in countries where Jews had political equality and economic opportunity, their Jewishness was rarely fully accepted. It remained a source of discomfort for many Gentiles and a sign of difference that limited Jews' social acceptance and career choices. Simply put, the position of Jews in society was widely thought to constitute a problem, and the term "Jewish problem" or "Jewish question" flourished in Europe from the 1840s until the Nazis attempted to solve it through a genocidal "final solution." Like Jewish politics in general, Zionism took on varying forms as it responded to the separate components of the Jewish "problem."

Two Key Terms: Prochronism and Parachronism

Zionist activists were reluctant to admit the resemblance between their project and previous and parallel attempts by Jews to solve their manifold crises. In this sense, Zionism was anachronistic in two contradictory ways: it was *prochronic* in its projection of modern Jewish nationhood into the ancient Jewish past, but it was also *parachronic* in its neglect, dismissal, or obscuring of earlier Jewish political projects that played an important role in Zionism's origins.

Zionist ideology is prochronic in its depiction of Jews as a nation, anchored in the biblical Land of Israel, that maintained its unity across millennia of dispersion. There are two components to this depiction—typological (the nation) and geographical (the Land of Israel). In the Pentateuch (the first five books of the Hebrew Bible), God promises to make Abraham the patriarch of a "great nation" (*goy gadol*) and commands the

Israelites to form a "sacred nation" (*goy kadosh*). In the textual canon of rabbinic Judaism from the Hebrew Bible to the Talmud, the major codes of Jewish law, and the Hebrew liturgy, Jews are described as the "people of Israel" (*am Yisra'el*) or the "children of Israel" (*b'nei Yisra'el*). They are defined by common descent from the patriarch Jacob, whose name was changed to Israel after his struggle with an angel at the Jabbok River ("wrestling with God" = *yisra* + *el*) in Genesis 32.

Scholars have long debated whether nations are ancient or modern creations and whether a nationalist sensibility is "hardwired" into the human psyche or is the product of specific historical situations. In the battle between "primordialists" and "constructivists," the most famous and consistent proponent of primordialism was Anthony Smith, who applied his theories to the Jews.[3] Most recently, Azar Gat has revived Smith's arguments and developed them at length for a variety of ancient and medieval cultures, including that of the Jews.[4] The question, however, is not whether the Jews' textual corpus expresses commonality and continuity of group identity but what that "groupness" consists of. Until the nineteenth century, Jewish commonality was based in a sacred textual canon, observance of ritual commandments, and concepts of holiness and divine election. Many biblical and rabbinic commandments sanctify practices to render Jews holy or to proclaim the holiness of God.

An important form of premodern Jewish solidarity was the ransoming of Jews who had been taken prisoner in war, sold into slavery, or captured on the high seas by pirates. Jews were commanded to redeem their captive brethren lest the captives be forced to violate Jewish religious law or, even worse, convert to other faiths. As Adam Teller shows, this commandment was a source of global Jewish solidarity, uniting Jews with brethren across hundreds, even thousands, of miles.[5] But this shared identity had little to do with characteristics of modern nationhood, such as language, culture, and shared historical experience. World Jewry constituted a civilization, but it was divided into many subcivilizations that diverged in ritual observance, education, gender relations, and economic practices. Jews did not constitute or define themselves as a people in the modern sense of the word.

Paradoxically, the prochronism with which Zionist ideology treated premodern Jewish collective identity blended with a parachronistic treatment of Jewish modernity. Zionism presented itself as a remedy for assimilation, the loss of cultural distinctiveness as Jews blended or tried to blend into the societies of the countries in which they lived. It is true that over the course of the nineteenth century, legal emancipation and increased economic opportunities granted Jews in some parts of the world unprecedented social mobility, which led to reduced levels of religious observance and, at times, a complete abandonment of ties to Jewish communities and Jewish life. Assimilation, however, rarely reached such an extreme. Although conversion to Christianity was a subject of deep concern in Jewish communities, it was uncommon. In Russia, where Jews were not emancipated until the Revolution of 1917 and opportunities for assimilation were limited to a narrow upper crust, over the course of the nineteenth century, some 85,000 Jews converted to Christianity. This is a minuscule number given that by 1914 the Russian Empire's Jewish population was more than 5 million, not counting the 1.5 million who had emigrated over the previous three decades. Conversion rates were low even in countries where Jews were emancipated, such as Hungary, which was home to almost a million Jews in 1910 but registered only about twenty thousand conversions between 1867 and 1914. In Western Europe, particularly Germany, the figures were higher, but even there most Jews maintained formal membership in Jewish communities and observed the major holidays and life-cycle events. In the late 1800s, leading figures in German and Austrian Jewish life forcefully denied that Jews comprised a nation but also depicted Jews as a *Stamm* (literally, "tribe," but more accurately a culturally defined community).[6] In 1871, the main character in a French Jewish story described being bound to other Jews "by faith, by race, and by common misfortune. . . . Those for whom I pray daily, though they dwell apart in all countries of the globe, and to whom I am inextricably bound by ancient struggles from the past and the promised future that we invoke in all our prayers."[7]

International political intervention and philanthropy were important vehicles for the expression of collective Jewish identity. Modern Jewish politics can be traced to 1840, when Jewish leaders throughout Europe publicly protested the baseless accusation that Jews in Damascus had ritually murdered a Capuchin monk. In 1858, the abduction by Roman Catholic church officials of an Italian Jewish boy whose nurse had secretly baptized him led to another international Jewish protest and the formation of Jewish defense organizations in the United States and France. In subsequent decades, Western European Jews established schools and provided vocational training for poor or persecuted Jews in Russia, Galicia (Austria-Hungary's Polish territories), the Middle East, and North Africa. The most famous Jewish educational organization, the Paris-based Alliance Israélite Universelle, also bore a Hebrew name adapted from the Jewish liturgy: *Kol Yisrael Haverim* (all Israel is bound in friendship). The organization drove home this point via its motto, the talmudic phrase *"kol Yisrael 'arevim zeh be-zeh"* (all Jews are responsible for one another).

In 1881, pogroms in Russia and accelerating Jewish emigration from Eastern Europe catalyzed transnational contacts between these organizations exploring whether Jews should immigrate and, if so, to where. Most Jewish emigrants sought safety and opportunity in North America and, to a lesser extent, in Western Europe or South America. In this moment of international crisis, the Russian Jewish ophthalmologist Lev Pinsker published a pamphlet titled *Auto-Emancipation*, arguing that Jews cannot permanently escape persecution by fleeing from Eastern Europe. Pinsker insisted that antisemitism would flourish so long as Jews were not rooted in an autonomous territory. His ideas resonated with Jewish nationalists eager to promote Jewish settlement in Palestine. And even though many aspects of Pinsker's pamphlet were radically different from the Jewish philanthropic discourse of the time, that discourse shared with Pinsker a profound sense of *klal yisra'el*, the bonds linking Jews across the globe.[8]

Zionism's prochronistic views about the nature of Jewish nationhood and its parachronistic neglect of the context from which Zionism emerged also characterized its representation of the Jews' relationship with the Land of Israel. Jewish connections with the Land of Israel are ancient and deep, but they should not be equated with Zionist goals to settle Jews in the land and configure it as a Jewish homeland. Rabbinic Judaism venerates the Land of Israel, but there has been a wide range of opinions on whether it is religiously commanded to live there. Talmudic sources emphasize that the mass return of Jews to the Land of Israel will occur only in the days of the Messiah and that attempting to initiate this return prematurely is a sacrilege. Underlying this concept is a theological passivity formed by two cataclysmic historical events: the destruction in 70 CE of the Second Temple in Jerusalem during a Jewish revolt against Roman rule and the decimation of Jewish communities in Judea in 132–135 CE in response to another failed rebellion, whose commander had messianic pretensions. The Talmud speaks of oaths, sworn by Jews to God in the wake of this calamity, that they would neither rebel against the nations of the world nor initiate a mass return to the land of Israel.[9]

Until the twentieth century, Palestine's Jewish community was minuscule and splintered. Jews of Iberian and Central and Eastern European origin (*Sephardim* and *Ashkenazim*, respectively) had separate religious institutions and raised money within their own communities abroad. Long-resident Afro-Asian Jews (*Musta'aribun*) formed yet another component of Palestinian Jewry. Well into the twentieth century the Jews of Palestine were a collection of separate communities divided by place of origin, customs, and native language or languages.

In the 1700s the Jews of Palestine numbered about five thousand, some 2 percent of the total population. In the early nineteenth century, Jewish immigration to Palestine began to increase, and by 1880 there were about 25,000 Jews of a population of approximately 470,000. Over the course of the 1800s, Palestine's economy expanded as a result of modernization policies implemented by the ruling Ottoman Empire and improvements in transportation technology, which enabled the increased export of Palestinian agricultural products. Sephardic and Afro-Asian Jews, who were native speakers of Arabic and were familiar with the local political and economic culture, became involved in Palestine's commerce, whereas many of the Ashkenazic immigrants lived as religious scholars and depended on charity from abroad.

A sliver of the 2.5 million Jews who left Russia, Romania, and the Hapsburg Empire between the early 1880s and the outbreak of World War I emigrated to Palestine. Modest but steady immigration from neighboring Arab lands and Yemen took place as well. All in all, about 65,000 Jews emigrated to Palestine over this time. Some of the new arrivals in Palestine were fervent nationalists, but many were pious scholars like those who had immigrated in the past. Others came for more mundane reasons: Palestine's warm climate, relative proximity to Europe (which made for a cheaper journey than the transatlantic crossing), and employment opportunities, especially in the port city of Jaffa.[10] Among the God-fearing Jews who continued to move to Palestine at the turn of the century were widows and never-married women who were not allowed to study in religious academies (*yeshivot*) but who, no less than men, venerated the sanctifying qualities of dwelling in the ancient Land of Israel.[11] The pious immigrants, men and women alike, maintained the Jews' traditional self-image as a holy nation united by religious obligation, rather than a people united by language and culture. They came to the Land of Israel to live among its ruins, not to restore the Hebrew kingdoms of biblical antiquity.

Zionism did not emerge directly from traditional Jewish attitudes toward the collective (the children of Israel) or territory (the Land of Israel). Nor did it burst onto the world stage in the 1880s when Jewish migration to Palestine began to accelerate, or a decade or so later when Theodor Herzl founded the Zionist Organization in 1896. Instead, it had multiple sources, dating to the middle of the nineteenth century. The sources were primarily in Europe but were as likely to be found among the more prosperous and acculturated communities of Germany and Austria-Hungary as among the poorer and less secure communities in Russia and Romania.

"Forerunners" of Zionism?

Scholars of Zionism have devoted much attention to what they call the "forerunners" of Zionism—thinkers and activists who, before the establishment of the Zionist movement in the late 1800s, displayed a Jewish national consciousness, advocated a planned and organized migration of Jews to Palestine, or both. Although nationalist movements routinely assert continuity of the collective across time, Zionism's attempts to construct a liminal space between past and present—a metaphorical foyer to the nationalist movement—are unusual. They signal both Zionism's dependence on prenationalist, primarily religious forms of Jewish belonging and its awareness of its break with that heritage. Locating "forerunners" mitigates the sense of rupture and justifies Zionism as not only legitimate but also essential and the telos of Jewish history.[12]

Histories of Zionism usually limit their discussion of "forerunners" or "proto-Zionists" to Jews. Yet speculation about the restoration of Jews to Palestine was common in Protestant Christianity since the time of the Reformation. In early modern times, some Protestants saw the return of Jews to the Holy Land and their conversion to Christianity as necessary to bring about the end of this world and the final judgment of humanity. In the mid-1800s, liberal Protestants in the United States and Britain began to conceive of the millennium more in terms of universal peace attained through human activism, and they saw in the restoration of Jews to Palestine an essential component of attaining this idyllic state. Restorationist schemes became more concrete, taking into account factors like what John Price Durbin, chaplain of the U.S. Senate, described in 1845 as "the emptiness of the land with respect to population, indicating that Providence is making room for the sons of Israel." This dismissal of the presence of a native Arab population is striking, but so is the assumption that God was preparing for the Jews' return, perhaps imminently.[13] In 1854 the Anglican minister William Henry Johnstone published a book titled *Israel in the World, or, the Mission of the Hebrews to the Great Military Monarchies.* Detailed chronological tables demonstrated that the restoration of the Jews to Palestine was near and that it would be enabled by global Jewish financial power. Although such language was often employed by antisemites, Johnstone saw the Jews' alleged power as a positive force that would crush despotism and establish world peace.[14]

Twelve years later, a more celebrated figure, Jean-Henri Dunant, founder of the International Red Cross, wrote that conflict between Europe's Great Powers over the vacuum left by the declining Ottoman Empire could be ended by promoting European investment in and immigration to the Middle East: Jews would take the lead in the revival of Palestine, which would become a neutral political entity like Switzerland. Such efforts would mark the end of "the system of forcible conquest by fire and sword" and put in its place "a pacific conquest by civilization."[15] According to Dunant's expansive vision, the restoration of Jews to the Holy Land would put an end to war and inaugurate a new era of universal brotherhood. It is no coincidence that at the First Zionist Congress Theodor Herzl sang Dunant's praises and described him as a "Christian Zionist."[16]

These Protestant dreams and schemes were filled with compassion for the Jews—what Anthony Ashley Cooper, the seventh Earl of Shaftesbury, described in 1839 as "a mighty change [that] has come over the hearts of the Gentiles." According to Shaftesbury, rather than persecute the "ancient people of God," Christians now seek the "peace of the Hebrew people" and, via an "approximation of spirit" between members of the two faiths, can work jointly to return the Jews to Palestine.[17] Proposals like Shaftesbury's multiplied over the following decades. Otherworldly millenarian zeal lay under the surface of their rhetoric, but as humanitari-

anism became the normative moral force in the Western world—leading
to momentous acts like the abolition of slavery and serfdom, the emancipation of Jews, and the signing of the Geneva Conventions—Christian
Zionism began to communicate in the reigning language of the time.

In 1891, William Eugene Blackstone, a prosperous businessman in
Chicago and a devout evangelical Christian, presented President Benjamin Harrison with a petition decrying the persecution of Russian Jewry
and justifying their return en masse to Palestine as a moral necessity.
The petition was endorsed by some of the United States' most prominent
citizens, including the chief justice of the Supreme Court, the Speaker of
the House of Representatives, the industrialist John D. Rockefeller, the
banking magnate J. P. Morgan, a mix of Jewish and Christian clergy, and
the editors of scores of major newspapers.[18]

The Zionist movement was created by Jews, but from the start it
was dependent on support from the Christian world. Restorationism was
therefore a prerequisite for the success of Zionism. It is harder to establish, however, whether Christian ideas influenced the nineteenth-century
Jews who championed a return to the Land of Israel. It is difficult indeed
to trace any such external influences on the disciples of the eminent
rabbi Elijah of Vilna (1720–1797) who moved to Palestine in the early
nineteenth century. Some decades later Rabbis Zvi Hirsch Kalischer
(1795–1874), Yehuda Alkalai (1798–1868), and Yosef Natonek (1813–1892) all
wrote in favor of a mass return of Jews to the Land of Israel, but they
hailed from Prussian Poland, today's Bosnia-Herzegovina, and Hungary,
respectively—geographically and culturally distant from the realm of
Anglo-American Protestants. It may be that direct influence was scant or
nonexistent but that the men were all influenced by the dynamic spirit of
the age: a sense of progress and possibility stimulated by revolutions,
nationalist movements, and technological change, combined with messianic zeal.

Alkalai and Kalischer rejected rabbinic Judaism's political passivity
and called for large-scale Jewish settlement in the Land of Israel. Their

rationale was in part philanthropic: they wished to improve the lives of impoverished Jews, both in Europe and in Palestine itself, by combining immigration with the development of crafts and agriculture. The rabbis also believed, however, that the act of immigration, settlement, and rendering Jews economically productive would herald the beginning of the messianic age. Alkalai's and Kalischer's plans for Jewish immigration began in the years leading up to 1840, a year that had messianic significance according to some interpretations of rabbinic literature.[19] The rabbis were clearly influenced by European nationalist movements of the time. Alkalai and Rabbi Akiva Yosef Schlesinger (1837–1922) combined Jewish nationalism with ultra-Orthodox religious observance; they venerated Hebrew not only as a sacred tongue but also as a bond uniting the Jewish people. Schlesinger praised the rabbinic dictum that Jews had preserved themselves over time by retaining Jewish languages, distinct names, and ways of dress. Invoking nations like Greece, Serbia, and Romania, which attained sovereignty thanks to intervention by the Great Powers of Europe, Alkali and Schlesinger called on them to restore the Jews to their ancient homeland.[20] In his 1862 book *Derishat Tsion* (Seeking Zion), Kalischer castigated Jews for their lack of bravery and resolve in comparison with the "Italians, Poles, and Hungarians, who lay down their lives and possessions in the struggle for national independence, while we, the children of Israel, who have the most glorious and holiest of lands as our inheritance, are spiritless and silent. We should be ashamed of ourselves!"[21] (An analysis of the salience of shame in early Zionism is presented in chapter 3.)

Kalischer's bold words had little impact. Along with other rabbis (including Natonek), the financier Moses Montefiore (1784–1885), and the historian Heinrich Graetz (1817–1891), Kalischer joined a philanthropic society in Prussia that expended modest resources on Jewish settlement in the Land of Israel. Natonek and Schlesinger were involved in the purchase of land for an agricultural settlement, named Petakh Tikvah, that was founded in 1878 and failed shortly thereafter.[22] It was not merely their lack of tangible accomplishments, however, that caused scholars to declare them to be "forerunners" or "proto-Zionists," rather than simply calling them early Zionists. Although they adopted nationalist language and compared the Jews to small peoples in Europe, their conception of the essence of the Jewish collective was so deeply tied to religiosity and messianism that it does not fit closely with the more secular movement that developed at the end of the nineteenth century.

The concept of Orthodox "forerunners" is also problematic in that it gives pride of place to only one of the many strands of modern Jewish sensibility that were necessary preconditions for the birth of Zionism. Another precondition was Jewish engagement in the cultural politics of nineteenth-century nationalist movements. Over the course of the nineteenth century throughout Europe (and, late in the 1800s, in the Middle East), writers chronicled their nation's history and produced new editions of literary epics and new works of fiction and poetry. They not only exalted the alleged uniqueness and majesty of the national language but also standardized it, welding variants of a spoken vernacular into a literary medium; they modernized it as well, adding words to enable discussion of advances in science and technology. Jews also engaged in these efforts, but ironically, the movement with which these developments were associated was the opposite of a nationalist one.

This movement was the Jewish variant of the Enlightenment, the *Haskalah,* which began in Central Europe in the mid-1700s and lasted in Eastern Europe until the final quarter of the nineteenth century. Adherents of the Haskalah, known as *maskilim,* published the first newspapers and novels in Hebrew, wrote works of Jewish history, and translated European literature into Hebrew. Maskilim aimed to create new, robust forms of Jewish collective consciousness by improving Jews' positions within their own societies, modernizing their education, and expanding their understanding of the non-Jewish world. They aspired to create a refined modern Jewish culture that would be respected by Jews and Gentiles alike.[23] Many maskilim wrote in both Yiddish and Hebrew, because each language reached a different constituency: Hebrew for the male, learned elite and Yiddish for the general Jewish public.

Because the Haskalah aimed to integrate Jews into the societies in which they lived, Zionist ideology depicted it as its opponent, but in fact Zionism was deeply dependent on the Haskalah. Both movements sought to modernize Jewish culture and normalize the Jews' existence while retaining a strong sense of Jewish particularity. It is no coincidence that among the first Zionists were disillusioned Eastern European maskilim whose hope for progress was dashed by the rise of antisemitism and anti-Jewish violence in the late nineteenth century. Among these was Peretz Smolenskin (1842–1885), who was from Russia but spent the final seventeen years of his life in Vienna, where he edited a highly regarded Hebrew newspaper, *Ha-Shachar* (The Dawn). In a series of essays starting in 1872, Smolenskin insisted that the Jews both constituted a people and were inextricably bound with their lands of residence. Jewish peoplehood, he insisted, was real yet abstract and inseparable from the "spirit of Torah."[24] In 1880, however, Smolenskin acknowledged his desire that Jews eventually form a new society in Palestine. This vague concept solidified in 1881, when pogroms swept through the south of the Jewish Pale of Settlement, the area within the western Russian Empire where Jews were allowed to live without special permission. In a novel completed shortly before his death, Smolenskin wrote of a Russian medical student bitterly disillusioned by antisemitism who calls for vengeance, "not by might and not by power; not with the fist of the wicked and not with blood and murder, but rather by spirit." The novel ends with the student preparing to leave Russia for the Land of Israel, where his spirit will be elevated—and his body will be secure.[25]

In the mid-1800s, Russia, Romania, and Galicia were home to three-quarters of world Jewry, and late in the century, Eastern Europe would provide the demographic and intellectual ballast of early Zionism. Yet endemic poverty stymied Eastern European Jews' involvement in major philanthropic efforts on behalf of Palestine's Jews. The impetus for these efforts came from the West, leading to the third necessary precondition for Zionism, which represented a blend between the religious and "enlightened" approaches described earlier. In 1839, the Anglo-Jewish banker Moses Montefiore, who had amassed sufficient wealth to retire at an early age, undertook the promotion of crafts and agriculture among the poor Jews of Palestine. Montefiore's actions marked the beginning of a series of philanthropic interventions by British, French, and German Jews. The Land of Israel began to lose its traditional image as a sacred, static object to which diaspora Jews sent alms, with little thought about their donations making real change in the lives of the Yishuv's community of Torah scholars. Instead, it came increasingly to be seen as a decrepit entity in desperate need of loving care, provided by a firm and guiding Western hand that would elevate the political, economic, and moral condition of the population. At the same time, the growing involvement of Europe's Great Powers in Palestine—manifested in the establishment of consulates, churches, schools, and hospitals—made Jews uneasy about Christian proselytizing activity, especially among ill Jews in Catholic hospitals. Accordingly, in 1854, the first Jewish hospital was built in Jerusalem. In the same year, the British branch of the Rothschild banking family established a modern school for Jewish girls in Jerusalem. A German-language school for Jewish boys followed two years later. And in 1870, the Alliance Israélite Universelle opened an agriculture school, Mikveh Israel, southeast of Jaffa. The school quickly assumed pride of place in the Alliance's international school network, receiving more funding per student and more attention in Alliance publications than any of its other educational establishments.[26]

The spirit underlying these developments was given a voice by Zecharias Frankel, an eminent German rabbi and scholar, who wrote, "The time is behind us, in which cowardly, ignominious self-abnegation sought to suppress any mention of the Holy Land and a connection of Jews [to it]. We desire a spiritual connection, mediated and rooted in our faith, and we are not ashamed of our faith, so there is nothing in this attachment that can be brought as an accusation against us." Palestine, Frankel wrote, is the central point that can unite "Oriental" Jews, who "cling" to the Holy Land "with pious love," and Jews of the West.[27] Like the leaders of the Alliance, Frankel placed Palestine at the center of a transnational Jewish solidarity, but his sentiments, lacking reference to a shared history, culture, and political vision, were not overtly nationalistic.

Jewish philanthropic projects in Palestine, such as increasing European and American tourism in the Holy Land, depended on technological innovations like steamships and railroads, which made travel to Palestine faster, safer, and more affordable than ever. The conviction that the world was rapidly advancing toward new heights of prosperity and amity was common among Jewish activists in Western and Central Europe. One of these figures, Moses Hess (1812–1875), was the only member of the camp of famous Zionist "forerunners" who was not religiously observant. A pioneer of socialism in Germany and an associate of Karl Marx and Friedrich Engels, Hess returned to his Jewish roots in middle age and in 1862 published a tract titled *Rome and Jerusalem*. The book excoriates Jewish assimilation, asserts the unique capacities of the Jewish people for compassion and solidarity, and envisions an eventual return of Jews to the Land of Israel. Hess saw the spirit of a beneficent God in technological triumphs like the Suez Canal (which was under construction at the time of writing) and the building of railway lines linking Europe and the Levant. At some point in time, Hess wrote, French diplomatic support and Jewish philanthropy would enable the founding of Jewish colonies "reaching from Suez to Jerusalem and from the banks of the Jordan to the coast of the Mediterranean." Jewish "capital will again bring the wide stretches of barren land under cultivation"; their "labor and industry will once more turn the ancient soil into fruitful valleys."[28] Once Palestine is restored, "there will arise no new domination of any race and the equality of all world-historical peoples will follow as a necessary result."[29]

Hess's book received little notice at the time of publication: his fame as a Jewish nationalist thinker would come in the twentieth century. The same cannot be said of Heinrich Graetz, who was one of the most popular Jewish writers of the nineteenth century. Graetz's work combines all three of the preconditions for Zionism laid out thus far: religious and messianic sentiment, an appreciation of the nation as a historical phenomenon, and philanthropic activism on behalf of the Holy Land. Graetz deserves close attention not only as the most significant Jewish nationalist of the mid-nineteenth century but also as a key figure in the placement of Palestine at the center of his nationalist program.

In an essay written in 1846, Graetz laid out the themes that would run through his eleven-volume *History of the Jews* (1859–1893). The Land of Israel, Graetz wrote, was the Jewish nation's spiritual body, just as the Torah was the source of its soul. The crossing of the Jordan River under the command of Moses's successor Joshua, as related in the Hebrew Bible, constituted the birth of Israel as a nation, rather than a collection of tribes with a common God. The Jewish nation was immortal, Graetz claimed, because of the messianic hope for the Land of Israel. The centrality of the land was also apparent from the periodization for Jewish history that Graetz proposed in this essay and in his subsequent work. The first era began with the formation of ancient Israel and ended with the Babylonian Exile, the second included the return to Palestine and the Second Temple period, and the third era extended from the destruction of the second Jewish commonwealth to the present.

In 1872, Graetz traveled to Palestine, and although he was distressed by the conditions of the Jewish community in the Holy Land, the country's landscape affected him deeply, and he was thrilled by the Alliance's agricultural school. Shortly after returning from Palestine, Graetz added to his chapter on the conquest of Canaan several pages of dithyrambic prose extolling the beauty and fertility of the Holy Land. The significance of this section was greatly magnified in the 1887 three-volume *"volkstümliche"* (popular) abridged edition of the history, in which an entire volume is devoted to antiquity, thus giving the Holy Land more attention than in the full-length version. Even more important, the description of the Holy Land is moved from an excursus after chapter 2 to the very beginning of the first volume.

The volume begins:

> A land that lies on the coast of the murmuring sea, that presents a variety of towering mountains, hillcrests, plateaus, and deep valleys, moves its people, if it is not entirely obtuse, to deeds that go beyond the everyday. This land displays special natural particularities— regular rainfall and regular seasons, a high average temperature and as a result luxuriant fertility and lush growth of flora, little fog, mainly clear and transparent air during the greater part of the year—and otherwise still more features that attract attention, which stimulate its dwellers to uplift and awaken them to the unfolding of their own spiritual life.[30]

Graetz goes on to describe the Land of Israel as infusing spirituality into the nation of Israel, awakening in it an "indestructible conviction" of its call to greatness and to a fate different from any other people.

Graetz bears the influence of the talmudic saying that "the air of Eretz Israel creates wisdom" (Bava Batra 158B) and of medieval writers such as Yehuda Halevi and David Kimhi who wrote of the Land of Israel as a source of physical health and moral elevation.[31] He is also speaking the language of nineteenth-century romantic nationalism, which idealized the natural beauty of the land and associated it with its people's virtue and nobility of character; for example, the lyrics of the Czech hymn "Kde domov muj," written in 1834, connect the land's roaring waters, rustling pines, and fields of blossoms with "serene souls in vigorous bodies, of clear mind . . . and with a strength that frustrates all defiance." But Graetz goes further. Building on a passage in Leviticus 18:28 in which God warns the Israelites that if they "defile the land" it will "vomit" them out, Graetz presents the land as sentient, animate, and capable of independent moral judgment: "Upon the settlement of the Israelites, the land henceforth received not only another name, but also another character. It was a holy soil that became the inheritance of God. . . . The holy land was endowed with a sensibility, as if it felt the people's behavior, be it pleasing to God or forgetful of Him."[32]

The inseparability of geography and morality is highlighted in the following pages of detailed description of the land's topography, climate, flora, and fauna. Graetz describes the land as richly fertile, with abundant freshwater, good air, and, unlike later Zionist imagery, few swamps. It is a healthy land that "engenders a powerful breed of men."[33] He presents the land as a microcosm of the global ecology, harmoniously combining cold and warmth, the oaks of the north and the palms of the south. Despite his obvious debt to nature imagery in romantic literature and poetry, Graetz's tone is serene, connoting balance and contentment.[34]

Despite being a committed Jewish nationalist and clearly attached to the Land of Israel, Graetz did not want to initiate the messianic *shivat tsion* (Return to Zion) in his own time. Rather, he wrote, it must "slumber in the deepest corner of the heart."[35] Graetz was convinced that the purpose of Jewish existence was "to found a religious state which is conscious of its activity, purpose, and connection with the world."[36] But he was willing to defer that event to beyond the historical horizon, and even the pogroms and economic crises of Eastern European Jewry in the 1880s did not change his course.

Not all forms of Jewish nationalism were as Palestine-centric as Graetz's. In Eastern Europe, the concentration of millions of Yiddish-speaking Jews in the Russian Empire's Pale of Settlement (the western portions of the empire to which most Jews were legally restricted), in Austria-Hungary's eastern territories, and in Romania fostered the creation of diaspora nationalisms that called for Jewish cultural autonomy in situ. The General Jewish Labor Bund, founded in Vilna in 1897, was a socialist party committed to collaboration with like-minded organizations, yet within a few years after its establishment it developed a diasporic-nationalist orientation. Even when Zionism became a mass movement in the early twentieth century, Bundism and more bourgeois forms of diaspora nationalism were formidable competitors.

Any form of Jewish nationalism, however, faced considerable resistance. Many Orthodox Jews were cold to Graetz's romantic nationalism, seeing it as a type of idolatry, a subordination of divine commandments to nature and human acts. Many Jewish radicals dismissed Jewish particularism as a distraction from the imperative of leading a socialist revolution that would put an end to inequality, which was ostensibly responsible for antisemitism. Upwardly mobile, acculturated Jews preferred to concentrate on improving their situation in their homelands and denied the existence of a distinct Jewish nationality.

The four preconditions of Zionism discussed in this section—active messianism, the Haskalah's Hebraic cultural revival, pervasive romantic nationalism, and dynamic philanthropic involvement in Palestine—do not fully explain why Zionism emerged in the late 1800s and how it became a mass movement in the following decades. To answer those questions, we need to return to the concept, raised in the introduction to this chapter, of Zionism as being a family name with multiple given names. Both historical actors and latter-day observers have applied the word "Zionism" to widely varying approaches to solve a diverse array of problems affecting late nineteenth-century Jewry (see figure 1).

Taxonomies, Old and New

Conventional taxonomies of Zionism make use of terminology that was invented over the years from the fin de siècle to the 1930s. Four of these types largely disappeared after World War I:

Hibat Tsion—In the early 1880s, in response to pogroms against Jews in Russia, small societies sprang up throughout the world, but particularly in the Russian Empire and Romania, to promote the emigration of

Figure 1 Delegate card from the Fifth Zionist Congress (1901), designed by
Ephraim Moses Lilien (1874–1925). This image incorporates religious and
romantic-nationalist elements. The lower caption, taken from the Jewish liturgy, reads. "And may our eyes behold thy return in mercy to Zion."
Credit: David Matlow Herzl and Zionism Collection, Toronto.

Jews to Palestine. In 1884, a meeting of these societies in Katowice
(in today's Poland) adopted the umbrella name *Hovevei Tsion* (Lovers of
Zion), and the underlying sensibility behind this movement was known
as *hibat tsion* (love of Zion). In Zionist historiography, the hibat tsion
movement is associated with small-scale settlement activity, limited
resources, and a lack of effective, centralized administration. It is also
linked with romantic nationalist literature, as discussed in chapter 3.[37]

Political Zionism: In 1890, a young Viennese Jewish activist named
Nathan Birnbaum coined both the word "Zionism," by which he meant a
Palestine-centered Jewish nationalism, and the term "political Zionism,"
which meant a public political campaign on behalf of the attainment of
Zionist goals.[38] Theodor Herzl had never heard of either term when he
underwent a conversion to Jewish nationalism in the spring of 1895; in
fact, in his pamphlet *Der Judenstaat* (The Jewish State) published the

following year, he invoked Zionism in a negative way, associating it with heartfelt but unfocused feelings that needed to be channeled into and held in check by an appropriate organizational framework. Herzl, however, quickly came to appreciate the popularity of the word, and he adopted the term "political Zionism" to describe a two-pronged program. First, he founded the Zionist Organization (ZO), which had a permanent executive office, held regular international congresses, published its own newspaper, and created a bank, land-purchase agency, and other subsidiary institutions. Second, Herzl sought international diplomatic support—in the form of either a charter from the Ottoman Empire or a protectorate by one of the European Great Powers—prior to Jewish settlement in Palestine. Although Herzl's diplomatic ventures were largely unsuccessful, they continued after his death, and during World War I Chaim Weizmann succeeded in obtaining from Britain a declaration supporting the creation in Palestine of a Jewish "national home." The 1917 Balfour Declaration is often seen as political Zionism's greatest success.

Practical Zionism: During the brief period between the founding of the ZO and Herzl's death (1897–1904), he encountered stiff opposition to his diplomatic program from those who continued to support small-scale Jewish settlement in Palestine. This so-called Practical Zionist opposition continued into the years after Herzl's death, especially because Jewish immigration to Palestine was accelerating at that time. The ZO itself co-opted this desire for tangible accomplishments by engaging in modest land purchases and establishing an office in Palestine that assisted a variety of settlement ventures.

Cultural Zionism: Like other nationalists of the fin de siècle, adherents of the Hovevei Tsion movement believed that the health of a nation depended as much on the vigor of its cultural life as on its physical safety. Herzl's foremost critic, the essayist Asher Ginzberg (1856–1927) who wrote under the pen name Ahad Ha-Am (Hebrew for "One of the People"), attacked political Zionism as superficial and mechanical. Ahad

Ha-Am stressed the centrality of Hebrew letters, exploration of the Jewish textual heritage in light of present needs, and the cultivation of what he believed was a uniquely demanding and beneficent Jewish morality that did not sit well with the compromises and cruelties of politics. Ahad Ha-Am was but one of many Jews in Eastern Europe and Palestine who edited and contributed to Hebrew-language newspapers with a cultural-nationalist agenda.

In contrast, four other widely cited forms of Zionism flourished throughout the period of British rule in Palestine (1917–1948) and survived into the period of Israeli statehood:

Labor Zionism: The social radicalism that inspired the Bund and that led some Jews into revolutionary movements with no Jewish aspect also affected substantial numbers of Zionists. Parties and organizations with the name Poalei Tsion (Workers of Zion) cropped up in North America and in Europe at the fin de siècle. During the decade before World War I, small clusters of young radicals moved to Palestine, where they founded minuscule political parties and experimented with new forms of cooperative organization in both urban and rural settings. After the transition from Ottoman to British rule, what became known as the Zionist Labor Movement gradually became the hegemonic political force in the Yishuv, and it maintained that status until the 1977 Israeli elections, when the Israeli Labor Party fell from power. Before 1948 Labor Zionism and its supporters throughout the world were divided into multiple factions. The more radical groups were engaged with communal agricultural settlement, with one faction adhering closely to Marxist doctrine regarding the primacy of class over national solidarity. A more moderate approach, adopted by the most popular and powerful of the Zionist Labor parties, known in Hebrew as Mapai, welcomed private capital and viewed the creation of a productive urban working class as a Zionist national imperative.

Revisionist Zionism: The Balfour Declaration and its incorporation into the League of Nations' Mandate for Palestine raised great hopes among Zionists for mass migration to Palestine and its establishment as a Jewish national home. By the mid-1920s, however, the Zionist leader Vladimir Jabotinsky (1880–1940) and his allies were disappointed with what they perceived as the slow pace of Zionist settlement and British foot-dragging in promoting mass Jewish immigration, despite the pressing needs of Eastern European Jews. A Revisionist faction within the ZO was founded in 1925, and a decade later most of that faction withdrew from the ZO altogether to form a rival organization. Revisionism claimed to revive Herzlian political Zionism by demanding the prompt fulfillment of the Balfour Declaration and the establishment of a state with a Jewish majority. That state's boundaries were to include Transjordan, as well as western Palestine. Revisionists opposed both the diplomatic moderation of ZO president Chaim Weizmann and the social-democratic regime in the Yishuv led by David Ben-Gurion. Revisionism was more explicitly militaristic than Labor Zionism, and its youth group, Betar, venerated military uniforms and martial drills. When Israel was founded, Betar's leader Menachem Begin became the leader of Revisionist Zionism's successor political party Herut, which was the core of a succession of right-wing blocs that in 1973 became the Likud Party.

General Zionism: During the interwar period, in both the diaspora and the Yishuv the General Zionists formed a political party (more accurately, two slightly different parties) that claimed to be unattached to any specific religious or social ideology. General Zionism was characterized by an overarching nationalism, a reluctance to adopt an unambiguously liberal stance on civil rights or economic issues, and a self-presentation as a third way between Labor and Revisionist Zionism. General Zionism endured into the 1950s, and it briefly enjoyed considerable popularity before Israeli politics began a gradual movement toward consolidation into blocs on the Left and Right, with General Zionism and Revisionism linking up in 1965 to form a single political party. In 1973 that party consolidated with several small parties to form the Likud, which has dominated Israeli politics for most of the past forty-five years.

Religious Zionism: Although most Orthodox Jews at the fin de siècle opposed Zionism, some were attracted to it. Rabbis like Isaac Jacob Reines (1839–1915) saw in the Land of Israel a natural destination for poor and persecuted Jews and wanted to ensure that the society of the Yishuv would adhere to Jewish law as strictly as possible. A more radical and explicitly messianic approach, similar to that of Alkalai and Kalischer, was adopted by Rabbi Abraham Isaac Kook (1865–1935), who in 1921 was appointed by the British authorities to be the Yishuv's Chief Ashkenazic Rabbi. Until the 1920s the majority of the Yishuv was Orthodox, but it did not form an effective political front because it was divided between Orthodox Zionists and a larger community of anti-Zionist Orthodox Jews. During the interwar period, waves of immigration to Palestine of non-Orthodox Jews pushed Religious Zionism toward the political periphery, but either on its own or in conjunction with anti-Zionist Orthodoxy, it exerted significant influence over the role of religious authority in the public sphere. This status as both peripheral and central continued into the period of statehood. Religious Zionism was invigorated and transformed by Israel's conquest of the ancient biblical heartland during the 1967 Arab–Israeli war. More than any other original form of Zionism, Religious Zionism has remained active and dynamic to this day.

With the exception of Religious Zionism, these forms of pre-1948 Zionism have either declined into insignificance or mutated into new forms that are substantively different from their predecessors. Accordingly, we need more capacious and inclusive categories of Zionist sensibility to include aspects of the Zionist project from its origins to our own day. Recently, some writers attempted to provide these categories by distinguishing an older "crisis" Zionism—responding to existential threats to the Jewish people, the Yishuv, or the state of Israel—from a newer "aspirational" Zionism, which takes as a given Israel's advanced economy and (relative to the past) military security, leaving Jews free to focus on cultivating personal connections with Israel and promoting democracy and human dignity within the Jewish state.[39] This approach produces a lopsided model of Zionism, the vast bulk of which remains in one type or another of the "crisis" category, leaving democratically oriented "aspirational" Zionism to attract a very limited following among the Jewish public.

Another sweeping bifurcation of Zionism has been proposed by the philosopher Chaim Gans, who counterposes a chauvinistic and unjust "proprietary Zionism" with a moral, egalitarian Zionism that recognizes the Jews' attachments to the Land of Israel but dismantles Jewish ethnocratic domination.[40] In the twenty-first century, varieties of this latter approach became known as "Liberal Zionism," a term that rapidly gained currency in North America after the outbreak of the Second Intifada in 2000. It was used both by Jews seeking to reconcile their bonds to Israel with commitments to liberal values and by anti-Zionists who derided these Jews for allegedly trying to square a circle.[41] Terms such as "proprietary" or "liberal" are interesting for what they tell us about the Zeitgeist of early twenty-first century Zionism, but they are too broad and normative to serve as analytical tools.

In a 2018 anthology that purports to be a successor to Arthur Hertzberg's classic work *The Zionist Idea,* the historian Gil Troy attempts to develop a capacious framework that encompasses all forms of Zionism across the nineteenth through twenty-first centuries.[42] Troy justly criticizes Hertzberg and other writers who identified classic Zionism with individuals who were all male and Ashkenazic. To his credit, Troy draws on a more diverse body of authors than Hertzberg, but his conceptualization maintains most of the original, early twentieth-century forms of Zionism, even though some have reached dead ends and others have changed into forms that their founders would not recognize. Troy acknowledges change over time by referring to successive generations of what he calls "pioneers," "builders," and "torchbearers," but such terms are value-laden and lack analytical rigor. Moreover, Troy creates a new category of "diaspora Zionism," which conveys the impression that Zionism within and outside the Yishuv and state of Israel have been separate phenomena. The relationship between Israeli and diasporic Zionism has, in fact, been enormously complicated, with fluctuating levels of congruence, interdependence, separation, tension, and antagonism.

The continued application of classic Zionist categories is problematic not only because change over time calls their relevance into question. Those in the past who identified with one Zionist camp or another were unaware of or reluctant to admit commonalities between them and their mutual influence. This was particularly the case for Labor and Revisionist Zionism during the heyday of their internecine struggles during the 1930s and 1940s. The social and economic ideologies of the two movements differed profoundly, but their goals and methods diverged more in style than substance. During the Israeli state's first decades, Labor Zionism was still identified with the "Left" and Revisionism with the "Right," but later in the twentieth century, with the triumph of neoliberal economic doctrines the only substantive difference between Left and Right remained the fate of the Occupied Territories and questions of Palestinian statehood. Even then, all but the most extreme positions within the Zionist Left maintained the primacy of Jewish claims to a state within most of historic Palestine and were wary of, if not downright hostile to, extensive intermixing with the Arab population. Divisions within Zionism between the Left and Right are real yet fluid and epiphenomenal.

Any division of Zionism into neat categories is, by definition, a heuristic: a series of ideal types that help us understand individuals and events. Members of a movement, party, or organization justify and conceive of their attachment to the collective in multiple, overlapping, and even mutually contradictory ways. The taxonomy I propose next should be seen as a list of eight ingredients that, in any specific historical situation, are blended to varying degrees. Moreover, across time and space some forms of Zionism are more or less dominant, new forms are created, and older ones die out altogether. A particular challenge in classifying Zionism is the relationship between its Israeli and diasporic forms. As an expression of collective Jewish ethnonationalist identity,

Zionism can be present anywhere Jews live, be they in isolated communities or a Jewish state. The radically different circumstances under which Jews in and outside Israel live—the former as a dominant nationality within a sovereign state and the latter as an ethnoreligious minority—influence the relative weight and salience of the various types of Zionism outlined here.

———•———

Philanthropic Zionism is a compassionate attachment for Jews who seek refuge or dwell in the Land or State of Israel. This attachment is expressed primarily through donating money, fundraising, or providing social services on a voluntary basis. As we saw earlier, it was an important component of support provided by Orthodox Jews for the early Zionist movement. Not all individuals who adopted this approach accepted the principle of Jewish nationhood that is often assumed to be an essential element of Zionism. Rather, they spoke of various forms of group identity that fell short of outright nationhood. In early twentieth-century Germany, for example, the economist Franz Oppenheimer aptly summed up this sensibility when he differentiated Zionists in Eastern Europe, who had what he called a "national consciousness" (*Volksbewusstsein*), from those in the West, who had a "group" or "ethnic" consciousness (*Stammesbewusstsein*).[43]

During the 1920s in the United States, a group of elite Jews who were eager to contribute to and raise money for the Yishuv did not feel comfortable identifying with a distinct Jewish nationality nor wanted to call themselves Zionists. The Zionist Organization's president, Chaim Weizmann, sought to win their support by giving a new meaning to wording in the League of Nations' Mandate for Palestine, which was confirmed by the League on Nations Council in 1922. The Mandate called for a "Jewish Agency as a public body for the purpose of advising and cooperating with the Administration of Palestine." At first, the ZO was considered to be that "Jewish Agency." In 1929, however, Weizmann successfully negotiated the expansion of this body's executive to include both individuals affiliated with the ZO and so-called non-Zionists.

Another important American Jewish source of support for the Yishuv was Hadassah, the Women's Zionist Organization of America. It adopted the term "Zionist" without qualms, but its approach was strongly philanthropic, focusing on the provision of medical care, education, and other social services, primarily to Jews but also to the Arabs of Palestine. Throughout the interwar period Hadassah was the largest Zionist organization in the United States, with membership totals that dwarfed those of the Zionist Organization of America.[44]

Since 1948, philanthropic sensibilities have continued to feature strongly in diaspora Jewish feelings about Israel. Donating money has been one of the most common means by which diaspora Jews express their bonds with the Jewish state. In the Western world, vastly more Jews give money to Israel than visit it for extended periods, let alone move there. The main difference between recent and past forms of philanthropic Zionism is the increasing comfort Jews feel in asserting their ethnic distinctiveness. Still, as Noam Pianko has shown, Jews in the world's largest and most prosperous diaspora community, the United States, are not likely to speak of themselves as constituting a distinct nation but instead use the vaguer language of "peoplehood."[45]

Hebraic Zionism is an expression of Jewish nationalism through use of the Hebrew language, devotion to that language's development and dissemination, and the belief that the flourishing of Hebrew and the revival of the Jewish community in the Land of Israel are mutually dependent. A romantic attachment to language was common among nineteenth-century nationalist movements, and Zionism was no exception. The rise of Hebrew journalism in Central and Eastern Europe predated Zionism, but Hebrew's revival was strongly associated with Eliezer Ben-Yehuda's emigration to Palestine in 1881 and his determination to make Hebrew into a modern vernacular. Moshe Leib Lilienblum's and Ahad Ha-Am's exquisitely crafted Hebrew essays and the stirring Hebrew poetry of the likes of Menachem Dolitzky and Naftali Herz Imber were hallmarks of the Hovevei Tsion.[46] In the final years of the Ottoman Empire, Middle Eastern Jews such as Abraham Elmaleh were prominent in the development of Hebrew education in both Palestine and adjacent countries.[47] In the interwar period and throughout most of Israel's history, Zionism was inseparable from the zealous cultivation of Hebrew. New immigrants were not considered truly Israeli until they mastered spoken Hebrew, and a cultured person was expected to be familiar both with its traditional and more modern forms and to be able to use them in formal communication.

Although both spoken and written Hebrew are well anchored in contemporary Israel, the acceleration in recent decades of economic and cultural globalization has considerably weakened Hebraic Zionism. Immigrants from the former Soviet Union in the 1990s were the first in Israel's history not to be expected to abandon their mother tongue and immediately embrace Hebrew. In contemporary Israel, English is increasingly used in the spheres of business and higher education.

In the diaspora, Hebraic Zionism was fostered by a community of dedicated writers and educators who made Hebrew into an important element in Jewish education worldwide. Hebraic Zionism was always, however, a minority movement. Even in interwar Poland, where the Hebrew educational system was the most developed in the diaspora, only about one-fifth of Jewish children attended the Zionist and Hebrew-oriented *Tarbut* schools. (The rest went to state schools, Yiddishist schools, or those run by the ultra-Orthodox political party Agudat Yis-rael.[48]) Over the course of the history of Israeli statehood, diaspora Jews (not counting Israeli ex-patriates and their families) with a command of modern Hebrew are not often found outside Jewish institutions. Hebraic Zionism has survived in Jewish day schools, where Hebrew is treated with reverence as both a sacred and national tongue, but few day school students master modern literary Hebrew. A more circumscribed deriv-ative of diaspora Hebraic Zionism is a sense of wonder when hearing

Israeli children speaking Hebrew.[49] This is an expression of romantic nationalism, like that of substate or state-seeking European nationalists whose languages were historically marginalized (e.g., Catalans, Basques, Welsh, Irish). In Europe today, however, parents tend to favor bilingual education—in both the dominant national language and the minority vernacular—for practical reasons such as educational and career opportunities.[50] Such pragmatic thinking, however, does not play a major role in Hebrew education in the diaspora.

Statist Zionism's distinguishing characteristic is a focus on Jewish self-determination as the keystone supporting all other forms of Zionism. One sees glimmers of it already in the mid-1800s; in 1863, Moses Montefiore baldly stated in an interview that "Palestine must belong to the Jews, and Jerusalem is destined to be the seat of a Jewish empire.'"[51] In 1877, during the Russo–Turkish war the Russian maskil Judah Leib Gordon speculated that the Ottoman Empire might soon break up and that a Jewish homeland could be created in Palestine. Ben-Yehuda went further, reasoning that just as Russia was helping Serbia and Bulgaria attain independence from the Ottoman Empire, it might do the same for the Jews and Palestine. Lilienblum alluded to Jewish statehood in an essay written shortly after the outburst of pogroms in Russia in 1881. All these writings preceded Pinsker's pamphlet *Auto-Emancipation*, not to mention Herzl's *The Jewish State*.[52]

Initially, Statist Zionism did not necessarily demand a sovereign state for Jews in Palestine. The ZO's Basel Program, affirmed at the First Zionist Congress in 1897, called for a Jewish "national home, secured by public law," not a state. Herzl himself was willing to accept alternate arrangements for Palestine, such as a designated Jewish province of the Ottoman Empire or a Great Power protectorate, and in 1931 Weizmann said he would accept a Jewish demographic minority in British-administered Palestine. During the late 1920s, Jabotinsky supported dominion status for Palestine within the British Empire at a time when the dominions did not yet have full control over their foreign policy. (Jabotinsky said that "statehood" could be the same as the "state of Kentucky" or the "province of Ontario within the Dominion of Canada.") During the 1920s and 1930s David Ben-Gurion was a statist in the sense that he wanted a well-organized, autonomous Yishuv with centralized power in the hands of the Jewish Agency Executive, which as of 1935 he controlled. Ben-Gurion assumed Palestine would become a Jewish–Arab federation until a prolonged Palestinian Arab revolt in the mid to late 1930s convinced him that this was impossible. Still, it was only in 1942, before the full scale of the Holocaust's devastation had occurred and was not yet fully known, that Zionists formally demanded a state in the entirety of western Palestine to accommodate what they thought would be millions of refugees after the war.[53]

The destruction of two-thirds of European Jewry in the Holocaust left Zionists psychologically crushed and in immediate need of a homeland to house the survivors. Few survivors wished to continue to live in the continent that had become a graveyard. The countries in the western hemisphere were not keen to accept the survivors en masse. Last but not least, after experiencing the consequences of complete powerlessness the survivors longed to live in a state where Jews could determine their own fate. At the 1946 Zionist Congress, two-thirds of the Zionist Organization's executive endorsed Jewish statehood in part of Palestine, a call that was legitimized by the United Nations in the following year.[54]

The establishment of the State of Israel and its stabilization and securitization during its first two decades were vast challenges. Israel's first prime minister, David Ben-Gurion, coined the term *mamlakhtiyut* (statism or republicanism) to describe the need for a powerful, centralized government and sufficient resources to absorb mass migration from Europe, the Middle East, and North Africa. Although statist Zionism's goals were ambitious, they were also pragmatic, allowing for flexible, variable approaches to the relationship between church and state, economic policy, international relations, borders, and even the form of government.[55] From their beginnings the ZO and the State of Israel were procedurally democratic, and from 1985 Israeli Basic Laws (the equivalent of constitutional articles) emphasized Israel's dual obligation to be a "Jewish and democratic state."[56] For many diaspora Jews, especially in the United States, Israel's democratic character was an essential moral justification for their Zionism. In the twenty-first century, however, the quality of Israeli democracy substantially eroded. Prime Minister Benjamin Netanyahu and many of his supporters displayed little respect for democratic norms, such as the balance of powers and the subordination of politicians to the rule of law. In a survey from 2016, three-fourths of Israeli Jews opined that Israel's Jewishness and democracy were compatible, but two-thirds of Religious Zionists stated that in a conflict between the state's Jewish and democratic character, they would prioritize the former.[57]

Israel's territorial conquests in 1967 strengthened the Israeli state immeasurably but paradoxically threatened to weaken Statist Zionism. The dynamism and enthusiasm that had fueled the construction of the Israeli state shifted to settlement of Jews in the Occupied Palestinian Territories, especially the biblical heartland of the West Bank. For the religious settler movement, the significance of the ancient Land of Israel, reaching from the Jordan River to the Mediterranean, eclipsed that of the State of Israel, which had been established on only a portion of that land. Nonetheless, most Israeli Jews remained Statist Zionists in the sense that the state was the sole unifying institution in a country made up of Jewish subcommunities divided by ethnicity, religiosity, income level, and political orientation. The West Bank Jewish settlements were popular for their affordable housing, new infrastructure, and many amenities, all funded by the state.

Well into the twenty-first century, the word "Zionism" signified the Israeli state's paradoxical blend of vulnerability and strength, achievement and unfulfilled purpose. The same dual definition of contemporary Statist Zionism as a celebration of the state's very existence and a belief in its permanent impermanence has had currency in the Jewish diaspora.

"Israelism" would be a more accurate description of this sentiment, but the idealistic, spiritual, and aspirational associations of the word "Zionism" assured its ongoing use.

Catastrophic Zionism is an extension of Statist Zionism that demands Jewish statehood to ward off an imminent cataclysm threatening the survival of the Jewish people. Although there were elements of catastrophic thinking in the writing of Pinsker and Herzl, they approached Zionism as a solution to multiple Jewish problems—immaterial, as well as material—and even though they depicted a grim Jewish future they did not foresee utter destruction. The founder of Catastrophic Zionism was the eminent writer and critic Max Nordau (1849–1923), who reacted with horror to the mass slaughter of Jews in Poland, Russia, and Ukraine during the civil wars that followed the end of World War I. For Nordau, the immediate and massive emigration of Eastern European Jewry was an existential imperative. During the 1930s, Jews in Poland found their living situation increasingly intolerable and turned to Zionism not out of nationalist idealism but rather out of desperation.[58] Vladimir Jabotinsky echoed these feelings, although he did not imagine anything on the scale of the genocide that between 1941 and 1945 destroyed two-thirds of European Jewry.[59]

After the Holocaust, Catastrophic Zionism featured a paradoxical combination of fear for the survival of Jews outside Israel and those in the State of Israel itself. There have been many motivations for post-1948 Jewish immigration to Israel, but fear for one's safety and livelihood has been among the most important. This rationale continued into the twenty-first century; in France, increasing antisemitism and lethal terrorist attacks against Jews spurred some 50,000 Jews to move to Israel between 2000 and 2020. Conversely, Jews the world over saw the Arab–Israeli wars between 1948 and 1973 as pushing the state to the verge of destruction. In subsequent decades, attacks on or within Israel by Palestinian militants and the Lebanese Shiite militia Hezbollah did not threaten the state's existence, but they mobilized diaspora Jewish support for what was perceived as a country under constant assault. This perception escalated into doomsday fears in response to Iraqi leader Saddam Hussein's missile attacks on Israel in 1990 and Iran's determination to develop nuclear weaponry.

Nonetheless, in the early twenty-first century, Catastrophic Zionism began to weaken among world Jewry. In Western Europe, despite exhortations from the Israeli government to "come home" in the wake of terror attacks (especially in France), the overwhelming majority of Europe's Jews, including those in France, chose to stay put.[60] In the United States, despite a spike in antisemitic incidents, including the murder of eleven Jews at a Pittsburgh synagogue in 2018, few Jews outside Orthodox communities contemplated immigrating to Israel. Younger Jews whose sense of ethnic identity was weaker than that of their parents and who questioned Israel's treatment of Palestinians grew less likely to uncritically defend the country's military and security apparatus.

A catastrophic view of Jewish history and existential fear for Israel's safety have been prominent in Israel from the time of the state's establishment in the wake of the Holocaust and the traumatic 1948 war. Israeli political culture veered between pride to the point of hubris in Israel's military might and panic when Israel came under attack or underperformed militarily. Associations between Arabs and Nazis were common in Israeli political discourse and popular culture alike. (In the twenty-first century, Iran has assumed the place formerly held by Egypt and the PLO as an alleged source of existential threat and torchbearer of the Nazis' genocidal ambitions.) The fears for Israel's safety that undergird Catastrophic Zionism were promoted by Israeli regimes, beginning with Israel's first prime minister, David Ben-Gurion, but especially under Likud prime ministers such as Menachem Begin, Yitzhak Shamir, and Benjamin Netanyahu.

Transformative Zionism assumes that the Jewish people must undergo a series of far-reaching changes, that the Zionist movement is the only means by which those changes can occur, and conversely that only Jews who have undergone this transformation can ensure Zionism's success. (The Hebrew phrase that nicely captures this dialectic is "*livnot u-lehibanot*," to build and be built.) Theodor Herzl is usually pigeonholed as a political Zionist, but he was also a founder of Transformative Zionism, because he believed that centuries of oppression, on the one hand, and more recent pressures on Jews in Western lands to assimilate, on the other, had robbed the Jews of honor and dignity. A Jewish state, he thought, would restore both by raising Jews to the same level as other nations in the world. Herzl and his close colleague Nordau established other common tropes in Transformative Zionism, such as the Land of Israel's capacity to make Jews healthy, bronzed, and muscular—a marked contrast to antisemitic stereotypes, which Herzl and Nordau both internalized, of diaspora Jews as physically frail and overwrought.

During the interwar period, both Labor and Revisionist Zionism were transformative movements; each demanded that Jews change in multiple ways, although the two movements' emphases differed. For Labor Zionists, transformation was to begin with what was known as "occupational restructuring"; that is, moving Jews from their traditional concentrations in commerce into agriculture or industry. This idea was central to the Haskalah, which internalized Gentile criticisms of Jews as economically unproductive, and was intensified by radical critiques of capitalism. Revisionist Zionism, in contrast, celebrated the Jews' historic role as pillars of the bourgeoisie, but its adherents valorized no less than Labor Zionists what was known as a "new Jew" or "new Hebrew." For Labor Zionists, new Jews would be unpretentious but cultured workers, loyal to their workplaces or agricultural settlements, their union, party, and, above all, the Zionist state. Revisionism preached its own variety of virtue (what Jabotinsky called *hadar*, a Hebrew word connoting nobility of character). Both movements deemed modern Hebrew to be a mobilizing and moralizing force, and both produced great Hebrew writers and zealous defenders of the tongue. Perhaps most important, the two movements shared the belief that diaspora Jews had lost the ability to defend themselves and that armed self-defense would be both a practical necessity and a moral value in and of itself.[61] Revisionism placed more emphasis on the aesthetics of militarism—uniforms, parades, and martial rhetoric—than Labor, but both movements were equally likely to proclaim, as was commonly heard after the Holocaust, "Jewish blood is not free for the taking *(dam yehudi lo hefker)*."

Transformative Zionism was the hegemonic cultural force within the Yishuv and among global Jewry throughout most of the twentieth century. It invented a self-serving chronology of Zionist settlement that became dogma. To this day, Zionist historiography speaks of Jewish immigration to the Land of Israel between 1882 and 1948 as having come in five "waves of ascent" *(aliyot,* sing. *aliyah,* from the biblical Hebrew word for the ascent from Palestine's coastal lowlands to Jerusalem, which is about 2,500 feet above sea level). The "First Aliyah" of the 1880s and 1890s is said to have consisted of nationalist Jews, many of whom maintained traditional Jewish observance and a handful of whom had socialist leanings. A "Second Aliyah" between 1904 and 1914 was similar in overall composition but contained a larger core of radical youth who would become the founders of Labor Zionism. The Third, Fourth, and Fifth Aliyot between 1918 and 1939 provided the bulk of the Yishuv's population by the start of World War II.

Just after World War I, however, Zionists used a different classification altogether, with the First and Second Aliyot referring to Jewish returns to the Land of Israel after the Babylonian Exile, and a third wave consisting of modern Jewish settlement. During the 1920s, Labor Zionists divided the modern settlement period in half, deeming the First Aliyah as incapable of bringing about national rebirth in contrast to the Second Aliyah, of which they were a part, which had the idealism and drive to fulfill Zionism's promise. The relationship between the Second and First Aliyah was like that between the New and Old Testaments in Christian theology: the former fulfilled the potential of the latter and, in so doing, supplanted it.[62]

Transformative Zionism sought to overcome the wounds inflicted on the Jews, and those that Jews had inflicted on themselves, over millennia of exile from the Land of Israel. Its project to "overcome" the diaspora (*lishlol et ha-golah*) was popular in the diaspora and the Yishuv alike. Although less than 5 percent of the Yishuv's population lived on collective agricultural settlements (*kibbutzim*), they became the hallmark of Labor Zionism. Diaspora Jewish youth were drawn to movements that trained them for emigration and life on the soil. The *sabra*, the plainspoken, rough-hewn but good-hearted native-born Israeli, was as much a cultural icon in the diaspora as in Israel itself. In Israel, the military assumed paramount value for defending the nation and molding a new generation of confident and courageous Jews. Diaspora Jews, in turn, derived vicarious pleasure from the triumphs of the Israeli armed forces and the sight of Jews in uniform, service weapons slung over their shoulders.

Transformative Zionism declined in Israel before it did in the diaspora. The austere and egalitarian economic values of Labor Zionism were already under attack by the 1960s, as Israelis longed for the comforts of the affluent Western countries with which they identified. The overthrow of Labor hegemony in 1977, the installation of the Likud in power, and economic crises in the mid-1980s inflicted severe blows on the national trade union (the Histadrut) and the kibbutz movements. In the 1990s and 2000s, the Israeli economy boomed, and high tech became its leading sector. In 2010, Israel became a member of the Organization for Economic Co-operation and Development (OECD), a consortium of the world's wealthiest countries, and in 2021 its per capita gross domestic product was higher than that of the United Kingdom or France. As Israeli society grew more prosperous it also became more materialist, individualist, and inequitable, with one of the highest levels of income inequality in the OECD. The decline of Israeli Transformative Zionism was not limited to its Labor variant; the civic virtue and nobility of character that

Jabotinsky considered to be the hallmarks of Revisionist Zionism were notably lacking in twenty-first-century Israeli politics.

Diaspora Jews have been slow to abandon Transformative Zionism, because there is great romantic power in the notion of *aliyah* as a sea change. But in our own day, to the extent that diaspora Jews move to Israel, they maintain their previous lifestyles. They do not Hebraize their names, as was done in the past, or seek to reinvent themselves as children of the land. Jewish tourists in Israel find much to marvel at, and even the sight of a soda can with Hebrew lettering can be inspirational for youth visiting from abroad. The IDF remains a source of admiration and fascination. Jewish tourists often compare Israeli society favorably with their own. But the visitors are spectators, not participants, and few form lasting bonds with the country.

Ethnic Zionism is a form of Jewish nationalism that invokes the Land of Israel more as a symbol of collective identity than a sacred object or homeland. It is a means of making oneself feel at home in, rather than estranged from, a diaspora homeland. Ethnic Zionism's origins lay in the multinational atmosphere of fin de siècle Central Europe, where Jewish distinctiveness was taken for granted by many people, Jews and Gentiles alike. In pre-1914 Galicia, attachment to Zionism could as easily entail a cultivation of Yiddish as Hebraic culture, and an assertion of rights as a national minority as much as yearning to emigrate to the Land of Israel.[63] Zionism's origins in Turkey were similarly explorations of new, secular forms of Jewish collective belonging.[64] In interwar Czechoslovakia, Jews identified as Zionists to demonstrate that they were not ethnic Germans, who were seen as the most formidable obstacle to the consolidation and stability of the new state.[65] During the same period, Ethnic Zionism in the United States often manifested in a mild sense of Jewish peoplehood, akin to the forms of nineteenth-century Jewish solidarity discussed earlier. In Poland, however, where Polish nationalism was fierce and frequently hostile to non-Polish minorities such as Jews and Ukrainians,

Ethnic Zionism was no less strident. Polish Jews were particularly receptive to Jabotinsky, whose slogan "every man a king" restored Jewish pride on both the individual and collective levels.[66]

In the post-1948 United States, Ethnic Zionism has provided a means of displaying particularity without the awkwardness of presenting oneself as a hyphenated American. Back in the 1920s, Supreme Court Justice Louis Brandeis equated Zionism with American political values, and until the early twenty-first century most Americans saw Israel as a model democracy, a scion of the United States itself. Therefore, a Jew could claim that embracing Israel automatically entailed an embrace of America.[67] After the 1967 war, this sentiment intensified due to a concurrent strengthening of U.S.–Israeli relations and the diplomatic isolation of Israel by much of the international community. Ethnic Zionism was also influenced by the growth of the Black, feminist, Hispanic, and Indigenous identarian movements during the 1960s and early 1970s.

In recent decades, Ethnic Zionism has been characterized by tourism to Israel (particularly the Birthright program that provides cost-free, structured trips for Jewish youth), the branding of Middle Eastern food as "Israeli" and serving it at Jewish social gatherings, and the consumption of Israeli television programs, films, and music.[68] The use of Hebrew words and phrases in Jewish summer camps, which a team of sociologists terms "Hebrew infusion," is designed to inculcate Jewish identity.[69] In all these forms of Ethnic Zionism, connections with Israel are manifold and essential, but its ultimate beneficiaries are diaspora Jews themselves.

Ethnic Zionism assumes a different appearance in the state of Israel, where "Israeli" takes the place of "Zionist" as a statement of collective Jewish ethnonational identity. Using the word "Israeli" in this way overlooks the fact that one-quarter of the state's citizens, and half of all those who live under Israeli control, are not Jewish. It both illustrates the dominance of Jews in Israeli society and leaves room for Israeli Jewish subethnicities, such as Ashkenazim, Sephardim (in the precise sense of Jews of Iberian origin), or Jews of Middle Eastern, North African, or Ethiopian origin. In contrast, when Israeli Jews use the word "Zionist," it indicates nationalistic pride, patriotism, or allegiance to values claimed to be in the best interests of Israel's Jewish citizens. In 2016, approximately three-fourths of Israeli Jews agreed that the word described them very or somewhat accurately.[70] The term has been used by both advocates and opponents of settlement in the West Bank, and between 2014 and 2019 a coalition of Israeli center-left parties was known as the "Zionist Camp."

Natan Sharansky, who was imprisoned in the former Soviet Union for Jewish activism before becoming a major political figure in Israel, has written that "our strongest glue is our Judaism, whether it be understood as a nationality, a faith, a response to antisemitism, or peoplehood."[71] By "Judaism" he means Jewishness (*yahadut* in Hebrew), which he defines in multiple ways but primarily as ethnonational; he also presents antisemitism as a centripetal force maintaining Jewish identity. In doing so, Sharansky continues in a long Zionist tradition, dating back to Herzl, who, on different occasions over the course of a few months in 1895, defined Jews in terms of religion, race, historical experience, and historical consciousness. "The only thing by which we still recognize our kinship is the faith of our fathers" was countered by a claim that Jewishness had "nothing to do with religion" and that Jews were "of the same race." Elsewhere he wrote of Jews as a "historical unit, a nation with anthropological diversities. . . . No nation has uniformity of race." Finally, in 1896 Herzl came up with a definition that he retained for the rest of his brief life and that has implicitly been employed by the Zionist project ever since. Rather than dwell on Jewishness as a state of mind or system of belief, he proposed "a quite moderate definition of nationhood. . . . We are a historical group of people who clearly belong together and are held together by a common foe. That is what we are, whether we deny it or not, whether we know it or not, and whether we desire it or not."[72]

Sacral Zionism is a belief that the Land of Israel is both sacred and sanctifying but that it and the Jewish people as a whole require the institutions of modern statehood. It has been most prominent among modern Orthodox Jews—those who strictly observe Jewish law but also embrace many aspects of secular culture. Historically, many *haredim* or ultra-Orthodox Jews rejected Zionism as blasphemous, hubristic, and imitative of Gentile nationalisms. Ultra-Orthodoxy's relationship with Zionism, however, was always complicated, with strident rejection being less common than subdued enthusiasm or conditional support. In the diaspora, a variant of Sacral Zionism has flourished in the Reform, Conservative, and Reconstructionist denominations of Judaism, for which Israel is not only the national home of the Jewish people but also a source of personal, spiritual elevation and a vehicle for the betterment of all humanity. In a different vein, since the 1980s American evangelical Protestants have proclaimed the state of Israel to be a divine instrument, enabling the settlement of Jews in the Holy Land that is a precursor to the Second Coming of Christ.

Sacral Zionism can be divided into two forms: *halakhic* and *messianic*. Halakhic Zionism refers to the integration of religious observance with acceptance of the principles of modern Jewish nationalism. This approach was taken by supporters of the first Jewish agricultural colonies in the late 1870s and early 1880s. In 1902, it was institutionalized with the founding of a Religious Zionist faction within the ZO known as Mizrahi, a portmanteau of *merkaz ruhani* (spiritual center).[73] For Mizrahi, as for Jews who moved to Palestine during the nineteenth century, there was a particular sanctifying value in performing those rabbinic commandments, such as tithing, that could only be fulfilled in the Land of Israel. Mizrahi also sought to ensure that the growing Jewish community in the Land of Israel would adhere to rabbinic law as much as possible. In 1935, it won two major concessions from the Jewish Agency Executive, which was the Zionist movement's proto-government: the rabbinate could control matters of personal status such as marriage, divorce, and burial, and Zionist public institutions would honor the sabbath and kosher dietary laws. A similar agreement was made twelve years later, on the eve of the UN decision to partition Palestine into Jewish and Arab states, with the ultra-Orthodox, non-Zionist political party Agudat Yisrael.[74] Orthodox political parties would have demanded the same in a Jewish state in any location in the world, because they would have felt empowered to demand a level of influence denied to them in typical diasporic circumstances.

The second form of sacral Zionism is messianic. Arthur Hertzberg claimed that all forms of Zionism derived from "the messianic impulse and emotions of the Jewish tradition."[75] Precisely because this concept purports to explain everything, however, it explains nothing. All modern political movements (except bona-fide conservatism) can be said to be messianic if defined in terms of bringing about the improvement of the world. Sacral Zionism's messianism is more specific, limited at first to marginal figures like Alkalai and Kalischer in the mid- nineteenth century. During the interwar period, Abraham Isaac Kook, the first Chief Ashkenazic Rabbi of Mandatory Palestine, saw the economic and political labors of secular Zionists as paving the way for the Jews' messianic deliverance.[76] When Israel was established, the official prayer for the state, collectively composed by the Chief Ashkenazic and Sephardic Rabbis and the celebrated author S. Y. Agnon, cautiously described the state as "the beginning of the flowering of our redemption" (*reshit tsemihat ge'ulateinu*). In the wake of the 1967 Arab–Israeli war, with the conquest of the ancient biblical heartland of the West Bank and the Old City of Jerusalem, messianic Zionism became a major political force. The 1970s and 1980s were the heyday of the messianic settler movement, epitomized by the Gush Emunim (bloc of the faithful), led by disciples of Kook's son, Zvi Yehuda Kook.[77] Like the secular socialist idealism of Zionist pioneers from the early twentieth century, messianic Zionism has proven difficult to maintain over time. It has largely been replaced by a more common amalgam of religiosity with Zionism, to which we turn next.

Judaic Zionism is a fierce attachment to both the Land of Israel and the Jewish people, justified in terms of theological concepts, miraculous origin stories, and a sacred canon. On the surface, it resembles Sacral Zionism, but its essence is different. Its focus is neither the observance of ritual law nor the expectation of the Messiah but rather the location of theological meaning in the state and its armed forces.[78] During Israel's 2022 elections, Judaic Zionism was embodied by the alliance of a hawkish religious-Zionist party with the Jewish Power party, which was grounded in xenophobic and irredentist ethno-nationalism.

Judaic Zionism's raison d'être is Jewish spiritual uniqueness, and it distances itself from other nationalisms, even though it borrows heavily from the conceptual armory of secular Zionism. During the interwar period, a critical mass of Orthodox and even ultra-Orthodox Jews in the Yishuv esteemed the value of productive work and formed parallel organizations to those of the Labor Zionist mainstream. In 1948, Orthodox Jews searching for the God who had hidden His countenance (*hester panim*) during the Holocaust saw Israel's military victory as miraculous. This miracle, however, required human agency and had little to do with the theological passivity that had shaped traditional Jewish thought. In 1956, when Israel entered the Sinai Peninsula during a brief war with Egypt, the Israel Defense Forces' chief rabbi, Shlomo Goren, spoke ecstatically of the mutually symbiotic "spirit of Judaism and the machine gun."[79]

A famous sermon from Israel's Independence Day in 1956, "The Voice of My Beloved Knocks," by the eminent modern Orthodox American rabbi Joseph Ber Soloveitchik, epitomizes Judaic Zionism. The title, which comes from the biblical Song of Songs, is echoed in a section of the sermon where Soloveitchik speaks of the beloved knocking six times. Each "knock" is an earthly, material manifestation of the divine, a source of joy and pride, with no otherworldly or messianic goal in sight. Soloveitchik celebrates Israel's provision of a safe haven to persecuted Jews, its military victories and prowess, its gravitational power to attract wayward, assimilating Jews back to their faith, and its proof to Gentiles both that God has not abandoned the Jews and that Jewish blood "is not free for the taking."[80] A decade after this sermon, another one, delivered by the equally eminent Orthodox rabbi, Norman Lamm, spoke more directly about Judaism's messianic aims but was careful not to link the current State of Israel with redemption. Lamm demanded that his public recognize that they live in exile and would benefit from aliyah because Israel offers not only "greater opportunity for the practice of Judaism" but also "more *Yiddishkeit*" (Jewishness, broadly understood) "than any place else in the world."[81]

In the contemporary diaspora, Judaic Zionism is the dominant motif in many Orthodox day schools, where children are taught to love Israel and the Hebrew language and to consider the land as their—and only their—patrimony. Post-high school gap year programs in Israel strengthen these bonds, and most emigration of Jews from Western countries to Israel comes from the Orthodox community. Judaic Zionism generates a desire more for a life among Jews in an environment suffused with feelings of belonging than the fulfillment of halakhic requirements or the expectation of messianic deliverance. These feelings characterize the vast majority of modern Orthodox Jews in Israel, even those who live in West Bank settlements.

———•———

Not all forms of Israeli Jewish national identity can be classified within Zionist categories. The Young Hebrew or "Canaanite" movement of the 1950s championed an anti-Zionist Israeli nationalism that rejected any relationship with the Jewish religion or the Jewish diaspora. The historian Adya Gur-Horon and the poet Yonathan Ratosh envisioned ancient Israel as the center of a great Mediterranean civilization and called on modern Israel to restore the region to its pre-Judaic and pre-Islamic glory.[82] A more modest and pragmatic rejection of Zionism by Israeli nationalists came in the form of "Post-Zionism," a term first used in 1947 by Rabbi Abraham Isaac Kook's nephew Hillel Kook, who was active in Revisionist Zionist circles in the United States. Just after the UN vote to partition Palestine into a Jewish and Arab state, Kook wrote that in the future the Jewish state would chart its own course, independent from diaspora Jewry. Jews who wished to remain outside the Jewish state were free to do so, but Israel would have no obligations to them. Another Revisionist Zionist, Vladimir Jabotinsky's son Eri, used the term "Post-Zionist" in 1952 in a similar vein.[83]

In the 1970s and 1980s, Post-Zionism began to assume a different meaning, associated with liberal universalism and the rejection of Israeli nationalism. This variety of Post-Zionism was popular among some Israeli intellectuals and journalists during the 1990s, when the Oslo peace process appeared to promise a resolution of the Israeli–Palestinian conflict and the full integration of Israel into a post–Cold War, liberal, and democratic world order. This optimistic and universalistic form of Post-Zionism did not, however, survive the Second Palestinian Intifada (2000–2005), during which Israeli politics lurched strongly to the right.

Whether nationalist or universalist, Post-Zionism was secular. A far more popular form of non-Zionist Israeli identity is religious. According to a 2016 Pew survey, about one-third of ultra-Orthodox Jews in Israel self-identify as Zionist. A small minority of Israel's ultra-Orthodox Jews reject the state out of hand as an abomination and see themselves as living on the holy soil of the Land of Israel, protecting it by their very presence from desecration by a secular state. Most ultra-Orthodox Jews veer more toward non-Zionism than anti-Zionism, and their views on the State of Israel are complex and even contradictory. According to a 2020 survey, although the overwhelming majority of ultra-Orthodox Jews reject the authority of Israeli state institutions, 70 percent have a sense of belonging in Israel, and more than half feel "part of the state and its successes and failures."[84] Such individuals do not attribute sacral meaning to the state as do most national-religious Jews, but they appreciate the state's support for their religious institutions and its mastery over the biblical heartland of the West Bank and the Old City of Jerusalem. (The two largest Jewish settlements in the West Bank, with more than one-sixth of the total number of settlers in the territory, are ultra-Orthodox enclaves.)

Even more removed from state veneration are religious extremists who would like to rebuild the ancient Temple on the current site of the Dome of the Rock. Ultra-Orthodox non-Zionism, however, does not always veer toward the right. Rabbi Menachem Froman of the West Bank settlement of Tekoa combined messianism, disinterest in the state of Israel, and an openness toward Jews and Arabs living side by side within the entirety of the Land of Israel, within a single state or two, and united by a common Judeo-Islamic spirit.[85]

Conclusion

The eight types of Zionism laid out here all correspond with varieties of nationalism throughout the modern world. Nationalist movements cherish language, aspire to statehood, attract diaspora support, and hope to restore honor to a humiliated people. They are as likely to embrace religion as an essential national characteristic as to reject it as a relic of an oppressive past. The ideal Torah state of Sacral Zionism has much in common with Islamicist nationalisms, both Sunni (Hamas in the Palestinian territories) and Shiite (the Islamic Republic of Iran).

Any nationalism has distinct features, but Zionism's differences are different. Leaving aside the diaspora of Israeli Jews in North America and Europe, diaspora Jews are not immigrants or the descendants of immigrants from the Jewish state. The relationship between Jews worldwide and Israel cannot be easily compared with that of, say, Irish Americans and the Irish Republic, or Tamil Canadians and Sri Lanka. Moreover, although immigrant communities such as Irish or Italian Americans have historically been targets of ridicule and fear, antisemitic accusations of Jewish "dual loyalty" and of allegiances to Israel that clash with their obligations to their land of citizenship have been more persistent and malign. At the same time, diaspora Jewish bonds with Israel are particularly visible, enduring, and institutionalized. Many ethnic groups have

heritage schools, engage in homeland tourism, and support the homeland economically and politically, but Zionist education, philanthropy,
and political engagement operate at unprecedented and unparalleled
levels of activity.

The reason for this is not mysterious. The Zionist project faced the
challenge of having to create the preconditions for its very existence.
It constructed a state in a territory whose population in the early twentieth century was overwhelmingly Arab. Even if the territory had been
empty, Zionists would have encountered vast technical challenges in
absorbing mass immigration and constructing state institutions and a
national economy. But it was not empty, and the clash between Jews and
Palestinians, and by extension with much of the Arab and Muslim world,
became the leitmotif of the Zionist project.

The Israeli-Palestinian conflict frames or underlies political debate in
the state of Israel. In the same way, academic writing about Zionism is
dominated by questions of Zionism's original intentions toward the Palestinians, its responsibility for the dispossession of Palestinians in 1948,
and its colonization of Palestinian land—both within the State of Israel
and in the territories captured in 1967. We now turn to these questions.

PART II

STATE OF THE QUESTION

2   *Zionism as Colonialism*

Presenting Zionism as a form of nationalism is not particularly controversial. Staunch Zionists celebrate the connection. The neoconservative thinker Yarom Hazony's book from 2018, *The Virtue of Nationalism*, is a paean to ethnoreligious particularisms, of which he considers Zionism to be a shining example.[1] Zionism's critics, in contrast, tend to be skeptical of nationalism, and they see Zionism as a form of racist and atavistic tribalism.

There is a deep divide, however, between scholars who do and do not conceive of Zionism as a variety of colonialism. Debates about virtually every aspect of the history of Zionism and Israel boil down to clashing conceptions of the essence of the Zionist project—whether it has been one of homecoming and seeking asylum or one of colonial settlement and expropriation. Two key questions run through the debate over Zionism and colonialism. First, is Zionism inherently inclusive or separatist, open to the coterminous exercise of Jewish and Arab self-determination within historic Palestine, or determined to drive the indigenous Palestinians out of the land? And second, has Israel been willing to integrate into the Arab Middle East, or is it determined to dwell in isolation, buttressed by alliances and cultural ties with Western powers?

Palestinian characterizations of Zionism as a form of European colonialism date to the 1920s. For the Palestine Liberation Organization (PLO), founded in Cairo in 1964, the equation of Zionism with colonialism was of the utmost significance, so much so that the first in a series of pamphlets by its Research Center in Beirut was titled *Zionist Colonialism in Palestine*. The pamphlet, authored by the center's founder Fayez Sayegh, asserted that Zionism was not only a product but also the epitome of European colonialism. Characterized by virulent racism, xenophobia, and territorial ambition, Zionism, "unlike European colonization elsewhere," was "incompatible with the continued existence of the 'native population' in the coveted country."[2]

During the 1960s, associations between Zionism and colonialism gained global currency. As early as 1962, within the committees and General Assembly of the United Nations, the Soviet Union and Afro-Asian states linked Zionism with racism, apartheid, and colonialism. In the United States, protests against the Vietnam War and for African American civil rights escalated into radical movements for social change in which Israel was seen as a tool of U.S. imperialism and a mirror of American racism. The 1967 and 1973 Arab–Israeli wars, as well as Israel's alliance with apartheid South Africa, accelerated this trend. In December 1973, the General Assembly condemned "the unholy alliance between Portuguese colonialism [in Mozambique], South African racism, zionism [sic], and Israeli imperialism." Feminist movements of the era had a similar penchant for radical critique of Israel. In June and July 1975, at the UN's conference for International Women's Year in Mexico City, Third World and Eastern Bloc representatives called for an end to "imperialism, neocolonialism, racism, apartheid, and Zionism." Four months later, the General Assembly incorporated this wording into Resolution 3379, which also declared Zionism to be a form of "racism and racial discrimination."[3]

A more nuanced, academic analysis of Zionism and colonialism developed alongside political polemics. In 1973 the French Jewish scholar Maxim Rodinson published a short and influential book titled *Israel: A Colonial-Settler State?* In 1979 Edward W. Said's canonical article, "Zionism from the Standpoint of Its Victims," brought nuance, theoretical ballast, and elegance of expression to the Palestinian critique of Zionism, thereby bringing it to a global academic audience.[4] In many ways, the debate about Zionism and colonialism still operates within the terms that Said established. He began by summing up the European colonial project of the fin de siècle:

Imperialism was the theory, colonialism the practice, of changing
the uselessly unoccupied territories of the world into useful new versions of the European metropolitan society. Everything in those territories that suggested waste, disorder, uncounted resources was to
be converted into productivity, order, taxable, and potentially developed wealth. You get rid of the most offending human and animal
blight . . . you confine the rest to reservations, compounds, native
homelands, where you can count, tax, use them profitably, and you
build a new society on the vacant space. . . . These then are the gross
points that must be made about the connections between Zionism
and European imperialism or colonialism.⁵

Said then noted how in every respect Zionism followed a European colonial model. It sought or formed alliances with the Western Great Powers. It considered the natives to be backward and claimed they would in
time be grateful for Zionist developmental largesse. It dismissed native
resistance as the product of primitive passion or elite manipulation and
refused to see the natives as a national community with desires and rights
of its own. The institutions developed by Zionists in pre-1948 Palestine
emphasized political, economic, and social separation between Jews and
Arabs.

By this line of reasoning, all aspects of post-1948 Israel's treatment of
Palestinians fall into a colonial mold. The logic goes as follows: The 1948
and 1967 wars led to the expulsions or forced flight of a million Palestinians and varying levels of oppression of those who remained under Israeli
rule, be they citizens of the State of Israel or residents of the Occupied
Territories. The Palestinians are exploited for their labor, their lands and
homes have been expropriated by the state, and millions of Israeli Jews
live on formerly Palestinian-owned land. The limited autonomy that
the Oslo Accords of 1993 and 1995 granted to most Palestinians within the
Occupied Territories is itself a form of colonial control. Israel's trampling

of Palestinian rights is enabled by the United States, which Israel assists in its striving for geopolitical hegemony in the Middle East. In short, Israel is a settler-colonial state, and Zionism, which justifies the state's existence and actions, is a settler-colonialist ideology.

Settler colonialism is the movement of people from one territory to another, the creation by the newcomers of permanent settlements, and the expropriation or elimination of the native population. This process may or may not be sponsored by the immigrants' state of origin. The historian Lorenzo Veracini differentiates colonial environments, in which immigrants maintain separation from natives but exploit their labor, from settler-colonial environments in which the newcomers expel the natives altogether and assert an identity as true children of the land.[6] Veracini and many scholars in history, sociology, and anthropology have identified Israel as a settler-colonial state.[7] Since its founding in 2011, the online journal *Settler Colonial Societies* has devoted three special issues and numerous standalone articles to Israel/Palestine.[8] The settler-colonial paradigm features prominently in Palestinian scholarship on the history and current situation of Palestinians in the Occupied Territories.[9]

Not all critics of Zionism cleave to Veracini's distinction between colonialism and settler colonialism. Instead, the adjective "colonial" frequently appears in writing about Israel as a blanket pejorative and synonym for oppression. This chapter seeks to correct the imprecise use of this heavily fraught term. A critique of Zionist attitudes and Israeli practices can be factually correct while mistakenly conflating attitudes such as condescension or disregard, as well as actions such as expropriation, exploitation, and expulsion with the particular, time-specific practice of modern Western colonialism. Placing Zionism within the broad sweep of Western colonialism leaves unexplained many of its key aspects, such as the nature of Zionism's connection with historic Palestine.

A nation can engage in both settler-colonial and anticolonial practices. The eminent South African historian Hermann Giliomee describe the Afrikaners as "a colonized people and colonizers themselves" and as "anti-colonial freedom fighters" who became a global pariah, "the polecat of the world."[10] Anticoloniality is not the same as the struggle of an Indigenous people to free itself from an external oppressor, because Afrikaners, like a substantial majority of Jewish immigrants to late Ottoman and Mandate Palestine, had European roots and considered themselves to be both rooted in the land and tied to Western culture. That said, neither Afrikaners nor pre-1948 Zionists identified as scions of the colonizing power—unlike eighteenth-century American revolutionaries, who claimed both to be a new breed and fighters for the rights of true Englishmen.[11]

One final introductory point: Zionism and Israel are not identical. Zionism is a nationalist project that originated almost 150 years ago and whose relationship with colonialism is as variegated as the subforms that we examined in the last chapter. Linkages between policies of the Israeli state and colonialism are more clear-cut, but we need to determine, rather than merely assert, that these policies were formulated in the name of Zionism and what Zionism has meant to Israelis in positions of power.

Zionisms and Arabs

Zionism first arose in Eastern and Central Europe among Jews for whom Zion was a spiritual and cultural ideal. The early members of Hovevei Tsion were aware that Palestine was overwhelmingly Arab, and they had differing views about how Jews and Arabs could or should live together. The Hebrew writer Moshe Leib Lilienblum exuded concern for his fellow Jews and attachment to the Land of Israel but displayed no ill intent toward Palestine's Arabs. In essays from 1883 and 1884, Lilienblum evoked Jews' unassailable historic right to the land, as well as the economic advantages for all of living in a space that bridged three continents and was in need of agricultural and industrial development. (Such a statement is not necessarily colonial; during the second half of the nineteenth century Ottoman administrators were keen to improve Palestine's economic productivity.[12]) Palestine's Arabs, Lilienblum wrote, "acknowledge that Israel's right to the land of its fathers has not passed—this news is the best assurance for our future."[13]

In contrast, Lilienblum's contemporary Isaac Rülf, the chief rabbi of Memel, had a much harsher approach. He averred that Jews must "aspire, in whatever form and by whatever means, to regain our original homeland, the land of our fathers, and re-create the Jewish state." He asserted that the Jewish claim to the land was not merely historic but also was that of "the rights of the conquerors."[14] Rülf made his intentions toward Palestine's Arab crystal clear: "At this point we speak of settlement and only settlement. That is our immediate goal. We speak of it and only of it. But clearly, 'England is for the English, Egypt for the Egyptians and Judea is for the Jews.' In our land there is room for us. We will say to the Arabs: move on! If they do not agree, if they oppose with force—we will force them to move. We will smite them upon their heads, and we will force them to move."[15]

Each of the forms of Zionism discussed in the previous chapter has had the potential to embrace or reject the Arab Middle East. Each could accept or distance itself from colonial mentalities and practices. The Hebraic Zionism of Ahad Ha-Am was noncolonial in that it condemned Jewish sovereign authority in Palestine and displayed little interest in improving the lot of the natives in a Western paternalistic fashion. Yet a passion for Hebraic culture and hawkish political views could easily coexist, as was the case for Joseph Klausner, a scholar of Jewish history and Hebrew literature who during the interwar period was a committed Revisionist Zionist. Shortly after the 1967 war, pillars of the Hebrew literary establishment, such as Nathan Alterman, Shmuel Yosef Agnon, and Moshe Shamir, signed the "Manifesto of the Movement for a Greater Israel," which advocated Israeli settlement in the recently conquered territories.

Philanthropic Zionism can defer to the state on geopolitical issues and uncritically toe the government line. But during the interwar period, Hadassah (the Women's Zionist Organization of America) preached a humanitarian Zionism that emphasized Arab–Jewish interaction (e.g., on Hadassah-funded playgrounds) and provided medical care to both Jews and Arabs. Hadassah's head, Henrietta Szold, was an outspoken binationalist, although the Hadassah rank and file did not embrace her views.[16] To be sure, Szold's binationalism assumed a Zionist "civilizing mission" in Palestine, but it was a mission for the benefit of Jews and Arabs alike.

In its first decades, the Labor stream within Transformative Zionism supported Jewish settlement throughout the Land of Israel, but in the wake of the 1967 war, it called for territorial compromise so that Jews would not rule over the Palestinians. Labor Zionism traditionally presented itself as less likely than Revisionists to employ force against Palestinians, but in fact there was a spectrum of opinions within Labor. One of the first Labor parties, Ha-Po'el Ha-Tsa'ir (The Young Worker), was moderate on Arab issues, whereas the post-1948 party known as Ahdut Ha-Avodah (Unity of Labor), was more militant and committed to territorial expansion. Under the British Mandate, the kibbutz movement and party Ha-Shomer Ha-Tsa'ir (The Young Guard) was committed to socialism and binationalism, yet it justified its kibbutzim's expropriation of lands claimed by Arab villages with the argument that these acquisitions would strengthen the kibbutzim, thereby allowing them to lead the struggle for equal rights for Arabs and Jews alike.[17]

Of all the varieties of Zionism discussed in the first chapter, Statist Zionism is most clearly linked with colonialism because of the alliances its leaders sought with the West's Great Powers (see figure 2). At the turn of the nineteenth century, Theodor Herzl urged Britain or Germany to declare a Jewish protectorate in Palestine. During World War I, Chaim Weizmann and Nahum Sokolow played Britain and France against each

Figure 2 Postcard commemorating the German Emperor Wilhelm II's visit to Palestine in 1898. The Dome of the Rock, an Islamic shrine, is identified as "the Temple of Jerusalem." Sent by Theodor Herzl, who met the Kaiser during the visit, to Herzl's daughter Pauline. The message reads, "30 October 1898/My good Pauline, your loyal father hugs you tenderly/in Jerusalem." *Credit*: National Library of Israel.

other, eventually securing assurances from the British foreign secretary, Arthur James Balfour, that Britain would promote a Jewish national home in Palestine.

During the thirty years that Britain controlled Palestine (1918–1948)—mostly under a formal mandate from the League of Nations—Britain found in Jews a useful source of what Scott Atran has called "surrogate colonization."[18] In an era when Wilsonian concepts of national self-determination put older forms of settler colonialism in a bad light, Britain could benefit from the presence of Jews, whom they considered more advanced and better able to develop and secure the land than Arabs. Although British support for the Jewish national home waxed and waned over time, Britain benefited the Yishuv by providing infrastructural investment, military protection, and permission for the Zionists to build up proto-governmental institutions, including a militia.

Israel could not have defeated the Palestinians and neighboring Arab states during the 1948 war without diplomatic and material support from the United States, France, and the Soviet Union. In 1956 Israel colluded with two declining colonial powers, Britain and France, in a brief war against Egypt; after the war France became Israel's chief military supplier for a decade. Since 1967, the United States has been Israel's patron, providing more aid to Israel than it does to any other country, assuring that Israel maintains a strategic edge in the region. Despite some presidential administrations' mild and ineffectual protests, the United States has not stood in the way of Israel's ongoing control over and settlement of the West Bank (including East Jerusalem) and the Golan Heights.

As is explored in depth in Chapter 5, the Zionist project has always depended on the Great Powers. Dependence alone, however, does not make Zionism colonial. Anticolonial movements and postcolonial states have often relied on patron states to supply them with diplomatic support, military training, and armaments. During the decade after the end of World War II, China and the former USSR supported the Viet Minh's struggle against France in Indochina, and these superpowers did the same for North Vietnam in its war against the United States during in the 1960s and 1970s. Similarly, members of the Arab League helped fund Algeria's National Liberation Front during its war against France between 1954 and 1962.[19] The post-1945 world, moreover, cannot be divided neatly between Western states that always supported Zionism and Israel and non-Western ones that always took the side of the Palestinians. For example, without the Soviet Union's diplomatic backing and approval of arms transfers from Czechoslovakia, Israel may well have failed to defeat the Arab states in 1948.

By 1950 Israel was seated at the United Nations and recognized by some fifty states from every region of the world. Israel failed to secure an invitation to the conference of newly independent Asian and African states at Bandung, Indonesia, in 1955, but three years later it began a program of development work in sub-Saharan Africa that was a public relations success. It won the country an image as a model of postcolonial state-building, and leaders of national liberation movements and postcolonial states displayed flashes of sympathy for Israel along with solidarity with the Palestinians. Heads of new African states praised Israel for what they described as its successful resistance against the greatest colonial power before World War II, the United Kingdom. This positive image traversed the Sahara and spread to the Maghreb. During the 1950s Tunisian intellectuals saw in Israel a counter to the growing power of Gamel Abdel Nasser's Egypt over North Africa. The Egyptian Jewish writer Jacqueline Kahanoff wrote of a young Algerian who called himself Khalil and rented a room in Kahanoff's parents' home in Cairo during the mid-1950s. The lodger endorsed the Zionist claim to statehood, admired Labor Zionism for its institutions and Menachem Begin for his stand against colonial oppression, and saw Israel as a model for economic development. "Khalil" was in fact Ahmed Ben Bella, a leader of the National Liberation Front and the first president of independent Algeria.[20]

Zionism's strongest links with colonialism lie in attitudes and practices toward Palestine and the Palestinians. Zionism originated in opposition to Europe yet retained notions of European civilizational superiority. Zionism sought to remove Jews from countries where they were disparaged and persecuted, but animosity toward antisemites did not keep European Zionists from considering themselves to be part of European culture. Theodor Herzl called Europe "militarized and seedy," but he also promised that a Jewish state would be a "rampart of Europe against Asia, an outpost of civilization as opposed to barbarism." The state would boast all the amenities of Europe—"salted breadsticks, coffee, beer, familiar meats"—and the opera.[21] In Herzl's novel *Altneuland*, the only Arab character, Rashid Bey, was educated in Germany and is immensely grateful to the Zionists for lifting his people out of their Oriental torpor. Zionist settlers had faith in Western technology to revive a once-fertile land, which they saw as having been desertified. The first settlers of the 1880s disparaged local agricultural technology and insisted on using heavy European plows, even though they were ineffective in the light Palestinian soil.[22]

This *mission civilisatrice* became part of the warp and woof of twentieth-century Zionism, which displayed both compassion and condescension toward the natives. At the turn of the century, radical Labor Zionist youth, recently arrived from Russia, fretted about the veteran settlers' close economic relations with Arab workers, whom the Eastern European immigrants thought to be primitive and backward. A desire for cultural separation was manifest in the project to build the city of Tel Aviv, which was founded in 1909 as a suburb of Jaffa. As the city grew during the Mandate period, its population was almost entirely Jewish. Although Tel Aviv's residents spoke several languages—English when dealing with the government, a variety of Jewish vernaculars at home— Zionist leaders strove to make Hebrew its lingua franca. During the 1930s, its architecture changed from an eclectic style with Orientalist motifs to a Western, modernist "Internationalism" inspired by the German Bauhaus school.[23]

Nonetheless, during the late Ottoman and Mandate periods, there were many points of contact between Jews and Arabs in Palestine— through business dealings, social interaction in mixed cities such as Jerusalem and Jaffa, visits to sites holy to Jews and Muslims alike, and attendance at public events, such as the annual Purim parade in Tel Aviv. As Menachem Klein has shown, some Jews attended Arab schools, and there were intermarriages between elite Jewish women and elite Palestinian men.[24] Tami Raz has uncovered evidence of hundreds of intercommunal romantic relationships between Jews and Arabs of more humble backgrounds, living on the seam between Tel Aviv and Jaffa.[25]

Until the 1920s the majority of Palestine's Jewish population was of Middle Eastern origin. Some had roots in Palestine dating back many generations, and others were recent immigrants, particularly from Syria and Yemen. Was an Arabic-speaking Jew from Damascus less of a "settler" than one from Pinsk? Did the possession of Arabic as a mother tongue and ancestry in the Arab world make one an "Arab Jew," intimately tied to the land and its majority population in a way that European Jewish immigrants could not be? In his provocative book *The Arab Jew*, published in Hebrew in 2003 and in English three years later, Yehouda Shenhav answers unequivocally in the affirmative. In his view, Arab Jews were natives to the Middle East and had long been victimized by the Ashkenazic-dominated Zionist movement.[26]

Shenhav's arguments were refined and nuanced in subsequent work by Abigail Jacobson and Moshe Naor, who trace the struggles in Mandate Palestine of elite Afro-Asian Jews for political power. (Jacobson and Naor call these Jews "oriental," a direct translation of the Hebrew word *Mizrahi* (eastern), which has become the most common term in Israel to describe Afro-Asian Jews. (It should not be confused with the national-religious organization Mizrahi that, as we mentioned in the previous chapter, was a portmanteau for *merkaz ruhani*, or spiritual center.) Claiming that nativity and intimate knowledge of Arab ways went hand in hand, Mizrahi Jews presented themselves as the most effective mediators between European newcomers and Palestinian Arabs and as inherently more conciliatory than their Ashkenazic counterparts. Such self-presentations may well, however, have been forms of positioning and status-seeking. Depicting Mandate Palestine's Jewish population as divided between aggressive Ashkenazim and pacific Mizrahim is grossly inaccurate. As Jacobson and Naor note, Iraqi immigrants to Palestine, like Ezra Meni and Avraham Sharoni, used their Arabic-language skills to work for the intelligence services of the prestate Jewish militias.[27] In general, Mizrahi Jews in Mandate Palestine were no less likely to espouse Statist Zionism than their Ashkenazic counterparts. As Yuval Evri and Hagar Kotef argue, in pre-1948 Palestine, Zionist ideology both allowed for Ashkenazic-Jewish immigrants to imagine themselves as natives and for Oriental-Jewish natives to be reconfigured as settlers.[28]

European Zionists were far from united in touting separation from Arabs and Arab culture. In Central Europe, since the mid-nineteenth century Jews had played a significant role in the development of the academic study of Near Eastern civilizations, in which Islam was presented in a positive light, perhaps because of its historically more benevolent attitudes toward Jews.[29] In the early twentieth century, a coterie of European Jews, such as the artists Boris Schatz and Ephraim Moses Lilien, romanticized the Middle East and the Jews' historic links to it. A small but influential group of European-Jewish immigrants to Palestine acquired Arabic and developed close relations with members of the bureaucratic, mercantile, and landowning Palestinian elites.[30] In a very different claim of propinquity, Zionist activists, from Eliezer Ben-Yehuda to David Ben-Gurion, claimed that Palestine's Arabs were the devolved descendants of ancient Hebrews, in desperate need of assistance from their more advanced brethren.[31]

A complex web of relations between immigrants and locals characterized settler-colonial situations. As Liora Halperin has written, early Zionist settlers' assertions of respect for the natives assumed hierarchical relationships of knowledge and power—the settlers knew the natives in a way that the natives could not know them, and the settlers were employers in contrast to the natives who were employees.[32] In interactions between colonizer and colonized, the former appropriated aspects of native culture as a sign of "firstness" and rootedness in the land.

A hardening among the Yishuv's Jews of "Hebrew" versus "Palestinian" identities occurred in the wake of nationwide anti-Jewish rioting by Palestinians in 1929. According to Hillel Cohen, until that conflict, Jews with deep roots in Palestine—whose ancestors had come from Middle Eastern countries or the Iberian peninsula generations or even centuries earlier—were decidedly ambivalent toward their recently arrived coreligionists from Europe. Only after 1929, Cohen argues, did Jews in Palestine cohere into a uniform community.[33] Changes in male headgear point to the growing cultural separation. Until the 1930s Jewish and Arab men in Palestine often wore the Ottoman fez, but as sectarian tensions grew, Jews regardless of place of origin doffed the headgear, and Arabs donned the traditional Palestinian *keffiyeh*.[34]

During the 1930s and 1940s, with the worsening of tensions between the two communities, Jews came to see Arabs as not only primitive but also menacing and savage. Zionist propaganda insisted, however, that Palestine's Arabs were docile and eager to live in peace with their Jewish neighbors. As we see in chapter 3, this perspective was expressed by Zionist leaders in Palestine and communicated to American Jewish activists, who disseminated it to the public via a network of Jewish newspapers. Acknowledging the extent of local Arab opposition to Zionism would call into question the morality of the Zionist enterprise, so acts of violent resistance were attributed to either reactionary elites in Palestinian society or outside agitators. This optimistic viewpoint may well have been sincere, as well as instrumental—both a perception and a rationalization.

It did not, however, emerge unscathed from the bloody fighting of the 1948 war or raids by Palestinian guerrillas during the early 1950s. In April 1956 Israeli defense minister Moshe Dayan delivered a eulogy for Ro'i Rotberg, who had been killed on his kibbutz near the Gaza border. Dayan warned that among Palestinian refugees in Gaza, "a sea of hatred and desire for revenge is swelling. . . . Without the steel helmet and the cannon's maw, we will not be able to plant a tree and build a home. Let us not be deterred from seeing the loathing that is inflaming and filling the lives of the hundreds of thousands of Arabs who live around us. . . . This is our life's choice—to be prepared and armed, strong and determined, lest the sword be stricken from our fist and our lives cut down."[35] Yael Zerubavel has observed that, since achieving statehood, Israel has represented itself as an oasis in a desert or, as former IDF chief of staff and prime minister Ehud Barak put it in 1996, "a modern and prosperous villa in the middle of the jungle, a place where different laws prevail. No hope for those who cannot defend themselves and no mercy for the weak."[36]

Barak's quotation is notorious and is often cited as an example of Zionist condescension and bigotry. The context of his remarks, however, was the early years of the Oslo peace process, and he was speaking to an audience of American Jews whom he was attempting to convince of the negotiations' potential to bring about a lasting change in Israel's position in the Middle East. In his speech, Barak used a common stereotype that he himself may have held and thought would appeal to his audience. Yet the speech contained within it the seeds of that stereotype's dissolution in an approaching era of regional stability and prosperity. Conversely, a century before Barak made these comments, Herzl jotted briefly in his diary that poor natives would be removed from a future Jewish state. This statement, too, has received an enormous amount of attention, but it would have had little import had the 1948 war not led to the flight and expulsion of 750,000 Palestinians.[37]

For Israel's critics, Zionism's links with colonialism emerge less from sensibility or intentions than from action and outcomes: displacement, expropriation, forced departure and thwarted return, and the denial of individual rights and national claims. Throughout the Mandate period, land purchases displaced rural Arabs, although it is difficult to quantify how much peasant landlessness was the direct result of Zionist activity, rather than changes in land tenure imposed by the British, widespread rural poverty, and urban economic opportunity. The 1948 war brought about Palestinian dispossession on an entirely different scale, so much so that it became known throughout the Arab world as the Nakba, or catastrophe.[38] Historians may place Zionism's settler-colonial roots in the late Ottoman and Mandate periods, but the Nakba, the creation of some 300,000 more refugees during the 1967 Arab–Israeli war, and more than a half-century of disenfranchisement and oppression of the Palestinians in

the Occupied Territories have made associations between Israel and settler colonialism commonplace.

Settler Colonialisms and Native Sons

Settler colonialism is a global category. It includes former English settler
colonies that are long-lived, independent states (Australia, Canada, New
Zealand, and the United States) and regimes that no longer exist, such as
French Algeria (1830–1962) and twentieth-century South Africa under
apartheid.[39] The developmental arcs of these countries vary greatly, as
do the characteristics of their Indigenous communities, historical relations between settlers and natives, and the course of colonial rule. An
examination of these diverse cases demonstrates, as the pioneer social
historian Marc Bloch has observed, that the benefit of comparative history is yielding insight about difference, as well as similarity. Moreover,
in his brilliant book *The Comparative Imagination*, George Frederickson
cautions that comparisons can all too easily become abstract or simplistic and that their purpose should be the deeper appreciation of a single
country, rather than the construction of a model purporting to explain
the development of multiple societies.[40]

The comparands found in existing literature on Israel as a settler-
colonial state are states within the saltwater empires of Western European powers. Since the end of World War II, however, the expropriation
of Indigenous peoples' lands and the settlement there of members of the
dominant nationality have been common global practices. The Indone-
sian colonization of East Timor, Moroccan settlement in the Western Sahara, and the "Sinification" of Tibet are practices referred to by
Johannes Becke as "post-colonial state expansion."[41] Going back further
in time, one finds the most spectacular and horrific case of settlement
colonialism in the twentieth century neither in Western Europe's overseas empires nor in Palestine but rather in Soviet Kazakhstan during the
1930s. Under enforced agricultural collectivization, more than two million people, some half of the native population, died or were driven into

exile and were replaced by members of minority nationalities from across the USSR.[42]

There are several reasons why most writers who term Israel a settler-colonial state limit their comparative purview to Western examples. There is the long history of Western colonialism in the Middle East and of links between Zionism and the Western powers. Israeli political discourse has long emphasized Israel's status as a Western state: industrialized, affluent, democratic, and culturally linked to Europe and North America. Sympathizers with the Palestinian cause have often seen the former Soviet Union and China in a positive light as countering U.S. global hegemony and supporting anticolonial liberation movements. Soviet and Chinese practices of internal colonialism therefore receive little critical comparative attention. A similar logic and selective memory characterize those who express solidarity with postcolonial states worldwide. There are, in fact, good reasons to place Israel within a settler-colonial framework, but that framework requires considerable expansion, both geographic and conceptual, beyond what is commonly found.

Signs emerged during the 2010s of a new perspective on post-1967 Israel's settlements in the Occupied Territories that goes beyond simply describing the process as colonization. First, Veracini claims that a full-blown project of settler colonialism has not occurred because most of the Palestinians in the West Bank, unlike those within the territory that became post-1949 Israel, have remained in place. Israeli Jewish settlers in the Occupied Territories have not erased the natives but dwell both among and apart from them. Johannes Becke has also characterized the West Bank settlement enterprise as incomplete and at best partly successful; he calls it "enclave colonialism."[43]

Another aspect of the equation of Zionism and colonialism that requires consideration is the project of settler indigenization, which Veracini considers to be a common feature of settler colonialism. Scholars analyzing this process within the Zionist project describe it as both spontaneous and natural, on the one hand, and scripted and directed from above, on the other.[44] In a seminal article from 1991, Zali Gurevitch and Gideon Aran claimed that unlike other peoples whose nativity is natural and taken for granted, that of Israeli Jews is mediated, reflective, and overwrought; defined by doubt and insecurity; and bears both the legacy of diaspora Jewry's abstract, textual connection to the Land of Israel and the all too palpable scars of a long history of persecution.[45] The anxiety that Gurevitch and Aran locate at the center of the Israeli soul, however, has troubled other settler colonials. Particularly in their societies' early years, worry lest they meld with the aboriginals leads settlers to separate themselves, to marginalize or eradicate the natives, and to artfully extoll their own indigeneity. To demonstrate this point I broaden my focus from Palestine and look to three other cases: colonial New England, South Africa under Afrikaner and British domination, and French Algeria.

In seventeenth-century New England, the roots of American identity lay in the complex and troubling encounter with the environment and the native peoples. Puritan settlers feared that they would not succeed in creating a replica of England, tranquil and civilized, in their new environment but would instead succumb to the savagery of New England's harsh environment. Nature was cruel and terrifying: winters were lethally cold, and the forests were unimaginably vast, thick, and dark. Nature, rough and savage, was to be conquered, subdued, and exploited.[46] Early Zionist settlers, too, could dread the land of their ancestral yearnings, invoking the biblical description of the "land that devours its inhabitants" (Numbers 13:32)—this time through disease, heat, and arid, unforgiving soil. Yet compared with New England, Palestine's smaller size, relative population density, capacity for rapid environmental improvement brought about by the beneficent force of technology, and, most of all, its status in the Zionist imagination as the Jews' ancient patrimony softened and countered the environmental threat. In Palestine, as Boaz Neumann observed, nature was as much the Jews' lover as their nemesis.[47]

For the Puritans, as for the Zionists, native peoples were both human beings and objects of nature. Although some Europeans fantasized about the Indian as a "noble savage," Puritans were more likely to see the "Red Man" as cursed or even as the seed of Amalek, whose destruction was to be celebrated rather than mourned. As John Winthrop remarked on what he believed to be the "miracle" of the mass death of natives through disease, "If God were not pleased with our inheriting these parts, why did He drive out the natives before us?"[48] Puritans also conceived of natives as meliorable through Christianization, yet this process carried the perception of considerable risk because it demanded living among them, possibly falling into their "coarse" and "savage" ways, and succumbing to the sexual allure of their womenfolk.

Unlike South America, where European men came alone as conquerors and laborers, and frequently cohabited with native women, in Protestant colonial North America, immigrants came as families to set up model religious communities. (The famous case of John Smith and Pocahontas notwithstanding, in general a society that aspired to be a new Jerusalem discouraged open mixing with what were seen as latter-day Canaanites.) On the western frontier in the nineteenth century, Indian women were more likely to be objects of male sexual desire, precisely because European men on the frontier were often alone. White Americans' exclusionary racial identity did not cut off sexual encounters between whites and Indigenous peoples—all the more so between whites and Blacks—but the mestizo and mulatto service castes that developed in colonial South America did not find a counterpart in colonial America or the United States.[49]

For the early Zionists, in the decades before the Arab became clearly denoted as a political enemy, he could be not only an object of suspicion and a perceived carrier of the virus of Levantine indolence but also an object of pity, paternalistic affection, and even romanticized emulation—as demonstrated by the social, economic, and at times romantic contacts between the two communities during the period of the British Mandate. Love affairs between Jews and Arabs aroused great anxiety among Jewish and Palestinian elites alike but were few in number, and unlike so many colonial societies in the nineteenth and twentieth centuries, the native woman was rarely an object of sexual fantasy in the literature or art of the Yishuv.[50]

Homoerotic idealization of the Arab male was more common, in the form of either a hypermasculine Bedouin horseman or a Jew who had acquired the looks and bearing of one.[51] This literary trope reflected Zionists' fascination, even obsession, with the physical regeneration of the Jewish body, which was usually coded as male. The Zionist striving to achieve and assert masculinity was a response to the feminization of Jews common in the rhetoric of antisemitism, which depicted Jewish males as physically unfit, cowardly, and prone to stereotypical feminine behaviors such as hysteria, scheming, and treachery. In North America and elsewhere, European colonialisms offered young men opportunities to achieve fame and fortune in new environments. Fin de siècle colonialism embraced Social Darwinistic fears of degeneration of the body politic, with Asia and Africa seen as arenas in which to strengthen the nation through the conquest and exploitation of distant lands. But the centrality within Zionism of transforming the male Jewish body and the degree of apologetics and self-criticism that underlay this agenda were not typical in European colonialism.

Perhaps the most salient parallel between the colonial North American and Zionist experiences lies in the New World Englishman's simultaneous anxiety about and celebration of a loss of refinement caused by distance from the European homeland. In the late seventeenth century, the fiery preacher Cotton Mather described his son Increase as "a *tame* Indian, for so the Europeans are pleased sometimes to denominate the children that are born in these regions."[52] In a sermon delivered in 1686 at the age of twenty-six, Mather fretted lest the settlers fall into a state of "criolian [*sic*] degeneracy," a fate that could be avoided only by willfully, consciously performing an English identity.[53] Mather simultaneously lamented the roughness of his and his peers' manner and celebrated the directness and simplicity of their speech and character. The "American," as the colonists increasingly came to be called, was obliged to assert his Englishness through dress, furnishings, and high culture while maintaining the moral integrity of the plainspoken provincial.

Zionism expressed similar tensions and resolutions. Before 1948 the Zionist movement was dominated by European and American Jews, who took it for granted that the hegemonic high culture of the Jewish national home would be European, even if it embraced some aspects of Oriental material culture, such as cuisine. It celebrated the Palestine-born child of immigrants, the *sabra*, who remained attached to Western culture while being a native of the land who spoke plainly and honestly (the Turkish/ Arabic word *dugri* became Hebrew slang for straight talk), simultaneously taking pride in the sabra's knowledge of Arab ways and limiting contact with the natives. Two hundred and fifty years previously, Cotton Mather had championed seventeenth-century *dugri* while embracing Anglophilia as a prophylactic against "criolian degeneracy."

Unlike North America, South Africa did not witness a decimation of the native population. Although aboriginal pastoralists in South Africa were largely wiped out by smallpox and other diseases carried by white settlers, most of the Bantu-speaking farmers of southern Africa were immune to smallpox. The history of white settlement in southern Africa, therefore, was always characterized by being vastly outnumbered by the natives—a perceived demographic threat that in the early twentieth century was described as fear of "swamping."[54] The alleged need to restrict native access to land claimed by whites and to root Black Africans in particular territories led to the Native Lands Act of 1913, which institutionalized many long-standing practices of segregation and can be considered a legislative precedent for apartheid, which was formally implemented in 1948. Ironically the rhetoric of demographic threat intensified even during the period of apartheid, with the acceleration of white outmigration during the 1970s. The terror of being swamped led to a panicky rejection of *gelykstelling*, the equalization of the legal status of white and Black, the equivalent to what in Israel/Palestine today is described as a one-state solution.[55]

White fear led to the construction of a number of psychological defenses. Classic Afrikaner historiography refers to southern Africa as having been thinly populated at the time of the white invasion and of the Bantus as immigrants who arrived in substantive numbers only after the whites had established themselves. According to this story, the natives were therefore not really natives but newcomers, as opposed to the old-stock Afrikaners. Unfortunately for white South African nationalists, the Black population's allegedly tardy arrival did not prevent them from constituting a constant danger, one that was not swept away as in North America by disease and decisive warfare that reduced the native population there to remnants bottled up on reserves. The eternal quality of the white–Black conflict inhibited the production of favorable views of natives as "noble savages"—an image propagated in North America precisely when the native no longer presented a threat. As Frederickson observes, traditional enemies who remain dangerous are not romanticized.[56] The parallels with Zionist sensibilities are obvious: the notion of "demographic threat" and the propagandistic claims that, before the arrival of the Zionists, Palestine was a mostly empty land.[57]

Until the 1920s, when one spoke in South Africa of the "racial question," it referred to the Afrikaners and English, not whites and Blacks. Afrikaners and English settlers, and even Afrikaners themselves, were sharply divided along socioeconomic lines. In 1922 white laborers in the Witwatersrand region went on strike against white mine owners who preferred cheap Black labor. The strike provoked a ferociously violent response from the government, thus prompting the laborers to appeal to the international socialist community with the slogan, "Workers of the

World Unite, and Fight for a White South Africa."[58] The construction
of a unified Afrikaner ethnic identity was a product of the Great Depres-
sion and World War II, when lower-class Afrikaners lent political support
to Afrikaner agricultural and industrial capitalists in return for high
wages and social status. Tensions between Afrikaners and the British
were fully resolved, however, only after 1948 with the triumph of the
National Party, which implemented apartheid and the Afrikanerization
of the civil service and professions, thereby bringing the Afrikaners and
English into a similar socioeconomic position and creating a unified
white community.

The homogenization of subethnicities—the process of intellectual
and political fusion by which a coherent white South African identity
was invented—bears comparison with the invention of Israeli identity,
as does the idiosyncratic blend of internationalism and ethnocentrism
in both the Zionist and Afrikaner labor movements. As noted, long-
standing divisions between European and Middle Eastern Jews in
Palestine faded in the wake of Arab–Jewish violence from 1929 onward.
Tensions between Ashkenazim and Mizrahim flared up again after Israel's creation, with the persecution of Jews throughout the Middle East
and North Africa and the emigration of some seven hundred thousand of
them to Israel. A vast power and income inequity developed between
established Ashkenazic Jews and new immigrants from Europe, on the
one hand, and Mizrahim, on the other. Ashkenazic paternalism toward
Mizrahim and Mizrahi resentment toward Ashkenazim constantly sim-
mered and occasionally boiled over, as in the case of riots in the Haifa
neighborhood of Wadi Salib in 1959 and the Mizrahi Black Panther movement of the early 1970s.[59]

The rise of Israel's right-wing Likud party to power in 1977 and the
dominance of the Right in Israel for all but eleven of the past forty-five
years are in part the result of ongoing Mizrahi anger over what Likud
leader Menachem Begin, employing bitter understatement, called the
Labor Party's "certain degree of condescension" toward Jews of North

African and Middle Eastern descent.[60] From the 1980s to the present, Mizrahi activists have presented the Mizrahim as a colonized community, economically exploited and politically deprived, whose history was ignored and whose culture was demeaned under Ashkenazic Israeli hegemony. In 1988 the cultural critic Ella Shohat, in a display of both homage to and competition with Said, published an essay titled "Zionism from the Standpoint of Its Jewish Victims."[61] Even in the twenty-first century, substantial economic and educational gaps between Ashkenazic and Mizrahi Israeli Jews remain, but they are narrowing, and intermarriage between the communities is common. In Israel, a Jewish national identity that unites Ashkenazim and Mizrahim is dominant, even if not monolithic. The same could be said for whites of Afrikaner and British origin in apartheid-era South Africa.

I find particularly striking a third comparison—that between the Zionist project and French Algeria from the late nineteenth through mid-twentieth centuries. In the early 1900s, French administrators interpreted Algeria through classical literature on the Maghreb, literature that they read familiarly and intimately, not unlike Zionist readings of the Bible. Just as Zionists venerated biblical history, French military strategy in Algeria hearkened back to ancient Roman practices, and French scholars zealously pursued archaeological excavations of Roman ruins to cement the link between the ancient and modern Latin rulers of the land. The motley immigrants to Algeria from the northern Mediterranean who became the *pieds-noirs* were called the "Latins of Africa," said to comprise a new race—fair of form, committed to hard labor and to reviving the land from neglect at the hands of ostensibly indolent and fanatical Arabs and Berbers. The archaeologist and writer Louis Bertrand saw the natives as devolved Latins, preserving only shards of the Roman heritage. In Algerian cities, street names evoked ancient Rome and modern France; Arab or Muslim names were rare.[62] There are obvious parallels between all these phenomena and Zionist aspirations for a global ingathering of Jewish immigrants, simultaneously inventing and restoring an ancient nation, as well as Zionist views of Palestinians as the land's long-time residents but neither its stewards nor its owners.

By the late 1800s Mediterranean settlers in Algeria were calling themselves "Algerians" or "the Algerian people" and expressing this identity via a distinct, earthy French dialect. This new collective identity, like that of the new Hebrew nation arising in the Land of Israel, was created in astonishing speed, only a few decades after the onset of mass colonization. A sense of rootedness and unmediated belonging to the land characterized even the most sensitive and conciliatory member of the pied-noir intelligentsia, Albert Camus, who—like dovish Israeli intellectuals—struggled with the clashing demands of two peoples for a single land. Camus once claimed, "I have had a long affair with Algeria which will undoubtedly never end and which keeps me from being completely lucid about it. . . . [Algeria] is my true country." [63]

In his writings from the 1950s, Camus remained stubbornly Eurocentric, imagining an Algeria rooted in the mists of the Greco-Roman past rather than in 1,300 years of Muslim civilization. Yet he was a principled, uncompromising enemy of pied-noir chauvinism and condemned the French authorities' brutal oppression of the Algerian national movement no less than the terrorist tactics of the National Liberation Front. Camus systematically deconstructed the chauvinistic and radical anticolonial arguments deployed by each side against the other. He depicted an Algeria of two nations bound not by history or shared experience but by a common love of the land, by desire, and, most important of all, by suffering, *angoisse*. "In Algeria," he warned darkly, "French and Arabs are condemned to live or to die together." [64] Late twentieth-century Israeli writers, such as David Grossman, Amos Oz, and A. B. Yehoshua, often wrote in this vein.

The discussion thus far demonstrates numerous points of contact and commonality between the formation of national identities in settler-colonial contexts, including the Zionist project. The settler-colonial model casts a new light on aspects of Israel that, according to its internal monologue, are unique. For example, although some European immigrants to Israel learned Palestinian Arabic, for the most part the process of indigenization entailed mastering Hebrew, a language of ancient Middle Eastern origin that had been transformed into a modern literary language and vernacular in Europe. Similarly, pied-noir settlers in Algeria spoke French, not the Arabic vernacular of the Muslim majority, and cleaved to French literary and popular culture, whereas white South Africans spoke Afrikaans or English and looked down on native vernaculars. In all of these circumstances, becoming a native meant creating a subculture that was separate from both the immigrants' lands of provenance and the lands of settlement but that was far closer to the former.

Another manifestation of Israel's status as a collective of indigenized colonials is its long-standing self-description as the only democracy in the Middle East. Its democratic spirit may derive less from the intentions of its founders or deep-seated Judaic values than from Israel's status as a settler-colonial state that, like the United States and South Africa, has developed as a frontier democracy. Frontier societies are based on an inextricable mixture of inclusion and exclusion—inclusion of whites and exclusion of natives and, in some cases, slaves. They are new societies, free of the heritage of graduated privilege and social hierarchy that continued to weigh heavily in the Old World. Within the bubble of the enfranchised community, freedom of expression is protected, even cherished, and the state operates according to the rule of law.[65]

Nonetheless, each of these contexts possesses distinct features or characteristics common to only a portion of the total sample. There are also significant economic differences that have collective psychological consequences. In post-1948 Israel, the Arab minority has not constituted an indispensable component of the workforce. The same is true even for the Arabs of the West Bank and Gaza, who, when Israel conquered the territories in 1967, provided an abundant supply of cheap labor. During the 1970s and 1980s Arabs from the territories were omnipresent as menial laborers and appeared to be pillars of the construction sector, but the Palestinian Intifada that began at the end of 1987—a movement intended, as per the literal meaning of the word, to "shake off" Israeli rule—demonstrated how easily Israel could shake off Arab labor, replacing it with guest workers from the Philippines, Romania, and Thailand.

The Israeli economy's relative imperviousness to the withdrawal of native labor separated it from South Africa, whose entire history was stamped by the dependence of white elites on native labor in agriculture and mining. The importation in the mid-1800s of Indians to Natal as sugar workers or of Chinese mine workers a half-century later never constituted a feasible alternative to native labor, despite occasional musings by Afrikaner nationalists for a complete separation between Black and white. The creation of semiautonomous Black homelands in the early 1900s derived from a desire to prevent male laborers from settling permanently in towns and to keep them as transients whose families lived in the homelands. The constant threat that African labor would lead to an erosion of white wages led white workers in the 1930s to demand a guaranteed wage superiority of at least eleven to one.[66] Apartheid was a response as much to an economic as a cultural crisis, a policy opposite from the split market that was a Labor Zionist ideal. Arab labor was widespread in the Yishuv during the Mandate's first two decades, but it declined markedly during and after the Palestinian-Arab Revolt of 1936 to 1939.

In the early twentieth century, Arabs outnumbered Jews in Palestine by a factor of ten to one, about the same ratio as that of Blacks to whites in South Africa. But the radical Zionist youth in Palestine did not want to profit from the Arab's body or to be a master of any sort of slave. As Boaz Neumann tells us, their hearts overflowed with desire, which was overwhelming, primal, and intoxicating. The Zionist youth desired that the land desire them; they were suffused with a heartfelt, even if fanciful, sense of homecoming. European colonists elsewhere did not build a collective identity based on personal psychic transformation. They conquered and loved the land but were not infatuated with it, nor did they aspire to melt into its landscape. For the Zionists, according to Neumann, Arabs were not merely perceived as indolent and static in keeping with classic colonialist stereotypes but they also lacked a vital life force and were too natural and organically linked with the soil to be its faithful husband; instead, they were undifferentiated extensions of its flora and fauna.[67]

To return to the question posed at the outset of this section, Zionism was the only form of settlement colonialism that was also a project preceded and structured by an ideology. The motley Dutch, German, and Scottish settlers who comprised the Afrikaner republics did not arrive with a coherent national identity. Afrikaner national consciousness developed organically, as a product of immigration and shared experience. Well into the twentieth century, the Afrikaans language lived in the shadow of Dutch, only replacing its European parent in 1925 as an official language of state. The first Afrikaans novel was published only in 1913; the Afrikaans Bible appeared twenty years later. In the Maghreb, the transformation of sundry Mediterranean communities into French Algerians was quick yet unchoreographed, and the pieds-noirs' dialect, *pataouète*, although featured in speech in popular novels, was not a literary medium in and of itself.[68]

Zionism, in contrast, was a coherent nationalist ideology, drawing on two competing and overlapping language-based nationalisms centered around Hebrew and Yiddish. Both modern Hebraic and Yiddish literary culture developed outside a Zionist framework or even a Jewish nationalist one. As Shachar Pinsker has shown, the late nineteenth-century pioneers of modern Hebrew literature were European coffee house cosmopolitans, born in Russia and more likely to be found in Odessa, Berlin, Vienna, or New York than Tel Aviv.[69] The Hebrew-language activists who made their way to late Ottoman or Mandate Palestine carried with them an advanced literary language that was unlike a creole such as *pataouète* or Afrikaans. The rudiments of the language were familiar to the vast majority of Jewish immigrants to Palestine.

Along with knowledge of Hebrew came familiarity with the Jewish textual tradition's devotion to the Land of Israel; as Gurevitch and Aran put it, in Jewish culture, Eretz Israel was not merely a "a place" but rather "the Place."[70] Jews in Palestine, later Israel, have mediated their perceptions of their surroundings through a textual screen.

From the beginnings of Zionist settlement through the State of Israel's formative decades, it was impossible for any but the most separatist anti-Zionist Orthodox Jews to avoid an educational and cultural network dedicated to fostering a structured Zionist identity. Schools, youth groups, newspapers, radio, workplaces, and public gatherings were all sites for the inculcation of a form of Jewish nationalism that conceived of itself as regenerating the Jewish people in its ancient homeland and via its ancient vernacular. Israeli nation-building was as rapid as the growth of the pied-noir community in Algeria, but the former was far more directed and purposeful, its linguistic base vastly richer, its culture more enduringly adhesive. In time, Israelis developed their own organic self-consciousness, akin to that of any people that shares territory and experience, as well as common enemies. In modern Palestine, ideology was a powerful accelerant that quickened and deepened the process by which immigrants became natives, outlanders became Indigenous, and Jews became Israelis.

Conclusion

Our comparative examination of colonial indigenization places Zionism within a settler-colonial matrix while allowing for its particularities, like a celestial body with an eccentric orbit around its sun. Those particularities include the heritage of the Holocaust, which accounts for the cohesiveness and endurance of Israeli Zionist identity and the determination of Israeli Jews to resist pressure to withdraw from the Occupied Territories and foster the creation of a Palestinian state. Whether Zionism's particularities or its commonalities with other forms of settlement colonialism are more important is largely a function of the observer's disciplinary position and political commitments. Engaged scholarship is not necessarily bad scholarship: most of the academic writings on which this chapter has drawn were produced by engaged individuals whose work is often of great merit.

Nonetheless, something is missing. The questions underlying this chapter, like its predecessor, are about Zionism's most essential and salient qualities. With few exceptions, however, our discussion has been about practices, actions, ideas, and opinions. But thought and action are predicated on and in turn generate emotion. As promised in the introduction, the remaining chapters of this book will present a new interpretation of Zionism through the lens of emotion. Many of the actors, events, and actions we have encountered thus far will appear again but in a new light.

PART III

IN A NEW KEY

3 *Zionism to 1948*

PASSION AND SOLIDARITY

Nationalism is a form of collective identification through emotional community. People may be indifferent to nationalism, but when they do identify with a nation, they feel that it defines and sustains them and that whatever endangers the nation endangers themselves. The matrix of emotions sustaining nationalism is vast, consisting of myriad varieties of the fulfillment or frustration of desire—the former including love, pride, hope, and yearning and the latter encompassing disappointment, fear, anger, and hatred. The affective valence of the matrix shifts constantly, its elements bonding and breaking apart, waxing and waning, and moving between the center and periphery of consciousness. Like other forms of nationalism, Zionism is sustained by a potent and labile bundle of emotions.

Not only Zionism but also modern Jewish politics as a whole can be interpreted as an expression of fear and anxiety. Beginning in 1840, when Jews in Damascus were persecuted in the wake of false allegations of the ritual murder of a Capuchin monk, and intensifying later in the nineteenth century, fear for the physical safety of Jews in Eastern Europe, the Middle East, and North Africa fostered international Jewish philanthropic activity and political lobbying of the Great Powers. In the early twentieth century, fear for Jewish survival motivated Territorialism, which sought a refuge for Jews anywhere in the world. Anxiety about the spiritual and cultural future of the Jews in the face of assimilatory pressures and growing irreligiosity inspired both secular Jewish nationalism and Orthodox political movements. During the Russian pogroms of 1903–1906, the socialist Jewish Bund played a leading role in armed self-defense.

Emotions such as love, pride, and the desire for honor were also present in Jewish politics, and future-oriented emotions such as yearning and hope formed the base of socialist movements, including Bundism. But Zionism was distinct in the prominence of passionate, embodied love and the interweaving of territory with collective solidarity. From the mid-1800s until the establishment of the State of Israel in 1948, an abstract romantic attachment to the Land of Israel gradually condensed into a more material, bodily, and erotic love of the blossoming Jewish national home. The growth of the Yishuv elicited admiration, even awe, among diaspora Jews, including many who did not overtly identify as Zionist. The interlacing of love for a concrete object (the Land of Israel) with identification with an abstract collective (the people of Israel) is pre-1948 Zionism's most salient emotional feature.

Terms of Endearment

"Love" is not so much an emotion as an emotional category connoting profound attachment and a sense of personal fulfillment through contact with the beloved. Aristotle conceived of love as romantic (*eros*), companionate (*philia*), parental (*storgē*), or spiritual (*agapē*). In nineteenth-century Europe, philia and storgē were often subsumed under the category of "sentimental" love—a bond that, at low levels of intensity, promoted empathy and humanitarianism but, at higher levels, produced intimate bonds of affection, esteem, and nurturing. The characteristics of romantic love also varied considerably depending on its intensity. It could refer to something as mundane as sexual pair-bonding or as exalted as the yearning to merge with another soul, nature, or the divine. Failure to attain that union could lead to utter despair. In sentimental love, in contrast, the bond was already forged, which in part accounts for the relative stability of its emotional register.

In classical Hebrew, the word *ahavah* could mean any of the Aristotelian types of love, yet the word *hibah*, derived from the word *hov* (bond), expressed feelings of affection, cherishing, and holding something dear.

The fact that in the late 1800s Palestine-centered Jewish nationalism was called *hibat tsion* (love of Zion) and its adherents called themselves *Hovevei Tsion* (Lovers of Zion) suggests a prominent role for a love that approximated European sentimentalism.[1]

We begin our account of the modern love of Zion with Abraham Mapu's pioneering Hebrew novel *Ahavat Tsion* (1853). As befits a work of mid-nineteenth-century fiction, love was its central theme. Mapu's novel is set in the biblical kingdom of Judah and tells the story of the passionate love between two beautiful adolescents, Amnon and Tamar. The novel owes an obvious debt to the biblical Song of Songs: both texts are intensely erotic and recount feverish, frustrated searches by lovers for their soulmate. Yet the novel is a quintessentially modern piece of literature, which uses the ancient Land of Israel as a backdrop for what Naomi Seidman calls "powerful, conflicted, and transgressive sexual impulses."[2] Love *of* Zion is secondary to love *in* Zion.

In the beginning of the novel, a friend of Tamar's father Yedidiah says to him, "Zion is the home of everything beautiful; therefore, let your daughter be one of her beauties, and bloom like a rose on the hills of Zion." Yedidiah then intensifies the erotic implications of the comment by replying, "She will bloom if she is planted in a garden which is fed with the dew from heaven."[3] This "garden" is Zion; as in the Hebrew Bible, it refers both to the city of Jerusalem and, by synecdoche, the Land of Israel as a whole. Noting the collapse of the northern kingdom of Israel, the novel contrasts the "gloomy and desolate" Samaria with the "beautiful and bright" Zion, "blooming in the splendor and glory of the king who rules there."[4] The association between Jerusalem and fertility is highlighted by Mapu's choice to begin and end the book at the time of Sukkot, the autumn harvest. Tamar and Amnon find and fight for their love amidst this riot of pastoral beauty, enveloped by the warmth of the Middle Eastern sun.

The novel assumes a territorially coherent Land of Israel, whose components are knitted together through intertwined positive emotions such as love, joy, and valor. It includes Bethlehem ("I loved you in Bethlehem, I longed for you in Zion," writes Tamar to Amnon) and the Carmel mountain ridge, where gardeners are "singing and laughing joyously" and the peasants in the fields feel "God's hand upon them in all seasons of the year" while their "handsome, buxom wives spin the wool and flax for clothes for the household."[5] When the country is threatened and goes to war, Amnon says, "The farmers will leave their fields, the priests their altars, the Levites their services, the mechanics their work, even the judges their benches, and, like one, they will all volunteer as soldiers to help their land and their king."[6] The fervent romantic love between Tamar and Amnon is linked to a robust and courageous love of country. The novel, however, is not a call for Jewish restoration to Palestine. Rather, it is a celebration of erotic love so long as it is underpinned by moral integrity, loyalty to the community, and faith in the divine. Eros is legitimized by agapē and both flourish in Zion, but the novel's goal is to bring about the consummation of the lovers' earthly passions.

Mapu's *Ahavat Tsion* is removed from the love rooted in storgē and philia, the love between family members and like-minded friends, which leads to concerted actions toward collective goals. In chapter 1, I placed Moses Hess's *Rome and Jerusalem* (1862) within the context of proto-Zionism because of its assertion of Jewish nationality and call for a Jewish return to Palestine. Underlying the book's political content, however, is a personal account of emotional awakening, repeatedly expressed through the language of love for family. "After an estrangement of twenty years," Hess writes at the beginning of the book, "I am back with my people."[7] Hess claims that his return was sparked by an encounter with a Jewish woman grieving for a personal loss: "It was only when I saw you in anguish and sorrow that my heart opened and the cover of my slumbering, national feeling was thrown off. . . . Such love . . . such infinite love for family can have its seat only in a Jewish heart."[8]

Throughout the book, maternal and familial love are held as the highest forms of feeling and as the cherished possessions of the Jewish people, which shunned the "gross sensualism" of Baal worship in antiquity and the ascetic "spiritual-love-Christianity" in the Middle Ages. Jews alone expressed "the living, creative force and universal history, namely, the organ of unifying and sanctifying love."[9] This love, like that of parents for their children, is unconditional: "Real, strong love, the love which dominates body and spirit alike, is always blind. . . . It is not the perfection and excellent qualities of the beloved which are the object of love's desire, but the beloved being as it is, with all its good and bad traits."[10] For Hess this all-encompassing, unconditional love binds Jews to each other and to the Land of Israel.

Heinrich Graetz felt similarly; his historical writings are replete with a passion that is simultaneously fervent, pious, and tied both to the Eretz Israel of the present and the ancient past. When Graetz began to write works of Jewish history, he had a negative model in the form of Isaac Jost, whose nine-volume *History of the Israelites from the Time of the Maccabees* (1820–1829) and subsequent publications were pioneering works of scholarship and immensely erudite; however, they were also cold, clinical, and highly critical of rabbinic Judaism. Ludwig Philippson, a prominent German rabbi and moderate reformer, accused Jost of lacking pride, and the London-based *Jewish Chronicle* called for a history "written in the spirit of *truth*, but not less in the spirit of *love* towards the Jewish nation."[11] Graetz's historiographical oeuvre was a fervid response to that challenge. Graetz filled his writing with "all historical remembrances . . . that seize my heart with a vast power and bring to life the full glory of the Jewish past, render it resplendent, and instill into me an ecstasy of pain."[12] The phrase "ecstasy of pain" (*Wollust des Schmerzens*) has powerful Christian, and especially Pietist, associations, describing the individual's internalization of rapturous suffering to cement bonds with the community of the faithful.

Graetz is often stereotyped as writing a *"Leidens—und Gelehrtengeschichte"* (a history of suffering by the Jewish masses and the scholarship of a minuscule rabbinic elite). But his work is more complex than that.[13]

When Graetz narrates Jewish suffering, he does so to evoke within the reader pride that the Jews have overcome, survived, flourished, and created. As he wrote in an essay in 1863–1864, Israel was at the time of the Babylonian Exile a "stunted, despised, spat-upon, downtrodden slave," but it is in fact a "Messiah-nation" destined for greatness, as foretold by the biblical prophet Isaiah: it is a light unto the nations.[14] The Jews who maintained their identity while languishing in Babylonian captivity were able to do so because of the intensity of their love and mourning for Zion.

Graetz eagerly anticipated his journey to Eretz Israel in 1872. Two years earlier, he had written that he would not write the volumes of his *History* on ancient Israel in "this foundational time, rich in grace, from Moses to Jeremiah, from the burning Sinai to the smoking ruins of Jerusalem and from the Babylonian captivity to the Maccabean fighters, until I have seen the setting of these occurrences with my own eyes."[15] Shortly after arriving in Palestine, an excited Graetz wrote to Hess (the two were close friends), *"Einah domah shmiyah le-ra'yah!* [Hearing about something is not comparable to seeing it in person!] Climatically, it is a wondrous land and truly wrought to be a promised land."[16] Atop Mount Hermon in the far north of Palestine, Graetz remarked that the landscape does not induce terror as do mammoth mountains or vast chasms; its effect on the soul is "gentle and mild," filling one with "soothing sensation of the lovely, the familiar, and the intimate."[17] This language epitomizes the ethos of mid-nineteenth-century sentimentalism, the depth of whose passion was conveyed precisely through its tenderness and moderation.

Graetz enjoyed a large and loyal Jewish audience, so one must assume that his sentimentality struck a responsive chord in his readers' hearts. However, a far more celebrated writer, George Eliot, made an arguably even more important contribution to the late nineteenth-century love of Zion in her last novel *Daniel Deronda* (1876). The book had a profound effect on Jewish readers, whether in its original English or in one of its many translations. Zion makes only a cameo appearance in the novel, but its presence, in the minds of Eliot herself and her Jewish readers, was greater than its screen time. Zion is a symbol for nobility of character, authenticity, pride in one's origins, and solidarity with one's community. These feelings are experienced by the novel's title character as he undergoes a protracted process of discovering his own Jewishness. Central to this process are both Deronda's love for Mirah, a virtuous Sephardic Jewess whom he marries at the novel's end, and his friendship with her brother Mordecai, a consumptive scholar with vast Judaic erudition and a febrile messianic vision.

About halfway through the novel, at a gathering of autodidact artisans, there is a lively debate about whether distinct nationalities should persist or assimilate into a culture of universal humanitarianism. Mordecai passionately expatiates on the beneficial particularity of nations in general and of the Jews in particular. He calls for the restoration of the Jews to Zion, to "a republic where there is equality of protection, an equality which shone like a star on the forehead of our ancient community and gave it more than the brightness of Western freedom amid the despotisms of the East."[18] In this republic, "the outraged Jew shall have a defense in the court of nations." In chapter 1, we encountered Red Cross founder Henri Dunant's vision of a restored Palestine as the guarantor of world peace; here Mordecai declaims that "the world will gain as Israel gains. For there will be a community in the van of the East which carries the culture and sympathies of every great nation in its bosom, there will be a land set for a halting-place of enmities, a neutral ground for the East as Belgium is for the West."[19] At the end of the novel, Deronda and Mirah sail off for Palestine to realize Mordecai's universalist and humanitarian vision. They are able and willing to undertake this vast task because of the strength of the bond between them, which is that of an idealized bourgeois marriage based on endearment, mutual respect, partnership, and commonality of temperament. The virtuous love of husband and wife will lead to the redemption of the Land of Israel and, in turn, of humanity itself.

The novel had an electrifying effect on Jewish readers. Translated extracts appeared in Hebrew newspapers and evoked widespread acclaim. It caught the eye of Hayim Guedella, a Jewish financier in London who was the great-nephew of Moses Montefiore and chair of the General Committee of Turkish Bondholders of Ottoman Sovereign Debt. Guedella proposed, in both the Anglo-Jewish and Hebrew press, that the empire's debt be paid off with funds to be provided by Jews in exchange for the purchase of Palestine from the sultan. Eliezer Ben-Yehuda read portions of the novel in Russian translation with, according to the Zionist publicist Nahum Sokolow, "great love, and their impact upon him was very great, and they endowed him with the spirit of hope and courage, and of wondrous awakening."[20] In 1884 the Warsaw-based journal *Ha-Asif* wrote that the novel "like lightning brightened our night."[21] In turn David Frishman's translation of most of the novel into Hebrew in 1893 reached a generation of readers not unlike those who had devoured Mapu's *Ahavat Tsion*—young, talmudically literate Jewish men who sought new forms of identity and new heroes to emulate in their quest.

Frishman was agnostic vis-à-vis Zionism, but he praised the novel for its depiction of "the people of Israel and its future, the return to Zion, and the revival of the Israelite nation."[22] The book's methods, he wrote, were as emotional as they were cerebral. He compared it favorably to Gotthold Ephraim Lessing's Enlightenment tale of toleration, *Nathan the Wise*: "This is not a philosophical work alone, like the book that Lessing wrote, it will not grab the reader by his heart because of its scholarship alone, but rather from the many visions and depictions that come with the book, which will pull in the heart of the reader." Nonetheless Frishman was impressed by Eliot's "powerful logic based on theories of the psyche and of cause and effect." He marveled that Eliot, born and raised among the English gentry, grasped the essence of Jewish nationhood (*le'umiyut*) and was deeply learned in Jewish literature (more so "than some of the learned of Israel themselves"), with knowledge of the ancient canon, the writings of medieval poets and scholars like Judah Halevi, Solomon Ibn Gevirol, and Moshe Ibn Ezra, and recent Jewish historical writing.

To maintain the novel's emotional impact on the Hebrew reader, Frishman condensed the book by one-third, reducing to a bare minimum its other main story line: the life of haughty Gwendolyn Harleth, her unhappy marriage to Lord Grandcourt, and her unrequited love for Deronda. Frishman explained that the sections of the book about the English aristocracy would be of no interest to Hebrew readers, who were not familiar with the game of roulette (the novel begins with Gwendolyn gambling in Baden-Baden) or other aristocratic pastimes like "shooting projectiles at a target and seeing who will miss and who will not miss" and riding horses to see whether "my horse will beat yours." Most importantly, Frishman claimed, Hebrew readers would be indifferent to a love story between two Gentiles. If the girl is named Rebecca or Sarah, Frishman opined, the Jewish reader will be absorbed, but not if her name is Ophelia or Gwendolyn.

Daniel Deronda fostered among its Jewish readers feelings of self-respect, honor, and, above all, pride that so illustrious an author had devoted a novel to Jews and treated them with familiarity and sympathy. These moderate and dignified feelings were blended with sentimental love in early Zionist poetry. For example, the popular hymn "Ein Hauch Weht Durch die Lande" (A Breath Wafts through the Land), was written around 1900 by Leon Kellner, a Galician Zionist activist and professor of English philology in Czernowitz. Emphasizing fortitude, steadfastness, courage, and faith, the poem announces to its readers:

A breeze wafts through the land
A mild, gentle wind
It awakens slumbering hearts
It arouses old and young
You, breath of life and ever young, You ancient, mighty God . . .

He bears on eagle's wings
The small and loyal remnant
O'er mountains, valleys, and seas
To the ancient craggy nest
Father, ever young, You ancient, mighty God
The rocks do not frighten us
Nor does the desert glow
With our sweat, and with our hearts' blood
We water Your sacred land, You ancient, mighty God.[23]

Toward the end of the nineteenth century, a more volcanic form of love of the Land of Israel became prominent in Eastern European Jewish culture. As the political and economic situation of Russian and Romanian Jewry worsened, Jewish nationalism flourished, Jewish immigration to Palestine increased, and Hebrew poets began to interpret the redemption of the Jews in the Land of Israel with heightened anticipation that assumed embodied and even erotic dimensions. As the sentimental love of Zion became more sensual, it branched off in two directions: one emphasizing the anticipated fulfillment of desire and the other bemoaning unrequited passion.

Both could be found in the poetry of Menachem Mendel Dolitzky, a Polish Jew who attained fame as a bard of Jewish nationalism. His 1886 poem "On the Hills of Zion," which won a competition sponsored by the Moscow chapter of Hovevei Tsion for a Jewish national hymn, features the children of Israel being reunited with their beloved mother, rejuvenating her and returning to an Edenic womb:

Arise, O aged mother, put on the raiment of glory!
We have returned to you, entwining in your soil
We have brought building tools to you to rebuild your ruins
Spades in our hands to open the furrows . . .
Receive, beloved mother, your immortal sons
Make them forget their exile, show your face to them

Remove the garment of captivity, and desire them, for they are your
children.[24]

This joyful expression of the fulfillment of longing competed with a venerable Jewish tradition of mourning for Zion, as expressed in Dolitzky's
1888 poem "If I Forget Thee," an homage to Psalm 137:5 ("If I forget thee,
O Jerusalem, may my right hand forget its skill"):

Zion, my perfect one, Zion, my dear one
My soul longs for you from afar
May my right hand forget its skill if I forget you, my beauty,
Until the pit in my tomb shall close its mouth upon me
May my tongue cleave to my palate till I die
If I do not remember you, O desolate daughter of Zion
May my heart wither from illness and affliction
If my hot tears for your affliction will dry . . .
I will not forget you, Zion, I will not forget you, my perfect one,
You, so long as I live, my hope and my calamity,
And when I die, my lips will be keening for you, O my beauty,
    in my grave.[25]

Among the Jewish public at the fin de siècle, in the contest between
two representations of the emotional bond between the Jewish people
and the Land of Israel—vigor versus lassitude, the lover who seeks and
attains the beloved or the one who passively mourns and yearns—the
latter won out. Naftali Herz Imber, the most famous of the early Jewish
nationalist poets, wrote in both veins. "The Watch on the Jordan" (1886)
is fiercely proud and militant, in keeping with Imber's claim to be "the
only Hebrew poet who wrote poetry like a man and not like a lachry-
mose woman."[26] The poem was popular among the first Jewish agricultural settlers in Palestine. However, his far more somber poem,
"Tikvateinu" (Our Hope), written in or around 1878, attained global popularity and—in an abbreviated form—became the Zionist and later the

Israeli national anthem under the title "Hatikvah" (The Hope). The first stanza and refrain of the poem speak of a "Jewish heart, within a true Jewish soul, its eye glances yearningly to Zion. Our hope is not yet lost, the ancient hope to return to the land of our fathers, the city where David encamped."[27] The passivity reflected in these lines is maintained throughout the poem's other eight stanzas. Several refer to weeping and mourning by a "daughter of Zion" for the destruction of Jerusalem and especially the Temple.

Around 1905, Yehudah Leib Maimon-Cohen, a Jewish schoolteacher in Jaffa, changed the last three lines of the refrain to "The hope of two thousand years to be a free people in our land, the land of Zion and Jerusalem." Doing so softened the text's messianic allusions, yet even in its revised form, the poem's evocation of sadness, longing, and stasis stood in direct contrast to "The Watch on the Jordan" and other poems beloved by the early Zionist settlers, such as Hayim Nahman Bialik's 1894 ode to the joy of constructive labor, "Birkat Ha-Am" (Blessing of the People).[28] Samuel Cohen, a resident of Rishon le-Tsion, a Jewish settlement in Palestine, set "Tikvateinu" to the melody of a Romanian folk song that may have also inspired the Czech composer Bedrich Smetana's 1874 piece "The Moldau." "Tikvateinu" was sung at the Zionist Congresses of 1900 and 1903, and its popularity soared in the following years.[29] The emotional message of the song, appealing to the sadness, hopes, and fears of Jews in the diaspora, was more poignant than the pastoral hymns favored by the colonists in Palestine.[30]

As its title indicates, "Tikvateinu" intertwines two powerful political emotions: yearning and hope.[31] The twentieth-century German philosopher Ernst Bloch wrote of hope as a "principle" centered around "anticipatory consciousness" or the "not yet." For Bloch longed-for utopias took many forms: "happiness, freedom, non-alienation, Golden Age, Land of Milk and Honey, the Eternally-Female, the trumpet signal in *Fidelio* and the Christ-likeness of the day of resurrection which follows it." Religious or secular, otherworldly or materialistic, hope is the human striving to live "without expropriation and alienation" via a form of homecoming to a place where, paradoxically, they have never been.[32] This process of homecoming is arduous and depends on faith. More sober and somber than mere optimism, hope is an emotion in the subjunctive mood, an acknowledgment of an unreal condition but a refusal to countenance despair in attaining it. In a poignant essay, "Towards a History of Jewish Hope," the eminent historian Yosef Hayim Yerushalmi explored the constant tension within Jewish civilization between hope and despair and notes that, despite the powerful messianic element in the Jewish tradition, "by no means have all [post-biblical] Jewish hopes been eschatological." Yerushalmi attributed hope to nineteenth-century assimilation and Zionism alike: both "craved an end to Jewish exile, the latter by an actual return to Zion, the former by transforming the lands of exile into Zion."[33]

Our discussion thus far has presented a transition within European Jewish belles lettres during the mid- to late nineteenth century from a sentimental to a romantic love of Eretz Israel, with the latter taking the form either of a joyous encounter with the beloved by a determined, dynamic lover or a passive yearning for yet hopeful anticipation of reunion. In the political writings of early Zionists, that emotional intensity was still present, but it had a different valence, presenting the restoration of the Land of Israel as a means of assuring the Jewish people of safety, well-being, and self-respect.

Honor and Dignity

Lev Pinsker's famous pamphlet from 1882, *Auto-Emancipation*, was a call for Jews to act swiftly, boldly, and courageously to alleviate the depredations of antisemitism in Eastern Europe. Jews must demand that the nations of the world grant "our independence, allow us to take care of ourselves, give us but a little strip of land like that of the Serbians and Rumanians."[34] Likewise a pamphlet published in the following year by Isaac Rülf, an activist in the Hovevei Tsion and the chief rabbi of the German city of Memel, called on Jews to display "resolve" and a "desire for freedom." Like Pinsker, Rülf believed that only thus could Gentile contempt for Jews be replaced with regard: "If they can't love us, at least they should have to respect us."[35]

Whereas standard accounts of Zionism usually juxtapose the approach of the Hovevei Tsion with that of Theodor Herzl, in fact the two were very similar on the emotional level. On the one hand, the Hovevei Tsion favored immediate Jewish settlement in Palestine, which Herzl opposed; he thought that the Jews' right to settle in the land en masse had to be recognized first by the Ottoman Empire or some other Great Power. This need for international recognition was the essence of Statist Zionism, which aspired to place Jews as equals among the community of nations. Herzl also did not share Hovevei Tsion's passion for the Hebrew language and culture. Yet, Pinsker and Rülf, no less than Herzl, saw in Zionism a means for Jews to overcome the shame of passivity and to restore their honor by becoming masters of their own fate. All three longed for the respect of the nations of the world. More than the Eastern European Jews who represented the bulk of the Hovevei Tsion, Herzl sought Gentile favor as well as respect, because he spent his life in countries where emancipation had been extended to Jews but had remained tantalizingly incomplete. Herzl's adoration of the German emperor Wilhelm II—to the point that Herzl once dreamed that the two men were alone in a small boat on the high seas—had no parallel in Russian Zionists' feelings about the tsar. Yet despite these differences, and despite Herzl's superior organizational and leadership qualities that led to his successful convening of the first Zionist Congresses, Herzl's message of solidarity and unity in his pamphlet The Jewish State—that "we are one people—one people"—was axiomatic, if not painfully obvious, to the Hovevei Tsion.[36]

The main difference in emotional messaging between Herzl and Eastern European Zionists was one of form rather than content. In The Jewish State, Herzl presents himself as a supremely rational human being who has not embraced Zionism as an ideology but has simply discovered it as a fact of nature. The pamphlet's prose is lapidary in its brevity, hardness, and brilliance. It offers a cool, apparently detached diagnosis of and cure for a deadly and heretofore ineradicable hatred. Yet there is a reservoir of urgency and sympathy underneath the text's straightforward presentation. It is the combination of superficial sangfroid and underlying desperation that makes the pamphlet so rhetorically effective. One of Herzl's closest allies, the celebrated writer Max Nordau, understood this perfectly when he read the pamphlet in February 1896:

> If you had never written another line . . . this brochure assures you a
> lasting place among heroes. Heroically, for a writer passionate about
> style—renouncing any showy language, the modest, austere terseness of the presentation; unspeakably heroic is the burning of all
> bridges behind you. . . . Henceforth you can only continue to act as
> you have—calling forth the deepest humanity from the reader. . . .
> Highly heroic is this more than brave, indeed, utterly fearless recognition of the ultimate feeling, which all Jews until now have born in
> the deepest recesses of their soul. . . . It was not your intentional
> effect that I would think primarily about the subjective—about you,
> and not on the work. But you must be able to empathize with me
> that I do this. For I do not know what will become of this work, but I
> do know that you have revealed yourself in this brochure.[37]

Like his language, Herzl's public persona—immaculately dressed and coiffed and uncommonly handsome, with a luxuriant black beard and deep-set, melancholic eyes—connoted prophetic insight, serenity without indifference, and composure without nonchalance. In his own lifetime, and even more so after his untimely death at the age of forty-four, Herzl's image served as an icon of the Zionist movement. His grave visage projected not only compassion for Jewish suffering but also hope, pride, and self-respect. The French Jewish writer Edmond Fleg was drawn to Zionism by Herzl's dedication, as well as the loyalty and attachment to the Land of Israel displayed by the Zionist movement as a whole.

Almost three decades after attending the Zionist Congress in 1899, Fleg recalled, "I trembled with emotion as I pictured the universal exodus which would bring them home from their many exiles to the unity that they had reconquered."[38]

A year previously Richard Gottheil, the first president of the American Zionist Federation, acknowledged that Zionism sought not to move all of world Jewry to Palestine but "to give back to the Jew that nobleness of spirit, that confidence in himself, that belief in his own powers which only perfect freedom can give. . . . He will feel that he belongs somewhere and not everywhere."[39] These same feelings informed the Zionist sensibilities of U.S. Supreme Court Justice Louis Brandeis, who wrote in 1915 that every American Jew should become a Zionist because it instills the "task of inculcating self-respect, a task which can be accomplished only by restoring the ties of the Jew to the Noble past of his race, and by making him realize the possibilities of a no less glorious future."[40]

At this point we must disentangle two closely related emotional dyads: shame and honor, on the one hand, and humiliation and dignity, on the other. Shame is both a publicly imposed disapproval of one's actions and an internalization of that disapproval. Shaming from without leads to self-loathing and a passive torpor. Honor has similarly external origins in a code of behavior that, if followed, bestows social capital and integrates individuals into the collective.[41] (As the biblical prophet Zepheniah said of the Jews who had been exiled from the Land of Israel, God "will give them praise and honor in every land where they have suffered shame" [3:19].) Throughout history men and women have both been accorded honor and victimized by shame, but for different reasons and in disparate ways. In nineteenth-century European nationalist movements, the nation was often represented as a shamed woman, but the ultimate shame, according to nationalist ideology, rested on men who had not been sufficiently loyal to her or willing to fight on her behalf. In Zionism the element of male shame was particularly prominent because of long-standing antisemitic accusations that Jewish men were feeble, cowardly, avaricious, devious, and disloyal—that is, they were lacking in the qualities of strength, courage, and honor that were traditionally associated with masculinity and were a hallmark of nineteenth-century bourgeois values. Herzl was painfully sensitive to such accusations, which he countered by cultivating a personality radiating rectitude, stamina, and selfless devotion to the Zionist cause.

Shaming often involves practices of humiliation, but those who perceive themselves as humiliated are just as likely to react with righteous anger as with self-blame and a sense of personal worthlessness. They are angry because despite being humiliated, they have retained their sense of self-worth; that is, their dignity.[42] Over the course of the twentieth century and particularly after World War II, throughout the Western world dignity began to replace honor as a cultural value. Much earlier, however, at the fin de siècle the most influential exponent of Hebraic Zionism, Ahad Ha-Am, emphasized the value of dignity rather than honor in Jewish public life. Dignity emerged out of a natural and healthy feeling of difference between Jews and others, a feeling that in turn led to self-protection and the cultivation of distinctive ways of life. Ahad Ha-Am keenly appreciated Jewish emotional needs and how Zionism satisfied them:

> It provides [an individual] an opportunity for communal work and political excitement; his emotions find an outlet in a field of activity which is not subservient to non-Jews; and he feels that, thanks to this ideal, he stands once more spiritually erect and has regained his personal dignity, without overmuch trouble and purely by his own efforts. . . . For it is not the attainment of the ideal that he heeds; its pursuit alone is sufficient to cure him of his spiritual disease, which is that of an inferiority complex, and the loftier and more distant the ideal, the greater its power to exalt.[43]

Whereas plays by Herzl and Nordau positively presented Jews who fight duels to defend their honor, Ahad Ha-Am felt that a sense of dignity should cause Jews to ignore antisemitic insults and take satisfaction in what he believed to be their moral superiority.[44]

Not all Hebraic Zionists shared Ahad Ha-Am's belief that to be "weak was superior."[45] The writer Micha Berdyczewski (1865–1921) was a self-styled Nietzschean who glorified ancient Israel's wars, particularly the revolt against Rome in 66–73 CE, in the belief that cultural vitality and military valor were inseparable. Likewise, in one of his most famous poems, "In the City of the Slaughter," Hayim Nahman Bialik excoriates the men of the Bessarabian city of Kishinev (today's Chișinău in Moldova) for not fighting back during the infamous pogrom of April 1903:

> Crushed in their shame, they saw it all;
> They did not stir nor move;
> They did not pluck their eyes out;
> They beat not their brains against the wall!
> Perhaps, perhaps, each watcher had it in his heart to pray:
> A miracle, O Lord,—and spare my skin this day![46]

The word "shame" appears ten times in the poem. Women appear only as the violated wives of cowardly men, who after the pogrom has passed ask the rabbi if they may still have sexual relations with them. Bialik's fulminations against the Jewish men of Kishinev derived not only from compassion for the destroyed community but also from his burning desire to kindle a new, activist, and proud spirit in his fellow Jews.

Internal Anxieties

In Europe, Hebraic Zionism could be just as focused on feelings of powerlessness and striving for empowerment as the overtly Statist Zionism of Herzl and Nordau. In the Middle East, where the political and economic position of the Jews was more secure than in Eastern or Central Europe, discussions of shame and honor, of agency and pride, were more muted. In general, Middle Eastern Zionism avoided the issue of Jewish statehood. As Ottoman subjects, Jews native to Palestine and its surrounding lands were in no position to advocate for dissolving the empire or handing Palestine over to a Jewish chartered company against the will of the government and the populace alike. Nor is there reason to believe that they wanted such things to occur. The writer and Hebrew educator Abraham Elmaleh was typical of Sephardic Jewish elites in late Ottoman Syria and Palestine in claiming that Zionism and Ottoman patriotism were fully compatible precisely because Zionism was an evolutionary, not revolutionary, cultural movement.[47] That movement promoted Jewish primary-school education in Hebrew, although the Egyptian and Palestinian Zionist activist Nissim Malul insisted that "there is no requirement for a nationalist person to know his language. The nationalist is one who experiences feelings of nationalism" or who engages in "nationalist deeds."[48]

What would these feelings and deeds consist of? For Malul, despite his acknowledgment that one could be a nationalist without knowing the national tongue, Zionism should strive to cultivate Hebrew literacy. And, he emphasized, it must present Hebrew as a Semitic language in kinship and symbiosis with Arabic: "As a Semitic nation we must reinforce our Semitic nationhood and not blur it within European culture. By utilizing Arabic we can create a real Hebrew culture, but if we blend it with European elements we will simply be committing suicide."[49] This position ran counter to that of European Zionists, who had mixed feelings about Zionism's interaction with Middle Eastern cultures. Some European Zionists, like Yehoshua Radler-Feldman (better known by his pen name, Rabbi Binyamin), promoted a Jewish return to the Orient as a reunion of Semitic brethren who would live in harmony within the Ottoman Empire's multinational structure. Yet, as we saw in the previous chapter, Orientalist stereotypes about Arab backwardness, indolence, and propensities for violence, as well as worry about "criolian degeneracy," were common among new Jewish immigrants from Europe to Palestine. Concerns about the Europeanization or Levantinization of Zionist culture demonstrate that anxiety as a political emotion has meanings beyond concerns for physical safety and that its source can be something much broader than an intentionally malevolent force.

An unexpected source of early Zionist unease was the initiative to create a capacious, supple literary Hebrew that could express complex thoughts and feelings. The dissemination of a modernized literary Hebrew and the development of a new vernacular Hebrew, to be spoken as a native tongue, were among the most important Zionist projects in the Yishuv at the fin de siècle.[50] Bialik worried, however, that whereas millennia of isolating Hebrew from the realm of the vernacular had maintained its literary majesty, the renewal of spoken Hebrew could destroy, as well as foster, a new Jewish culture.[51] Gershom Scholem, a pioneer scholar of Jewish mysticism, expressed related fears in 1926 in a letter to the philosopher Franz Rosenzweig:

> This country is a volcano! . . . More than anything else today we are concerned about the Arab. But much more sinister than the Arab problem is another threat, a threat which the Zionist enterprise unavoidably has had to face: the "actualization" [i.e., modernization, bringing up to date] of Hebrew. . . . Many believe that the language has been secularized, and the apocalyptic thorn has been pulled out. But this is not true at all. . . . It is impossible to empty out words which are filled to the breaking point with specific meanings.[52]

According to Scholem classical Hebrew is "fraught with danger" and contains the "hidden power" of messianism. Adhering to classical Hebrew would lead not to a healthy society but towards an abyss. Yet the Hebrew "spoken on the streets" of Palestine is a "ghastly gibberish," a "faceless lingo" as the result of secularization. Grave peril lies in either outcome: whether Jews successfully extract the "apocalyptic thorn" or limp along with it in place.[53]

In chapter 1, I introduced the concept of Transformative Zionism, which sought to change diaspora Jews into Hebrews rooted in the Land of Israel. Zionism was both defined and threatened by the Herculean challenge of changing the Jews' native tongue to Hebrew, their livelihoods to primary production, and their political loyalties to the Yishuv as a Jewish state in the making. Idealistic immigrants sought to slough off their diasporic identities by abandoning their given or family names for Hebraic ones via direct translations (e.g., Goldberg to Harpaz), poetic patronymics (e.g., Ben-Zvi, "son of the gazelle"), or associations with Jewish antiquity. (Shortly after emigrating from Poland to Palestine in 1905, nineteen-year-old David Grün, who would go on to become the preeminent leader of the Yishuv and early State of Israel, adopted the last name of Ben-Gurion, a leader of the ancient Jewish revolt against Rome.) These trends were clearly visible by World War I, especially among a cluster of perhaps two to three thousand Eastern European youth who constituted the pioneering core of the Zionist labor movement. They developed an ethos of overcoming and overthrowing the diasporic Jewish past, which they viewed with a blend of nostalgia, condescension, and discomfort. They set their sights on the future and their hearts on the rejuvenation of the Land of Israel.

The Interwar Period: The Institutionalization of Passion

Transformative Zionism enhanced the passionate romanticism of the Hovevei Tsion. The pioneer youth were divided politically—some were Marxists, others were Tolstoian agrarians, and, still others, Kropotkin-esque anarchists—but they shared a devotion to radicalism of a Russian hue and a burning will to create in Eretz Israel a new community based on Jewish labor and Hebrew culture. They had formed intimate social communities in their hometowns, and they brought to Palestine an adolescent intensity, filled with exuberance and prone to emotional extremes. To provide a particularly colorful example, a knot of young Jews from Bobruisk, Belarus, formed a *kvutzah* (small agricultural cooperative) on the Sea of Galilee during World War I. One of the group, Berl Katznelson, was eager to perform agricultural labor but had little capacity for it. While he devoted himself to Zionist ideology (and later became one of Labor Zionism's most important thinkers), he became romantically linked with another member of the Bobruisk group, the nurse Sarah Shmukler. During an outbreak of yellow fever in 1919, Sarah, who devoted herself selflessly to the sick, succumbed to the disease. At her funeral Katznelson howled in despair and leapt into her grave. He later married another member of the group, Leah Miron who had loved him all along and who was Sarah's closest friend.[54]

The pioneers' passions became the stuff of legend. In 1988 the Israeli author Meir Shalev published a novel about the pioneers, *Roman Russi*, whose title is deliberately ambiguous, meaning both "a Russian novel" and "a Russian love affair."[55] That affair was both interpersonal and between individuals and the land itself. In a landmark study of Labor Zionism's psychoemotional matrix, Boaz Neumann wrote of "pioneer desire" as "an anarchic flow, devoid of reason or purpose, neither a biological need nor a social demand nor an act of will."[56] Digging wells and sowing seeds, the young workers saw themselves as impregnating the land. Barren—that is, naked—hills and mountains would be covered and their honor and beauty restored through forestation. The pioneers' love for the land was both sexual and chaste—a search for purity—exemplified by the Zionist agronomist Yitzhak Elazar-Wilkansky's comment likening swimming in the Sea of Galilee to immersion in a mikveh (a Jewish ritual bath). In the poetry of Avraham Shlonsky, who worked on road building and construction in Palestine during the early 1920s, labor was a sacred act of devotion and sacrifice.[57]

The language of pioneer passion is that of male desire, yet Zionist women also expressed their love of the land and their desire, as per the Labor Zionist mantra, "to build and be built" (see figure 3). Only about 10 percent of the Zionist youth who arrived in Palestine during the decade before the outbreak of World War I were women, but that figure rose to 17–18 percent for the years just after the war.[58] One of the most eloquent of these women, the poet Rachel Bluwstein (commonly referred to by her first name) spent four years before the war in Palestine, working in the fields of two Jewish settlements. Rachel adopted a more

Figure 3 Stock photograph of female Zionist pioneers in Palestine around 1940. The arrangement of the women's bodies and the implements they are holding suggests that the photograph was staged and was made for publicity purposes. *Credit*: Alamy; photographer unknown.

modest tone than her male counterparts, but her attachment to the land was no less deep. As she wrote in 1926,

> I never sang your praise, my land,
> Nor did I embellish your namesake with epics of valor
> Nor with a spoil of battles;
> Only a tree—did I plant with my own hands on the quiet banks of
>   the Jordan,
> Only a path—did I clear with my feet across the fields.
> Indeed, very meager, I have known this, mother,
> Indeed, very meager, is your daughter's offering.[59]

A 1931 anthology of the writings of Zionist pioneer women is filled with stories of women striving to overcome the dual challenges of backbreaking agricultural labor and of men who dismissed the women's suitability for anything but household work. In the primitive conditions under which the workers lived, however, household chores were themselves difficult and exhausting. Batya Brenner joined a kvutzah and proceeded to fail at a succession of domestic tasks, but she doggedly stuck with them and was thrilled when she finally successfully baked bread for her comrades. "Who of my old friends in the shtetl back home knows what real happiness is? Who of them has lived through such a joyous day?" she declaimed in her memoir.[60] As with her male counterparts, Brenner's desire to work was a means of attaining honor and self-respect.

During the interwar period, young Jewish men and women formed scores of collective settlements—small and large, urban and rural, temporary and permanent. Working and living conditions were often harsh, and in the new rural settlements, food and potable water could be as scarce as malaria was omnipresent. The youth sought to overcome these challenges with revolutionary fervor, a spirit of altruism, and, most importantly, finding joy in labor and comradeship. The philosopher Hermann Cohen once said derisively of Zionists, "Those louts! They want to be happy."[61] In fact, there was little room in the pioneers' psyche for banal emotions such as quotidian happiness or contentment. Joy impelled young workers, exhausted after a day of hard labor, to folk dance late into the night. It was a cultivated frenzy.

The link between modern political movements and joy dates back to Friedrich Schiller's "Ode to Joy" (1785), which attained immortality when it was set to music by Ludwig van Beethoven in the final movement of his Ninth Symphony. The Zionist equivalent of Schiller's ode was "Hava Nagila" (Come, Let Us Rejoice), whose lyrics, although inspired by Psalm 118, were crafted in 1918 and set to an uptempo version of a traditional Hasidic melody.[62] The lyrics are a call for febrile rejoining: "Come, let us rejoice and be happy! . . . Come, Let us sing and be happy. . . . Awake, my brothers, with a happy heart!" In the song, happiness is more than a state of individual well-being: it is a surge of anticipation of the fulfillment of a deep-seated desire.

At Bitania, a labor collective near the Sea of Galilee founded in 1920 by members of the Marxist Zionist youth movement, The Young Guard (Ha-Shomer Ha-Tsa'ir), joy was directly linked to eros—not an erotic love of the land but erotic human attraction, which would be both acknowledged and sublimated into devotion to the community. Meir Ya'ari, Bitania's leader, was a charismatic figure who gathered his flock for intense, intimate, and prolonged conversations about their innermost desires and fears.[63] This was a therapeutic process, but its goal was not, as in Freudian psychoanalysis, attainment of a coherent and realistic sense of self-in-the-world so much as a joyous melding of self into the collective.

The opposite of joy is despair, an abandonment of hope. It can develop suddenly, in response to an overwhelming, crushing event or gradually as a product of an accumulation of disappointments. The history of Zionism is filled with disappointment—an emotion triggered by the failure to obtain an object of desire or, even worse, by the inability of that desired object to live up to expectations. From the beginnings of modern Jewish immigration to Palestine, there was always return migration among Jews who could not secure their livelihoods or found the environment too harsh, the surroundings too alien, or the existing Jewish communities too unwelcoming. Some of the foundational works of twentieth-century Hebrew literature, such as Y. H. Brenner's *Breakdown and Bereavement* (1920) and S. Y. Agnon's *Only Yesterday* (1945), narrate the travails and disillusionment of young arrivals from Russia to Palestine.

The more idealistic one was—the greater one's sense of mission to transform Eretz Israel and oneself—the greater the potential was for disappointment and despair. The adolescent pioneers struggled with their identities, their yearning for social inclusion and romantic fulfillment, and the contradiction between what they were and what they aspired to be. It could all be too great to bear. At Bitania the despair of one member,

Ernst Pollak, was so great that he shot himself. His body was found next to a copy of Fyodor Dostoyevsky's novel *The Brothers Karamazov* open to the section known as "The Grand Inquisitor," a lengthy disquisition on the limits of human freedom and capacity for good.[64] Isolated from society and ravaged by malaria, some members of the Bitania collective gave vent to their despair by engaging in occult practices, and their tombstones at the Kinneret cemetery bear mysterious satanic symbols.[65]

The immigrant youth were prone to disappointment or despair both because of the difficulties they faced adjusting to life in Palestine and the psychological burden of sloughing off their former selves as "diaspora Jews" and crafting a new "Hebrew" identity. In contrast, the native-born children of the Yishuv, the sabras, became symbols of national physical and mental health. Zionist literature praised sabra youths' lithe and tanned bodies (tacitly assuming they were the children of pale Ashkenazim rather than darker-complexioned Middle Eastern Jews). Their clothing was that of a European youth movement—khaki shorts and a short-sleeved shirt—with the addition of unpadded "biblical" sandals (*sandalim tanakhi'im*) and a casual and practical bucket hat (*kova tembel*). Unlike their psychologically intense and introspective predecessors, the members of the sabra generation were supposed to be self-possessed, pragmatic, and stoic while at the same time unquestioningly devoted to the development and protection of the Yishuv.[66]

The Labor Zionist poet Nathan Alterman depicts the stoicism of the idealized sabra in a poem written in December 1947 about two sabra fighters, male and female, emerging from a battle for the creation of a Jewish state:

Weary without end, deprived of repose
Young Hebrew curls dripping—
Silently come forward
And stand without moving.
No sign if they're alive or shot through

Then the people, spellbound, steeped in tears,

Say, Who are you? And the two

Answer in silence: We are the silver platter

Upon which you will have the State of the Jews.[67]

The repeated references to silence in the poem are telling. Silence bespeaks inner calm, strength, and dedication as opposed to the pathos and declamatory style of earlier generations of Zionists. When the sabras did speak, their language was directed to the tasks at hand and the means to accomplish them.

The sabra and the pioneer were ideal types that both represented and exaggerated reality. Most Jews in Mandate Palestine lived in towns and cities, not agricultural communities, and capitalist agricultural settlements flourished, especially in the citrus-growing regions near Palestine's coast. But there was an element of transformative zeal in even the more bourgeois forms of Zionism that dominated the Yishuv's towns and cities, especially Tel Aviv. Tel Aviv's leaders cultivated an ethos of what Hizky Shoham calls "urban Zionism," characterized by civic virtue and conviviality.[68] Bourgeois urban Zionism aspired to happiness, not Labor Zionist joy. Bourgeois happiness was a secular emotion, whereas the joy of redemptive labor was a secularized form of spiritual exaltation.

Interethnic conviviality was part of the fabric of urban Zionism. Until the 1930s Jews and Arabs in Palestine attended each other's celebrations (Arabs joined the Tel Aviv Purim parade, and Jews came to the festival of Nebi Rubin).[69] In contrast, the Labor Zionist sense of mission promoted a more wary view of Arabs that blended admiration, condescension, and disdain. The pioneers of the early twentieth century determined that Palestine's Arabs lacked the Jewish youths' passionate desire to work, improve, and "redeem" the land.[70] During the interwar period, Labor Zionist claims that Arabs had failed to steward the land and that Zionists had come to reclaim it were commonplace. Contempt for alleged Arab indolence combined with fear of the Arabs' alleged propensity for violence. These fears, stoked by intercommunal violence in Jerusalem in 1920 and Jaffa in 1921, escalated vastly after the riots of August 1929, when Arabs killed more than one hundred Jews throughout Palestine, and over the course of the Palestinian-Arab Revolt against the British and Zionists between 1936 and 1939.[71]

Despite the presence of such powerful negative emotions toward Arabs, textbooks in the Yishuv's schools and political pronouncements from the Yishuv's governing elite made a studied attempt to refrain from expressions of outright hatred of Arabs. Instead the Arab masses were portrayed as rather childlike and easily manipulated, thereby deserving of paternalist concern rather than rage.[72] A constant claim of Zionist propaganda was that Jewish immigration had brought great material benefit to Palestine's Arabs, a boon that threatened the traditional Palestinian elites, who were the true barriers to peace. Responding to the violence of 1929, the Histadrut stated confidently that violence between Jews and Arabs was only a passing phase because, in time, Arab workers would realize that their class interests were identical to those of the Jews.[73]

The Histadrut's cool, composed response to the 1929 riots reflected Labor Zionist efforts to craft an emotional regime that would mold the Yishuv population's response to crisis. Within that emotional regime, responding to violence with a steady resolve was a sign of strength and virtue, a triumph of Western sangfroid over ostensibly Levantine hotheadedness. During the Palestinian-Arab Revolt, this emotional regime demanded the exercise of what the Yishuv's Labor Zionist leaders called restraint (havlagah) when responding to Palestinian provocations. Application of the minimal force required to execute a defensive mission bestowed on Zionism what was called tohar neshek (purity of arms).[74]

The regime of emotional restraint was sorely tested by World War II. During the first three years of the war, residents of the Yishuv feared for their very existence. Because the British had ruthlessly suppressed the Palestinian revolt, there was little Jewish-Arab violence. But Palestine's

Jews anxiously followed the Axis armored corps' advance eastward across North Africa. Italian bombers attacked Tel Aviv and Haifa. An Axis invasion of Palestine and the destruction of its Jewish community appeared imminent.[75] In October and November 1942, the German defeat at El Alamein, Egypt, stopped the Axis advance, but the Yishuv faced another, no less inconceivable, tragedy.

Early in the war, Zionists assumed that, despite persecution, most of Europe's Jews would survive the hostilities and a Jewish state would become their shelter. In June 1942, an emergency Zionist conference at the Biltmore Hotel in New York City denounced the British government's 1939 White Paper, which proposed creating in Palestine a unitary state with an Arab majority, and instead demanded Jewish statehood. But the sense of triumph at Biltmore was crushed a few months later when news filtered in from Europe about the mass murder of millions of Jews who were to have found freedom in the Jewish state.

On November 27, 1942, the Yishuv's National Council declared three days of public mourning for the Jewish dead of Europe. As the war wore on, the Zionist leadership engaged in symbolic rescue activity, but it could do little to staunch the slaughter of two-thirds of Europe's Jews. The Yishuv's political parties bickered about their stances toward rescue, Britain, and the postwar future, and the two principal Zionist militias, the Labor movement's Haganah and the right-oriented Irgun, were bitter rivals. Yet all the Zionist factions shared an overarching and overwhelming sense of helplessness, loss, and anguish—an emotional palette contrary to the stoicism cultivated by the Yishuv leadership over the previous two decades.[76]

The behavior of the Jews in Palestine over the course of the 1948 Arab–Israeli war cannot be understood without taking into account both the trauma wrought by the Holocaust and the emotional regime that the Yishuv's governing bodies had created during the 1930s. During the 1948 war, for the most part Israel's political and military elites steered clear of calling for revenge or justifying murderous rage against the enemy. This public discourse does not, however, tell us what feelings lay inside the Jewish fighters' hearts, nor what they did to Arabs of their own accord, under orders from their superiors, or with the tacit support of the state's leadership.[77] Newcomers and veteran settlers alike felt that their backs were to the wall and that they had to give everything they had to the war effort because there was nowhere else to go. (By late 1948 one-quarter of the 100,00 Jews fighting in the recently established Israel Defense Forces were refugees from Europe, and many had been in concentration camps.[78]) Jews did not have the choice of fleeing unless they left by sea, which was possible only for some affluent city dwellers.[79]

During the winter of 1948, when fighting was mainly between Palestinian militias and Zionist forces, and the Palestinians temporarily had the upper hand, the Haganah carried out a series of public opinion surveys in Haifa. The surveys revealed that the Jewish civilian population's emotional state ranged from grim to optimistic, but that for the most part they were resolute, calm, and willing to endure substantial material sacrifice for the war effort. Their main fear was of civil war between the Haganah and the Irgun; primary sources of frustration were profiteering and an unequal distribution of wartime obligations among Jews.[80] Being in the eye of the hurricane, they were less likely to panic than to seek out meaningful action, like donating to war bonds, that gave them a sense of patriotic belonging and agency.[81] Nathan Alterman expressed this sense of determination and purposefulness in a poem in 1941, when he wrote, "How thin is the line between the verge of catastrophe and the eve of jubilation."[82]

For sabra youth, the commitment to the war and the newborn state was total and unquestioning. A ten-year-old boy from an Orthodox Zionist settlement wrote in a youth newspaper to an imaginary Jewish soldier: "If I were as old as you are, I would take a Sten [an inexpensive British submachine gun] in my hand and smite the enemies of our people. I try to conjure up your image as you stand with a roaring weapon in your hands, striking the enemy. Hebrew warrior! Be strong and of good courage! Be not afraid!"[83] Those "enemies" were the Palestinians, the Arab states, and by extension the perpetrators of the Holocaust, foremost among them, Germany. The fact that the Palestinian leader Mohammed Amin al-Husseini spent the war years in Berlin, broadcasting propaganda for the Nazi regime, made the connection between the Palestinians and the Nazis appear airtight.[84] Just as Labor Zionism channeled the passions of immigrant and Yishuv youth into the construction of the Jewish national home, Israel's hard-fought victory in 1948—in which one in every hundred Jews (and a much higher percentage of young ones) died—cemented the association of Arabs with the Jews' historic enemies, from the biblical Amalek to Adolf Hitler.

Zionism in the Diaspora: Solidarity as an Emotions Bundle

Zionist passion circulated throughout the world, but it fared better in some countries than in others. In interwar Europe, Zionism flourished where the political and social position of the Jews was fragile. Such was the case in Poland, home to Europe's largest Jewish community and the second largest in the world after the United States. Zionism was particularly popular in Poland's multiethnic eastern borderlands. The international Zionist pioneering movement He-Halutz established training farms where young Polish Jews lived in communal settings, experiencing the hardship, camaraderie, and intimacy of a Palestinian kvutzah.[85] The Revisionist Zionist movement's youth league Betar was also popular, simultaneously rejecting and embracing the ambient Polish environment by appropriating key aspects of Polish nationalism of the time, such as the striving for national dignity, a sense of historic victimization, a commitment to personal honor, and a predilection for paramilitary dress and drill.[86]

In the United States, in contrast, interwar Zionism was more ethnic and philanthropic than transformative, and its connection with the Yishuv was one of solidarity rather than passion. Solidarity is a bundle of action-oriented cognitive states, such as attachment, admiration, and obligation; in turn, they are nourished by a bundle of feelings including pride, compassion, and trepidation. Unlike pity, which places the provider of assistance at a remove from the beneficiary, solidarity requires a sense of commonality and proximity, as well as difference and distance. Unlike empathy, which involves an internalization of the feelings of others, solidarity is a manifestation of sympathy—an acknowledgment of another's travails while not suffering oneself.

American Jewish solidarity with Zionism did not require formal Zionist affiliation. At the end of the 1920s fewer than 2 percent of American Jews belonged to a Zionist organization. (Throughout the 1920s, German Jews were almost three times more likely to belong to Zionist organizations than American Jews, and they also emigrated to Palestine in larger numbers.) Four-fifths of those Americans who did identify as Zionists were members of Hadassah, the Women's Zionist Organization of America, which engaged in a wide range of medical, educational, and cultural projects in the Yishuv.[87] For leaders of Hadassah and its male counterpart, the Zionist Organization of America, such projects were humanitarian and embodied progressive American values: to be a Zionist was to combine philanthropic concern for Jews in Palestine and confidence in a robust future for Jews at home in America.

American Jewish concern and aid for Palestine's Jews, however, came from quarters far removed from the official Zionist movement. The riots in Palestine in 1929 sent shock waves through the American Jewish community. Rabbis of all denominations gave sermons condemning the violence and offering consolation to the bereaved. The Reform movement's historic opposition to Zionism as a form of nationalist particularism began to soften, and in 1930 "Hatikvah" was added to the Reform hymnal. Abraham Cahan, the editor of the popular Yiddish daily newspaper *Forwerts*, traveled to Palestine after the riots and wrote positively about the Yishuv, even if he did not embrace Zionism. Although many Jewish communists were fiercely anti-Zionist, others were more sympathetic and declared a day of fasting in memory of the victims. Henry Hurwitz, editor of the prestigious *Menorah Journal,* compared the "intense passion of the Jewish folk for Zion" to a "love affair."[88]

Over the course of the 1930s, the darkening position of European Jewry, a wave of Jewish immigration to Palestine, and the Palestinian-Arab Revolt further deepened bonds between American Jews and the Yishuv. In 1937 the Reform movement issued a new platform that praised the "rehabilitation of Palestine," which held "the promise of renewed life for many of our brethren." The statement went on to "affirm the obligation of all Jewry to aid in its upbuilding as a Jewish homeland."[89] In America's major cities, Jewish community newspapers reported in detail on the Palestinian Revolt and violence against Palestine's Jews.

During World War II, trepidation for the fate of Europe's Jews and anguish when news of their destruction became widely known led to an exponential increase in formal support for Zionism. Between 1939 and 1948, membership in Zionist organizations in the United States increased from some one hundred thousand to more than seven hundred thousand.[90] During World War II the patrician American Jewish Committee (AJC), which had fewer than four hundred members but exercised considerable influence over Jewish public life and had access to the centers of power in Washington, refused to formally identify with Zionism and ignored the Biltmore Program. However, after 1945 it embraced the creation of a Jewish state as a home for Holocaust survivors.[91] Zionism still had competitors and detractors within the American Jewish community, but after the war it became mainstream, if not hegemonic.[92]

The emotional intensity of American Zionism increased immeasurably in the wake of the Holocaust, which left American Jews grieving for lost loved ones, anxious for the surviving remnants of European Jewry, and burdened by survivor guilt. Henry Montor, vice chair of American Jewry's primary fundraising instrument, the United Jewish Appeal (UJA), knew how to appeal to these feelings to benefit his cause. At the outset of the UJA's 1946 campaign, Montor brought to Washington, DC, a contingent of survivors from the Bergen-Belsen concentration camp to meet a select group of 350 major donors. The donors, who had passed the war years in comfort and safety in the United States, were humbled, awed, and shamed in the presence of Jews who had been through hell. At the Washington event and similar gatherings throughout the country, the attendees were required to publicly declare their financial commitment to the campaign. The donors were mostly male, and Montor appealed to their masculine pride as they competed with each other for honor and status.[93] Fear of being belittled within one's immediate social circle, combined with compassion and guilt, made for a particularly powerful emotional formula for Zionist solidarity. The orchestrated performances of affect had remarkable results: a UJA campaign total of more than $100 million, three times the total from the previous year.

Emotional bonds with Jewish refugees in Europe were further intensified by the Zionist struggle for Jewish statehood in Palestine. American Jews greeted the United Nations partition resolution of November 29, 1947, with a blend of jubilation, pride, and worry for the Jewish state's survival in the face of Arab hostility. In May 1948, after Israel declared its independence, a University of Chicago student said at a youth event celebrating Israel's creation, "When I saw the flag of Israel rise in the air, I felt the crowd melt in a maze of collective emotion. We were as one."[94] The prominent rabbi Milton Steinberg issued a Jewish call to arms on behalf of the future Jewish state.[95]

While war raged in Palestine in 1948, the UJA raised the unprecedented sum of $150 million—the equivalent of $1.5 billion today. This amount was almost equal to all American Protestant, Catholic, and nonsectarian donations for overseas relief in that year.[96] Milwaukee-born Golda Meyerson (later Meir), head of the Political Department of the Jewish Agency for Palestine, was a consummate fundraiser whose speeches touched the heartstrings and opened the purse strings of her audiences. In Miami in February 1948, she proposed a clear division of labor between her audience and the Jews of Palestine: "This is your war, too. . . . But we do not ask you to guard the convoy. If there is any blood to be spilled, let it be ours. . . . Remember, though, that how long this blood will be shed depends on you."[97]

Meyerson's speeches appealed to solidarity interlaced with guilt for living in safety while the Jews of Europe had perished and now while the Jews in Palestine were under attack. A June 1948 UJA fundraising pamphlet played on these feelings. Large blood-red letters screamed "JEWISH BLOOD FLOWS AGAIN":

> But this time it's FIGHTING BLOOD! It's the blood of heroes. . . . Freedom blood. . . . It's the blood of Jews . . . flowing even as you read! Not the helpless, hopeless, hell of Hitlerism—today in Palestine Jews have a fighting chance. They're fighting for the freedom that generations hoped for, finally decreed by the United Nations. On every ambushed road, in every besieged village, through every deadly night and day, they're winning this freedom at last. . . . 1948 will tell the tale—whether Hitler's work will be finished for him, or whether the Land of Israel will rise as a new nation for those who wish it. It's entirely up to you—and you have to live with your conscience. Give now, and give as never before.

On another page, thin strips of block letters resembling a telegram blare, "You are safe . . . your family is safe . . . your future secure . . . But what if Jewish defenders are wiped out? What then O Americans? What Nazi plan comes next? Palestine Jews must not fail. You must not fail. . . . Give . . . Give . . . Give."[98]

The fundraising campaigns usually focused less on Israel's established Jewish population than on Holocaust survivors in Europe or newly arrived European Jews in Israel. Compassion for the survivors constituted the lowest common denominator that could motivate American Jews to give generously to Israel. When planning the 1948 UJA campaign, Montor consciously chose to concentrate fundraising efforts in the hands of organizations that represented all of American Jewry, rather than specifically Zionist ones.[99] This approach characterized a 1948 UJA fundraising film depicting the plight of Jewish refugees who had left Europe for Israel, only to be placed in tents in the desert because of a lack of housing. While pictures of human misery flash across the screen, a stern-voiced narrator scolds his viewers for not fulfilling their campaign pledges:

> Who is to blame? Did you have a share in putting these people into the tents, into these lines? . . . Perhaps the agencies of the United Jewish Appeal haven't done enough. . . . Or does the fault lie with American Jewry? . . . We must act now, today. *Cash* is the only thing that will get them out of these camps. *Cash* is the only thing that will give them a new home. *Cash* for the United Jewish Appeal will fulfill our promise that they shall not be homeless again.[100]

The film's attempt to induce feelings of both compassion and guilt in the viewer is transparent. The manipulation of emotion, however, is only successful if the recipient of the message is receptive to an emotional appeal. If the viewers of this film had felt no sympathy for Holocaust survivors, no qualms about dwelling in comfort in an American city while their coreligionists suffered in the sun-scorched desert, the film would have failed to achieve its goals. But the emotional message of this film hit its target.

American Jewish solidarity with Israel in 1948 took more active forms than giving money. About 1,200 American Jews volunteered to fight for Israel. They had a sort of anthem, lacking in the dignity and pathos of the poetry with which this chapter began but no less revealing. There were multiple versions of the lyrics, but the verses always ended with "Fight, Fight, Fight for Palestine!" The preliminary couplets included "O you sons of Moses/With your crooked noses" and "Save your dimes and nickels/For your kosher pickles."[101] The verses employed self-parody that superficially accepted diasporic Jewish stereotypes only to contest and invert them. The lyrics displayed a hybrid American and Eastern European Jewish culture that had little to do with the culture of the new Zionist community in Palestine.

In April 1948, four American volunteer fighters (known by the Hebrew acronym *machal*) composed a more serious and dignified version of the song.[102] In both its humorous and earnest forms, the song expressed pride in and solidarity with the Jews of Palestine, as well as a deep yearning for honor. It is no coincidence that the song was sung to Rudolf Friml's "Song of the Vagabonds," an ode to patriotic loyalty, to fighting bravely and dying for one's country.

The extent of American Jewish solidarity may be gauged from a study carried out in May 1948 by the sociologists Marshall Sklare and Benjamin Ringer. Their interviews of 230 Baltimore Jews revealed that 90 percent supported Israel's establishment, 95 percent supported Jews sending money to Israel, and 80 percent supported sending arms. Almost 40 percent responded affirmatively when asked, "If you could, would you yourself like to fight in Palestine?"[103] Only 5 percent expressed a desire to live in Israel, but most felt comfortable with Israel as a place "to give displaced persons a chance to live and rehabilitate themselves."[104] Synagogue attendance and other forms of religious observance, as well as knowledge of Yiddish, were factors that increased the intensity of attachments to Israel but did not affect overall support for Israel's establishment and the conviction that Jews were obligated to assist the state.

Half the interviewees claimed that, since the fighting had begun, they felt closer to the Jewish people, and another quarter said that they already felt tightly bound to the Jewish people and could not have become more so. The interviewers noticed that interviewees were wont to refer to Israelis in the third person rather than first person ("they" rather than "we"), suggesting that "'feeling closer' did not always represent intimate identification" with Jews in Israel.[105] It was precisely Israel's distinctiveness from diaspora Jewish self-images—its embodiment of pioneering values and military valor—that made it such a source of pride. And the compassion and guilt felt by American Jews toward their European brethren presupposed the chasm that divided the two communities— the one that flourished and the one that was destroyed.

Conclusion

In December 1947, the popular weekly radio program *The Eternal Light*, produced by the Jewish Theological Seminary of America and aired on NBC, presented a special broadcast to commemorate the UN partition resolution on Palestine. Starring two Jewish celebrities of Eastern European origin, the actor Paul Muni and the opera singer Regina Reznick, the program paid only brief attention to the UN's recognition of the Jews' right to statehood: "In Flushing Meadow 33 nations vindicated an ancient plan, and once again the people of Judea rises among the counsels of nations." Instead the focus of the program was on Holocaust survivors who would populate the new state and on the divine providence that lay behind the international community's actions. Throughout the long history of the diaspora, the Jews, "a people without grass or cattle" and with "no field to plow," had prayed to "become herdsmen again and tillers of the soil." But the plan for Jewish return would be limited to those "who of necessity would have to return or perish. A haven, a sanctuary, a refuge, a pledge redeemed." While Jews in Displaced Persons camps had been given "a new lease on life," "we who are in America shall bless them and shall make a prayer that they shall be happy in their land as we are happy in this, our land." Israel's establishment will herald a new era of global peace and brotherhood, but one that America's Jews will witness from afar.[106] The program invoked Jewish solidarity framed within a profession of American patriotism, heartfelt but measured pride, and joy tempered by solemnity and distance.

American Jewish solidarity with Israel differed from the sentimental and romantic love professed by the fin de siècle Hovevei Tsion or the volcanic, erotic passion of Zionist youth in interwar eastern Europe and Palestine. Yet these affective bundles shared much in common, including a striving for honor and for respect among the nations of the world. Moreover, as we shall see in the next chapter, in the years following

Israel's establishment, an enthusiastic and passionate love of the young state emerged among American Jews. This love was first expressed alongside, and then eventually surpassed, their anguish and guilt over the Holocaust and their compassion for persecuted Jews abroad as the most prominent emotion expressed in American Jewish public rhetoric.

4   *Zionism since 1948*

A GREAT ROMANCE

Eros had been present in Zionism since the period of the Hovevei Tsion and the early Labor Zionist movement. But only from the 1960s did a passionate love of Israel become a "feeling rule," a normative expectation within Jewish institutions such as synagogues, schools, and summer camps.[1] This love was the affective underpinning of a new form of Jewish collective attachment centered around support for Israel rather than ritual observance or faith in the divine.

According to the eminent political theorist Shlomo Avineri, "It is the state of Israel that unites more Jewish people all over the world than any other factor in Jewish life. For Jews the world over, Israel is not just an aggregate of Jewish individuals in need of assistance—it is the new *public* dimension of Jewish existence."[2] It has replaced the local Jewish community as the primary political unit with which Jews identify. In 1977 the rabbi and scholar Arthur Hertzberg noted the corollary to this new form of identification: "The only offense for which Jews can be 'excommunicated' in the United States today is not to participate in these efforts [to support Israel]. Intermarriage, ignorance of the Jewish heritage, or lack of faith do [sic] not keep anyone from leadership in the American Jewish community today. Being against Israel or apathetic in its support does."[3] Hertzberg himself saw in Zionism a means of heightening awareness of Jewish global citizenship and deepening Jewish literacy and consciousness. But for many Jews, attachment to Israel was not a means to an end but rather an end in and of itself.

The relationship between post-1948 Jewry and Israel may be described as a romance. In its simplest form, it is a love of Zion with a possessive and erotic element. Yet on another level it is a romance in the Shakespearean sense of the word: it is a tale of great quests and adventures, neither wholly tragic nor comic, in which extraordinary, miraculous events bring about the unification of loved ones across great distances and the worst designs of evildoers are foiled, yet loss and sorrow are never completely absent.

This chapter begins with an analysis of the changing emotional register of Zionism within the post-1948 Jewish world but devotes most of its attention to American Jewry, the largest and most influential Jewish community in the post-Holocaust diaspora. In contrast to pre–World War II European Zionism, from its beginnings American Zionism never displayed much interest in ideology. It was, however, permeated by pathos. The pathos engendered by the Holocaust made American Jewry's relationship with Zionism, which weaves together feelings of triumph tinged by tragedy, into a romance in the literary sense of the term. American Zionism's affective palette has always been multihued, and it was formed as much by events at home as in the Middle East. The origins of the romance date back to the years around Israel's establishment, and it continues to this day, although the balance of emotions that sustains it has changed over time.

The Zionist romance demands that Israel be worthy of an arduous quest. For Avineri this means that Israel must offer a superior "content and quality of life" than found in the diaspora, which discovers "in Israel such qualities as it lacks in itself." Passionate love for Israel is fueled by a sense of exception, difference, and awe. When that sense dissipates, Avineri worries, Jews wander away. If Israel becomes another Los Angeles, Avineri posits, it will not have "normative standing" among diaspora Jews. Similarly, its army, which has been a source of symbolic pride for generations of Jews, loses its luster if it becomes just another military force, engaged in violence and an occupation with dubious justification.[4]

These assumptions have been proven only partially correct. Israel is now an affluent, highly developed country, much of which does resemble Los Angeles or Miami, and increasing numbers of American Jews have become unsettled by Israel's treatment of Palestinians. Nonetheless, Zionism—manifested in public, ritualized displays of love for Israel—remains central to American Jewish public life. Even the frustration or hostility toward Israel expressed by a vocal minority of Jewish intellectuals, activists, and students in recent years can be understood as indicative of engagement, as well as disaffection.[5]

Israeli Zionism as Israeli Patriotism

During the early decades of the State of Israel, Zionism had multiple connotations. It referred to a patriotic attachment to the new Jewish state and a commitment to its security and economic development. Even the most humdrum occupations, such as factory labor, could be considered a "national task," but pride of place was reserved for agricultural settlement, especially in peripheral areas of the country, and for military service. David Ben-Gurion hoped to channel the spirit of voluntarism, which had sustained the youth movements, militias, and other institutions of the pre-1948 Yishuv, into the new era of statehood.[6]

The realization of Zionism, however, demanded more than the development of the state, because it was linked with a sense of mission to the diaspora. This mission to world Jewry was clear from the Jewish state's name: Israel, the biblical name for the Jewish people. Israel's raison d'être was immigration and what it still calls the "absorption" of newcomers—a process of settlement, socialization, and cultural transformation. Israeli Zionism was an ongoing revolution that could not survive without the continued existence of a diaspora, whose liquidation was, according to some interpretations, Zionism's ultimate goal. As the Israeli author A. B. Yehoshua wrote in 2017, "A Zionist is someone who accepts the principle that the State of Israel doesn't belong solely to its citizens, but to the entire Jewish people."[7] Early Israeli Zionism featured a particularly strong variety of an element common in modern nationalism: a sense of obligation by members of a nation to their co-nationals abroad.[8]

The Zionist goal of the "ingathering of the exiles" (*kibbutz galuiyot*) ran afoul of the actual encounter between those exiles and the established Jewish community in Israel. Holocaust survivors elicited a blend of compassion, pity, contempt, and disgust. Veteran Israelis claimed that the survivors were cowards for not having resisted their oppressors and had survived through immoral practices such as theft and collaboration. Disgust, the most embodied and sensory of negative emotions, characterized Israelis' responses to the survivors' foreign appearance, Yiddish speech, and the real or imagined stench of the camps.[9] The migration of more than five hundred thousand Jews from Middle Eastern and North African countries between 1949 and 1964 elicited even stronger negative feelings, laced with a paternalistic humanitarianism and a belief in Ashkenazic civilizational superiority.[10] In early Israeli political discourse, Holocaust survivors and new immigrants from Arab states were called "human dust," a term reminiscent of the Russian term "camp dust" used to describe those sent to the gulag. These negative evaluations coexisted with a commitment to subject the newcomers to a political education that would transform them into upright citizens and sturdy laborers.[11]

As Jewish immigration to Israel slowed in the 1960s, the externally directed aspects of Israeli Zionism gradually weakened. They returned to prominence from time to time, such as during the organized transport of Jews from Ethiopia to Israel in the mid-1980s and the mass migration from the former Soviet Union to Israel in the 1990s and early 2000s. Yet after Israel's conquest in the 1967 war of the ancient Hebrews' biblical heartland in what is widely known as the West Bank, Israeli Zionism became increasingly associated with territory and ethnicity rather than immigration.

Three months after the war ended, a group of some sixty prominent Israeli intellectuals published a statement in one of Israel's major newspapers claiming, "The Land of Israel is now in the hands of the Jewish people, and just as we are not permitted to forego the State of Israel, so

too we are enjoined to sustain what we have received from it: the Land of
Israel. . . . We are hereby committed faithfully to the wholeness of our
land . . . and no government in Israel shall ever forgo this wholeness."[12]
The statement's signatories came from both the Left and Right of the
Israeli political spectrum, and most were not religiously observant. They
were motivated by nationalist irredentism: the yearning for territory
that is believed to have been part of the people's patrimony. However,
over time secular irredentism and Sacral Zionism, which imputes holiness to the entirety of the Land of Israel, became inseparable.

Less than a week after the war's end, two hundred thousand Israeli
Jews poured into Jerusalem to celebrate the holiday of Shavuot and what
was called the reunification of the city. According to the *Jerusalem Post*,
"Every section of the population was represented. Kibbutz members and
soldiers rubbing shoulders with the [anti-Zionist, ultra-Orthodox] Netu-
rei Karta."[13] Thousands attended religious services at the Western Wall,
at the base of the Temple Mount at the Old City's eastern edge. (The
Arab residences near the wall, home to more than 130 families, had been
blown up by military personnel, who swiftly laid out a grand esplanade
to accommodate the throng of worshippers.)

The transition from Statist Zionism to one that sacralized territory
had been foreshadowed before the conquest of the Old City. Naomi
Shemer's song "Jerusalem of Gold," released just three weeks before the
outbreak of the war, was an homage both to Jerusalem's holiness and its
natural beauty. Filled with biblical allusions, the song depicted the Old
City and Temple Mount as deserted—although, in fact, the Old City
bustled with Palestinians and other non-Jews, and the Temple Mount,
known to Muslims as Haram al-Sharif, was the site of mass prayers at the
Al-Aqsa Mosque. The song quickly became a hit, even more so after
the war when Shemer appended verses describing Israel's triumphant
return to the wellspring of its being: "We have returned to the cisterns/
To the market and marketplace/A ram's horn calls out on the Temple
Mount/In the Old City."[14]

Most diaspora Jews were thrilled by Israel's victory in 1967 and what was called the liberation of Jerusalem's Old City. But this sense of shared fate was belied by the considerable differences in standards of living, social conventions, and values between Israeli and diaspora Jews. They literally did not speak the same language—few diaspora Jews had mastered modern Hebrew. Moreover, diaspora Jews needed Israel far more than Israel needed them. The IDF accepted volunteers from abroad with an eye toward encouraging their immigration, just as the Jewish Agency sponsored programs that brought Jewish youth to Israel for extended periods. Yet for most Israeli Jews who did not have familial connections to diaspora Jews, the latter were of little import.

In 2018 the chair of the Jewish Agency, Natan Sharansky, described Zionism in terms of "identity and mutual exchange" between Israel and the diaspora.[15] A few years previously, the prominent rabbi and educator Donniel Hartman asserted that Zionism demanded the common labor of Jews both within and outside Israel to determine their shared moral values and collective interests.[16] Yet it was not clear what benefit Israel gained from its interactions with diaspora Jews, aside from financial contributions and the lobbying of their governments on Israel's behalf. By the turn of the millennium, Zionism in the sense of carrying out a mission to the diaspora was relevant primarily within select Israeli government agencies and public–private educational partnerships directed toward Jews abroad. But elsewhere in Israel Zionism took on varied and even contradictory meanings. For the Religious Zionist community, it connoted the sacrality of the entirety of the Land of Israel. For most other Israeli Jews, Zionism, like the word "Jewish" itself, had a demographic and ethnic rather than ideological connotation.[17]

The anchoring of twenty-first-century Zionism in national rather than transnational attachment is demonstrated by the 2019 popular song, "A Tribe of Brothers and Sisters." The lyrics blend religious, classic Zionist, and contemporary themes ("From . . . Jerusalem in penitential prayers . . . /From the parties of Tel Aviv"). The official video of the song features thirty-five singers, a mix of secular and religious, Ashkenazic, Mizrahi, and Ethiopian—but all Israeli and Jewish.[18] (One is a convert to Judaism from Islam.) Although the song conflates Jewishness with Israeliness, it was warmly embraced by diaspora Jewish organizations. Participants in the Birthright program, which provides cost-free trips to Israel for diaspora Jewish youth, created an English-language version. Its participants identified with the Israeli members of the tribe, even if the Israelis did not reciprocate.

American Zionism after 1948: From Solidarity to Adoration

Efforts by American Jewish leaders to foster a sense of compassion, urgency, and guilt among the Jewish public did not stop after Israel's establishment. In 1949 United Jewish Appeal campaign posters depicted the immigration to Israel of survivors from Europe as "the greatest homecoming in history." A fundraising magazine advertisement showed a happy, healthy-looking Holocaust survivor holding a baby and saying, "Now I'm glad he was born." Eight years later the UJA responded to an exodus of Jews from Hungary with a poster that read "This Time We Can Save Them."[19] A commemorative UJA booklet from 1958 included images of UJA fundraising gatherings a decade previously, alongside photos of Israeli soldiers and political leaders, as well as new immigrants alighting from ships in Israel, dancing the hora, and defending new agricultural settlements.[20] All these fundraising materials described diaspora Jews as essential elements in Israel's creation.

Members of America's Jewish philanthropic and rabbinic elite were intensely committed to Israel. In 1941 a breakaway faction from the Reform movement's rabbinical association had formed an anti-Zionist group called the American Council for Judaism that, like the Reform movement in the late nineteenth century, defined Judaism in purely universalist rather than nationalist terms. Its fortunes declined rapidly after 1945, however, with the strengthening of American Philanthropic

Zionism. The American Jewish Committee (AJC) played a key role in this chain of events. In 1950 Jacob Blaustein, president of the AJC, forged an informal understanding with Israeli prime minister David Ben-Gurion that the AJC would mobilize political and economic support for Israel, but that Israel would neither intervene in the internal affairs of the American Jewish community nor impugn the legitimacy of American Jewish desires to live in and identify with the United States.[21] Some major benefactors of Israel shied away from calling themselves Zionists, but some of these "non-Zionists'" commitments to Israel were unshakable. In 1951 Lessing Rosenwald, son of the founder of the Sears, Roebuck and Co. department store chain and president of the anti-Zionist American Council for Judaism, was irked by "chauvinistic statements of the fanatical Zionists, claiming that Jews the world over owe a first allegiance and loyalty to the state of Israel."[22] Nonetheless, despite his pique, Rosenwald insisted that the AJC continue to support Israel via the Jewish Agency.

The influential American Jewish journalist Boris Smolar described Max Fisher, a real estate magnate in Detroit who advised a string of U.S. presidents on urban, Jewish, and Israel affairs, as "not a Zionist" yet "a most dedicated friend of Israel." That was an understatement. Between 1965 and 1967, Fisher was general chair of the UJA and led the Israel Emergency Fund drive during the 1967 war. By 1968 he had personally donated more than $1 million to the UJA and the Israel Emergency Fund and had served as chair or leader of virtually every major American Jewish philanthropy. He visited Israel thirteen times between 1954 and 1968.[23]

Fisher's trips to Israel were all within the framework of UJA-sponsored study missions. These missions, which catered to major donors, were not pleasure holidays but had intense, densely packed itineraries designed to fortify the visitors' Zionist commitments and instill a sense of partnership with Israel's governing and military elite. Highlights from the itinerary of the October 1967 mission, just four months after the war, exemplify both its goals:

October 19/20: Jerusalem's Old City and Western Wall.

October 21 (Shabbat): Optional aerial tour of the Sinai Peninsula to
   view sites from the 1956 and 1967 wars such as Sharm el-Sheikh,
   the Straits of Tiran, Mitla Pass, and the Bir Gafgafa airfield.

October 22: Half the group tours Gaza, with lunch on an army base,
   while the other half tours the Golan Heights. Both groups dine
   with Finance Minister Pinchas Sapir.

October 23: Dinner with Labor Minister and former military
   commander Yigal Allon.

October 24: Demonstration of the Israel Air Force; lunch with Chief
   of Staff Yitzhak Rabin.

October 25: Demonstration in Tel Aviv of products of the Maskit
   fashion house "for the ladies."

On subsequent days there were more opportunities to tour the Sinai and
visit schools, universities, and absorption centers for new immigrants.[24]
While the major donors could experience the thrill of helicopter rides, a
demonstration by fighter aircraft, and meals with legendary military
commanders, the mission experience was repackaged for workaday Jews
by filming portions of the events, adding titles and dissolves in the editing process, and making them available for home projection, accompanied by a narrative guide.[25]

   Reaching out to the Jewish public and stoking their commitments to
Israel were not easy tasks. The emotional and financial torrent of 1946
to 1948 was not sustainable. As Israel settled into the humdrum business
of absorbing immigrants and building institutions, the percentage of
funds dedicated to Israel in the annual campaigns of local Jewish federa-
tions declined. Few American Jews visited Israel, and fewer still moved
there. Yet they were still receptive to appeals for financial support. Once
again Henry Montor displayed philanthropic genius in conceiving of a
new means by which American Jews could express their distant yet sincere attachments to Israel—not by direct gifts but through the purchase

of Israeli governmental bonds. The bonds were something between an investment and a gift: they were paid off with interest at maturity and the interest rates were competitive, but the risk of default was considerable given the country's uncertain geopolitical situation. It was precisely the country's delicate position that attracted American Jews to Israel Bonds; it elicited a nurturing, almost parental love akin to the desire to help a needy child attain independence.[26]

As Dan Lainer-Vos has argued, Israel Bonds played on the social distance between American Jews and Israel. American Jews were both proud and in awe of Israel's fortitude and valor—feelings that David Ben-Gurion knew how to exploit when he journeyed to the United States in May 1951, bringing with him two Israeli naval vessels and a bevy of female IDF soldiers, to launch the first Israel Bonds drive.[27] The bonds targeted small givers, but those who bought more than $10,000 in bonds in a given year were given the title "Guardian of Israel," described by the campaign's literature as "a counterpart of Israel's shomrim or Guardians, . . . watch[ing] over the economic development of Israel."[28] Thus an American Jew who could not or would not live as an Israeli pioneer or soldier, could, through bond purchases, experience not only vicarious pride in Israel's accomplishments but also a personal sense of empowerment.

Throughout the 1950s and 1960s, news about Israel was widely disseminated in Jewish newspapers, synagogue newsletters, and rabbinic sermons. Synagogue gift shops carried Israeli-made ritual objects, such as candlesticks, cups for sacramental wine, and prayer shawls. Israeli art became fashionable for Jews who could afford it.[29] The emotional connection between American Jews and Israel was expressed through materiality—donating money to the Jewish National Fund to plant forests and irrigate parched desert soil, buying Israel Bonds to sustain the absorption of immigrants, purchasing Israeli crafts to be displayed in one's home, and experimenting with Israeli cuisine. A similar materiality informed Ben-Gurion's secularization of prophetic biblical language of Israel as a "light unto the nations," possessed of a mission to "make the desert bloom" and bring advanced agricultural and medical technology to the Third World.[30] As in the interwar period, American Jews could avoid charges of dual loyalty by presenting Zionism as a world-reforming enterprise with universal practical benefits.

In 1958 Leon Uris's novel *Exodus* injected a jolt of romance into this staid materialism. The book tells the tale of Ari Ben-Canaan, a native son and kibbutznik who fights for Israel's independence and gradually wins the love of a beautiful American Gentile nurse, Kitty Fremont. The book is often described as an epic, and indeed it meets many of the criteria of the genre in that it is lengthy, paints a broad historical as well as narrative canvas, and provides both a tale of heroic action and a foundational myth for a collective. But to be more precise, the novel is a *romantic* epic in its blend of tragedy and triumph, as well as its blatant sentimentality. In the novel Israeli men are courageous fighters but also sensitive and thoughtful. Ari is a more muscular incarnation of a staple of classic romantic fiction: the darkly handsome and brooding, even psychologically tortured male. (Imagine *Jane Eyre*'s Mr. Rochester, but bronzed and toting a Sten submachine gun.) In addition to heroic Zionists, the novel is littered with supercilious Englishmen and mendacious Arabs, all set against a landscape of literally biblical proportions.

Exodus was phenomenally successful: it topped U.S. best-seller lists for a year and to date has sold more than twenty million copies. In an engaging study of Uris's life and of the novel's production and reception, Matthew Silver analyzes the particular resonance of the novel for American Jews who, he argues, were provided with a set of images with which they would conceive of Israel for decades to come.[31] In fact the novel did not create so much as reflect and articulate preexisting sensibilities— otherwise, American Jews would not have found the book appealing. One of the novel's most prominent features is its explicit comparison between the birth struggles of the state of Israel and of the United States of America, with the Yishuv likened to the thirteen colonies, the Negev to the American frontier, and the British of the 1940s to the British of the 1770s. But these sorts of comparisons had already been made in the U.S. press a decade before, at the time of Israel's creation.

Uris's novel fulfilled American Jews' long-standing desires to integrate into American society while maintaining a particularistic Jewish culture. Scholars writing on this tension usually do so in ideological or theological rather than emotional terms. For instance, Michael Barnett's history of what he calls American Jewish foreign policies presents American Jews as sharing a liberal political theology that emphasizes universalism over tribalism and manifests its universalist commitments via a striving for social justice.[32] But it is doubtful that political theology attracted Jews to Uris's novel. We need to think less in terms of liberalism and universalism than American Jews' emotional needs for family and community, feelings such as shame and honor, or drives such as ambition and compensation.

The virile, strong, and courageous Ari Ben-Canaan was a source of both pride and reproach. Many of Uris's male Jewish readers had served in the military in World War II or the Korean War, and during and after those wars American Jewish organizations expended considerable effort disseminating images of tough, uniformed, and armed Jews fighting for their country. Yet the tragedy of the Holocaust ensured the survival of venerable stereotypes—enunciated as much by Jews as by antisemites—of Jews as passive and unwilling or unable to defend themselves against aggressors. Woody Allen, whose career as a stand-up comedian began two years after the publication of Uris's novel, reinforced long-standing images from fin-de-siècle Yiddish literature of the Jewish male as brainy but feckless, sexually inept, and apt to try to talk rather than fight his way out of trouble. Although by 1960 antisemitism was in decline and American Jews were experiencing rapid social mobility, the stereotype of the Jew as a hapless schlemiel was very much alive, and Ben-Canaan was its nemesis.

The gender-studies scholar Sikata Banerjee argues that colonized peoples were often stigmatized by colonizers as unsuited for civilized warfare by dint of being savages (as the British thought of the Irish) or effeminate weaklings (the British stereotype of Bengali males).[33] For nationalists in both Ireland and Bengal at the fin de siècle, Banerjee shows, military activity was not merely a means to the end of attaining independence but also a way of demonstrating masculine prowess through displays of raw strength, courage, and discipline, the quintessentially bourgeois "manly" virtues. In both cases that Banerjee analyzes, there was a place for women as rebels and guerrillas, but only until the attainment of independence, after which women were compelled to retreat to the spheres of family life and charitable activity. The multifaceted significance of armed struggle accounts for its importance in postwar national liberation movements throughout the world.

I am not claiming equivalence between the idealization of armed struggle in anticolonial movements and the American Jewish romance about Israelis in uniform. But if our focus is on perception and affect rather than material reality, then the insecurities of American Jews, vicariously reveling in Israeli military strength, bear comparison with the feelings of inadequacy expressed by oppressed peoples who had lived under immeasurably worse conditions. Such feelings are strongly gendered, with humiliated men seeking psychological compensation through the military, whether experienced directly or vicariously. But women in anticolonial movements have been no less insistent on the recovery of collective honor and dignity.[34] American Jewish men and women may have had different emotional responses to Israel's military, but Hadassah was just as likely as male-dominated Jewish organizations to claim, as per a 1956 Hadassah newsletter, that "Israel Needs Arms for Survival."[35]

Nonetheless it would be wrong to overstate the function of either Israel or the Holocaust in American Jewish life before the 1967 war: Israel was always present, but it was not central. When in 1966 *Commentary* magazine asked several American Jewish public figures about what it meant to be a Jew, neither Israel nor the Holocaust appeared in a prominent way.[36]

The 1967 war, however, elicited a flood of American Jewish support for Israel unseen since 1948. Although the greatest danger to Israel, Egypt's air force, was destroyed in the first hours of the war, and the war itself was over in six days, the sense of crisis did not fade. A month after the war's outbreak, the UJA Israel Emergency Fund had raised more than $100 million.[37] As in 1948, fundraising catalyzed the formation of intense fellowships of donors, both bonding and competing with each other in displays of generosity. Country clubs closed their golf courses during fundraising meetings.[38] Although most American Jews limited their support to giving money, ten thousand of them, alongside twelve thousand European Jews, hurriedly departed for Israel to volunteer—not as soldiers as in 1948 but as replacement workers for men called into battle.[39]

A month after the war, Smolar wrote in his weekly column,

> The American Jewish community will never be the same. . . . A new chapter has now been opened in the history of American Jewry. No longer can one now say with certainty that the interest of American Jews in things Jewish is declining. Suddenly masses of Jews, young and old, who never before thought much of their Jewishness stood up to be counted during the days when Israel was in a fight for its existence. . . . [The war mobilized] thousands and thousands of Jews who never wanted to be part and parcel of the Jewish community and who did not respond to calls of Jewish responsibilities. Many of these "self-discovered" Jews will respond from now on, after having been awakened by Israel's six-day war which shook them and shook the world.[40]

The previously apathetic had been mobilized, and those who were already supportive of Israel forged stronger, deeper ties. In 1966 two hundred major donors traveled to Israel on the UJA Study Mission; a year later, the number of participants more than doubled.[41]

In oral interviews carried out in 2013 and 2014, Jewish activists from the 1970s recalled their youthful experiences in Israel after 1967. Over and over again they referred to "falling in love" with Israel and the Hebrew language. John Ruskay, a peace activist who went on to become the CEO of the UJA-Federation of New York, recalled, "Israel represented for me—I was a teenager—every idealistic impulse and vision I had . . . it was beautiful. It was sort of more egalitarian or so it appeared." American Jewish life was "superficial" and "boring," but Israel was "kind of socialist, democratic, diverse, sexy. The land had been re-created. I was becoming aware of the Holocaust. This was but a moment after the Holocaust. Kibbutzim. It was just glorious."[42] Life in Israel was challenging, but precisely for that reason it was idealized as more authentic, altruistic, and meaningful.

After 1967 Israel assumed a greater role in American Jewish public life, education, and popular culture. Jewish youth groups and summer camps promoted bonds with and love of Israel by displaying the Israeli flag, singing Israeli folk songs, teaching Israeli folk dancing, and screening Israeli films. The summer camps employed Israeli counselors and encouraged the use of Hebrew—at times extensively—although its use was often limited to names for the camp's physical spaces and the main events of the day; for example, *hadar okhel* (dining room) and *mifkad* (assembly). Camps taught Zionist history through discussions and role playing, with campers reenacting confrontations with British soldiers over illegal immigration or fighting the 1948 war.[43]

Love of Israel even seeped into humor. In 1969 the writer and editor Bill Adler, whose bestsellers included *Kids' Letters to President Kennedy* and *What to Name Your Jewish Baby*, published *Jewish Wit & Wisdom*, which included a chapter on "Life and Laughter in the Promised Land." Adler wrote of Israel in language steeped in admiration of the country's achievements: "The Israelis are a happy people, and their land has already produced a crop of laughter that rivals the miraculous fruit and vegetable crops of the irrigated deserts. . . . You will find that Israel has contributed more than her share to the cause of Jewish humor."[44] Israelis, according to Adler, share the same Eastern European roots and the ironic, yet not cynical, approach to humor common among American Jews.

An initiative to incorporate Israel into two extended families, both American and Jewish, came from the writers Bob Booker and George Foster, whose comedy albums *The First Family* (1962) and *You Don't Have to Be Jewish* (1965) had been hugely popular. Shortly after the end of the Six-Day War, Booker, a Christian, and Foster, who was Jewish, released an homage to Israel titled *The Yiddish Are Coming! The Yiddish Are Coming!*[45] More than half the album's songs and skits were about the recent fighting. Featuring the same cast as the previous recordings, including the veteran actors Lou Jacobi and Jack Gilford, the album presented Israelis speaking Yiddish or New York-inflected English. Whereas Arab soldiers were depicted as primitive dolts, the Israelis were warm-hearted, quick-witted, ironic, fond of complaining, and dominated by their mothers—in short, conforming to stereotypes of Ashkenazic Jews.

Just as the album turned Israelis into diaspora Jews, so did it demonstrate solidarity between American Jews and Israelis. Its cover depicted the assembled cast of middle-aged Jews wearing eye patches like that worn by the country's defense minister Moshe Dayan, and the album featured a song titled "The Man with a Black Patch on His Eye" (see figure 4).[46] This song portrayed Dayan as a warrior with qualities reminiscent of his biblical namesake (Moshe is Hebrew for Moses), but the song's content was Americanized by a rollicking, country-western 4/4 beat:

Then Moshe raised his left hand and Moshe raised his right,
And soon the colonel's[47] army was runnin' out of sight.
But Moshe's brave Israelis were hot on the trail.
They captured so many Russian tanks they're going to have a sale.
The moral of this story, on this you can depend.
Every fight for freedom will win out in the end.
When democracy is threatened, brave men will proudly stand
Behind the man who's got the heart. A man like Moshe Dayan.[48]

Figure 4 Emulating Israel's warrior hero in 1967: the cast members of the 1967 comedy album *The Yiddish Are Coming! The Yiddish Are Coming!* sport eye-patches like that of Moshe Dayan.
Credit: Bob Booker.

Underneath the song's apparent insouciance lay awe and veneration, exemplified by the direct comparison of Dayan to the biblical Moshe, whose raised hands in Exodus 17:11 were an indication of Israelite military triumph. The song expressed elation in the wake of panic, all packaged in such a way as to display bonds between Israel, Americans, and Jews.

As we saw from John Ruskay's remarks, the post-1967 infatuation with Israel was accompanied by a sharp rise in public Jewish conversation about and commemoration of the Holocaust. The two were connected because American Jews had, before the outbreak of the war, feared for Israel's destruction, which Jewish leaders described as a potential second Holocaust. According to Michael Barnett, after the war American Jewish leaders began to think that the defense of the Jewish people and the prevention of another catastrophe lay entirely in the Jews' own hands: those of American Jews, whose task it was to give money to and lobby for Israel, and those of Israelis, who had the might to reshape the geopolitics of the Middle East. The paradoxical blend of empowerment and trepidation emerged even more strongly during the Arab–Israeli war of October 1973 when it took three weeks of heavy fighting for Israel to repel Egyptian and Syrian offensives in the Sinai and Golan Heights, and Israel's casualties were the highest since the 1948 war.

During the 1973 war, in addition to fearing for Israel's survival, American Jews faced worries at home. As the fighting raged, the American Jewish Committee monitored American talk radio shows and newspaper editorials, locating hotbeds of pro-Arab sentiment among Arab American housewives and college students. Acknowledging rising sympathy among Black activists for the Palestinian cause, as well as tensions between Blacks and Jews in the inner cities, the AJC noted "a substantial amount of antisemitism, both traditional and the Black variety," on talk shows in New York City.[49] The traditional variety included the views of Senator J. William Fulbright of Arkansas, who declaimed on radio that Israelis were "very rich, very strong, and very politically astute" and had thus been able to buy the votes of at least eighty members of the Senate.[50]

The specter of domestic antisemitism fueled by Jewish financial resources did not prevent American Jews from launching an all-out effort to assist Israel during the 1973 war. A new Israel Emergency Fund raised $100 million within a week.[51] The Federation of Jewish Philanthropies of Greater New York, which raised money for and administered social services within the New York area, agreed to merge its campaign with that of the UJA and to receive only one-ninth of the receipts. After the war the

New York federation, which had previously not been explicitly Zionist, undertook its own study missions to Israel.[52]

During the 1970s American Jews' sense of dual threat—to Israel and to themselves—inspired not only increased lobbying and donations for Israel but also demands from Jewish philanthropies for greater outlays on programs for Jewish education in the community and on college campuses. The slogan of the New York Federation's 1972 campaign was "It's not just education. It's survival."[53] Moreover an organized campaign on behalf of Soviet Jews wishing to emigrate had been launched in the previous year. The initiative was not only carried out without a specific directive from the Israeli government but it ran counter to Israel's stated desires to direct the emigrants solely to Israel as opposed to European destinations.[54] The American Jewish fierce love of Israel coexisted with solidarity with world Jewry, and at times the two clashed.

Escalating hostility to Israel in the international community in the 1970s led to the popularization of the slogan "Am Yisrael Chai" (The People of Israel Live). This phrase, which encompassed both the Jewish people as a whole and the State of Israel, nicely illustrates the meaning of Zionism to diaspora Jews at the time. It was an assertion of ethnic particularism, a commemoration of past suffering, and an identification with a young Jewish state that was sufficiently familiar to be an extension of one's own selfhood yet sufficiently different to be enthralling and alluring. Diaspora Jews simultaneously feared for Israel's survival and boasted about its military power. Israel was sovereign yet perceived as vulnerable and needing help from the diaspora. It was a place where Jews need never apologize for their identity, where Hebrew was literally shouted in the street, where a Jew would almost inevitably marry another Jew, and where assimilation in the Western sense was impossible. In these respects, the love of Israel was an aspiration for self-preservation.

Given that American Zionism rested on the pillars of affection and anxiety, the removal of either pillar could topple the whole structure. Unequivocal Jewish support for Israel dimmed, but only slightly, during

Israel's 1982 invasion of Lebanon, during which the IDF subjected Beirut to seven weeks of intense bombardment that killed thousands and abetted the Lebanese Christian forces' massacre of hundreds, if not thousands, of Palestinians in the Sabra and Shatila refugee camps. A very different kind of threat to Jewish support for Israel came from the 1979 peace treaty with Egypt. A month after the signing of the treaty, the New York federation campaign chair observed, "One of the problems confronting many solicitors appears to be the question of peace. They are finding resistance to the Campaign because Israel is supposedly at peace."[55]

The Israeli–Palestinian peace process of the 1990s was similarly challenging to Zionist activists. In 1996 a conference brought together an array of influential American Jewish officials and scholars to ruminate on the challenge of maintaining Jewish solidarity in the face of Israeli-Palestinian peace. Reflecting the spirit of that era, the social scientists Steven M. Cohen and Charles Liebman flatly asserted, "Politically and militarily, Israel is perceived as basically secure."[56] A diminishing sense of crisis, combined with Israel's growing economic maturity, led to a situation where Israel did not need nor want American Jewish money. An American Jewish leader attending the conference (but left unnamed in the conference proceedings) opined that fundraising for Israel must go on anyway, even if the Israeli government burned the money, because raising money was a vital means of preserving the American Jewish community.[57]

Four years after the conference, the Second Intifada erupted, and mainstream American Jewish organizations retreated to the language of fear and anxiety, solidarity with Israel, and suspicion, if not downright hostility, to the international community characterizing American Jewish public discourse during the 1970s. In 2002 Hillel International, whose chapters served the spiritual and social needs of Jewish college students, made Israel central to its mission. The motto of the newly founded On Campus Coalition, funded by Hillel and the Schusterman Family Foundation, was "Wherever we stand, we stand with Israel." Eight years later

Hillel drafted guidelines claiming Israel was a core element of Jewish life and a gateway to Jewish identification for students.[58] These were defensive measures, as the minute cracks in American Jewish unity regarding Israel that had formed in response to the 1982 Lebanon War grew wider after the onset of the Second Intifada in 2000. Although most American Jews continued to identify with Israel, the link between anxiety and solidarity with the Israeli government's actions began to fray.

Zionism at the Turn of the Millennium: Decline or Reconfiguration?

For diaspora Jews, donations to Israel are indications of personal commitment—if not to the State of Israel as a concrete reality, a place to which one feels attached, then as an ideal of Jewish solidarity and a symbol of the Jews' revival from the catastrophe of the Holocaust. People donate for complex reasons stemming from a wide variety of emotions. Positive emotions such as solidarity and compassion blend with negative ones such as guilt, shame, and fear. The negative emotions can arise from personal concern for Israel's safety or anxiety about peer pressure, social exclusion, or a loss of status in the community should one not support Israel as expected.

Over the 1990s and 2000s, American Jewish national fundraising campaigns steadily reduced the percentage of contributions going to Israel and retained more for domestic use. With the end of the Cold War, the ebbing of the mass immigration of Jews to Israel from the former Soviet Union, the Israeli-Palestinian peace process, and the prospering Israeli economy, Israeli leaders told American Jewish fundraisers that they no longer needed their money.[59] Nonetheless total American Jewish giving to Israel increased markedly thanks to the growth of family foundations and issue-specific Israeli organizations like the "Friends of" each of Israel's universities and major hospitals.[60] These developments reflected broader changes in philanthropic practices in the United States and by themselves said little about how American Jews felt about Israel.

Rising affluence may have been just as relevant for these increased donations to Israeli causes as deepening attachment. It is no coincidence that total American Jewish giving to Israel skyrocketed during the 1990s and much of the 2000s, a period of unprecedented economic growth in the United States and of dazzling riches for sectors in which Jews were heavily represented, such as financial services and real estate development. Giving to Israel spiked in the early twenty-first century during periods of violence and tension—the Second Intifada and when conflict flared in Gaza—providing eloquent testimony to an elasticity of the supply of funds that responds directly to the stimuli of emotions such as fear and solidarity.

That said, donations provide at best indirect evidence of feeling. Public opinion surveys can offer more direct insights. Surveys asking Jews how they feel about Israel fall into two varieties: those that ask respondents to rank attachment to Israel on a list of attributes of Jewishness and those that elicit responses to specific questions about respondents' levels of attachment to Israel. The former survey type nicely illustrates the uncertainty principle in that observable events are affected by the observation itself. The act of ranking or listing one's identification markers engenders an effort to think clearly and systematically about vastly different phenomena. Since the 1960s surveys of this type have consistently shown Israel as ranking in the middle of the pack of attributes of Jewishness. In a 2013 U.S. national survey, "caring about Israel" ranked behind preserving the memory of the Holocaust, behaving ethically, and pursuing social justice—and only one percentage point higher than "having a good sense of humor."[61]

The lability of human affect calls into question the usefulness of the artificial hierarchies called for in these surveys. People operate within bounded, yet flexible, affective fields. Surveys that ask people to describe their attachments to Israel in vague terms (e.g., "very attached," "somewhat attached") may therefore be more helpful. The general trend of these surveys has been gradually declining attachments, with a growing difference between those under thirty-five years of age and those over fifty. In a 2020 survey, one-quarter of American Jews described themselves as "very emotionally attached" and another third as "somewhat emotionally attached" to Israel. There were no substantive differences in attachment by gender or level of education, but the generational gap was indeed striking: more than over two-thirds of Jews older than sixty-five professed to be very or somewhat attached to Israel as opposed to less than half of those under age thirty. Intriguingly there was less of a generational gap regarding whether caring about Israel was an "essential or important part of what being Jewish means to them": 89 percent for those over sixty-five compared to 71 percent for those under thirty. The main difference was between those who considered Israel essential to their identity: 52 percent of those older than sixty-five considered it essential compared to 35 percent of those under thirty.[62] These figures appeared to indicate an emotional cooling rather than complete disengagement or indifference.

During the 2010s, surveys and anecdotal evidence sparked a debate about the future of American Jewish ties to Israel. On one side stood the journalist and commentator Peter Beinart, who believed that American Jewish youth were abandoning Israel because the occupation and oppression of the Palestinians contradicted their liberal values. On the other side the sociologist Theodore Sasson argued that young American Jews have historically been less attached to Israel than their elders and that young Jews may well gravitate to Israel as they mature.[63] The problem with Sasson's argument, however, is that the time horizon for the comparison of attitudes over time is too narrow to be a useful predictor. That is, Jews who came of age in the 1970s or early 1980s, and who appear to become more attached to Israel as they grew older, were products of a generation for whom the 1967 and 1973 wars were a living memory. In the 1990s the Oslo peace process could give young Jews a sense of hope and a belief that Israel embodied the liberal political values with which, according to Beinart, most were inculcated at home and school. In contrast, university-age Jews in the twenty-first century lived in a radically different environment—darker and more foreboding on virtually every front. The militancy and illiberalism of Israel's government under Benjamin Netanyahu (2009–2021) were unprecedented. As in the stock market, so in the accumulation of emotional capital: past performance is not necessarily indicative of future results.

Sasson's view was bolstered by the scale of the Birthright program, which between its inception in 1999 and the onset of the coronavirus pandemic in 2020 brought some 750,000 young Jews, the vast majority of them American, to Israel on brief organized tours. Birthright brought together small groups of youth to experience a series of intense, mutually reinforcing encounters. Feelings of pride, love, hope, fear, anxiety, and awe induced a kind of psychological vertigo as participants were presented with the entirety of Jewish history, culminating in the Holocaust and the establishment of the State of Israel, in ten days bursting with activity. As one Birthright participant put it, "Everything seems to have meaning, *everywhere*."[64] "Everything" could include not only major historical and religious sites but also objects as mundane as a soda can or t-shirt with Hebrew lettering.

The Birthright groups were ephemeral, dissolving with the end of the tour, but the aftereffects could be durable: follow-up surveys revealed that many Birthright participants kept in contact with each other and with Israeli soldiers, who usually spent time with the groups and whose presence was often considered by participants to be the most exciting part of the trip. A half-century earlier, Jews could read about Ari Ben-Canaan or see him on the screen, portrayed by the ruggedly handsome Paul Newman in the film adaptation of the novel. In contrast, in the Birthright program young Jews had the opportunity to spend several days in the company of young and attractive Israeli soldiers, who were intensely admired, sexually desired, or both by the group participants.[65] Birthright made abundantly clear the inextricable link between the erotic, emotional, and intellectual dimensions of diaspora Jewish attachments to

Israel. (One former Israeli soldier who took part in Birthright tours told me that, for soldiers who already had romantic partners, Birthright was considered a *bizbuz haktsa'ah*, a wasted allocation of human resources.)

By 2020 considerably more American Jews of all ages had visited Israel than they did a generation previously. In the mid-1990s only about one-quarter of American Jews had been to Israel. By 2020 the percentage of at least one-time visitors has risen to 45 percent, more than half of whom had gone more than once.

Among Orthodox Jews the figure was higher than 70 percent. This was but one indicator of Orthodox Jewish bonds with Israel, which showed no sign of defection or drift. More than 80 percent claimed to be highly or somewhat emotionally attached to Israel and that caring about Israel was an essential or important part of what being Jewish meant to them. These attachments were linked with religious faith: almost 90 percent of Orthodox Jews believed that the Land of Israel was given to the Jews by God. (Among American Jews as a whole, only about one-third shared that belief.[66]) In day schools associated with Modern Orthodoxy— those open both to secular and sacred education—the psalms of thanks-giving for holy days, the Hallel, were recited on Israel's Independence Day. It was common for Modern Orthodox Jews to recite the prayer for the State of Israel in synagogue and to incorporate into the grace after meals a reference to the Land of Israel as "the beginning of the flowering of our redemption" (*reshit tsemihat ge'ulateinu*), taken from the prayer for the state.

These practices were angrily rejected by some ultra-Orthodox Jews who found Zionism repugnant on theological grounds. But throughout the early 2000s, even among the ultra-Orthodox, who were historically non-Zionist Jews, connections with the state and with the Land of Israel steadily strengthened. In 2020 a party known as Eretz Hakodesh (The Holy Land), representing a variety of ultra-Orthodox Jewish groups including the historically non-Zionist Agudat Yisrael, ran a slate in elections to the World Zionist Organization ("World" was added to the

Zionist Organization's name in 1960). Even more remarkable than the party's platform, which called for "a strong and secure Israel," was the mere act of running for election to the WZO, membership in which presupposed acceptance of its 2004 platform that declared "the centrality of the State of Israel and Jerusalem, its capital, in the life of the nation" and listed its goals of "strengthening Israel as a Jewish, Zionist and democratic state"; "furthering Jewish, Hebrew and Zionist education"; and "settling the country as an expression of practical Zionism."[67]

Orthodox Zionists were far more likely to send money to Israel and immigrate there (settling both within the pre-1967 borders and the Occupied Territories) than other American Jews. Yet it is inaccurate to ascribe these actions to the demands of halakhic observance. Although the desire to perform commandments unique to the Land of Israel (*mitzvot taluiyot ba-aretz*) historically spurred some Orthodox Jews to emigrate, the vast majority of American Orthodox Jews were content to support the country from afar. Nor could American Orthodox Jewish attachments to Israel be chalked up to messianism. Theodore Sasson's interviews of Orthodox Jews in the Boston area revealed sensibilities about Israel that were not qualitatively different from those of Jews from other denominations. They framed their support of Israel in terms of the Jews' need for a safe haven and a response to global, especially Arab, antisemitism.[68] In 1966 the towering figure in American Modern Orthodoxy, Rabbi Norman Lamm, praised Israel's existence not as a harbinger of the messianic era so much as a guarantee of the Jews' demographic survival. More than a half-century later, a sermon by Rabbi Sammy Bergman of Toronto's Modern Orthodox Shaarei Shomayim synagogue blurred the connection between Israel's establishment and divine redemption. The process, he cautioned, might be slow, uneven, and strewn with horrific events. Jews, he said, are commanded to be optimistic, enthusiastic, and, above all, hopeful about the messiah's arrival but not to assume it. Jews are ordained to live in a state of chronic anticipation, of gratitude for gifts past rather than the expectation of riches to come.[69]

The same modesty of expectations characterized the bulk of Orthodox American Jews who moved to the Occupied Territories in the late twentieth and early twenty-first centuries. A vocal and visible contingent of Orthodox American Jews, inspired by messianic beliefs, were enthusiastic supporters of the settlement movement of the 1970s and 1980s. Nonetheless, as Sara Hirschhorn observed in the 2010s, the majority of American Jews in the West Bank settlement movement identified as liberals, not zealots.[70] For such individuals, there was more to living in the West Bank than the fulfillment of biblical prophecy. A belief in a divinely promised land may have dictated the destination for immigration, but the settlers' underlying drives included a yearning for personal fulfillment and a high material quality of life in nurturing communities, a beautiful landscape, and government-subsidized housing.

Insight into what Israel has meant for Orthodox Zionists lies in Gurevich and Aran's essay, "On Place," which I referred to in chapter 2. Gurevich and Aran center the essay around the tension within the Zionist project surrounding the conception of the Land of Israel as both sacred territory and secular space; that is, between what they call "Place" and "place." Many Orthodox American Jews have melded "Place" and "place" in the tradition of what is known in the scholarship on rabbinic Judaism as realistic messianism. This is the view, attributed in the Talmud to R. Shmuel (Berakhot 34b) and reiterated by Maimonides, that "the only difference between this world and the days of the Messiah is with regard to servitude to foreign kingdoms alone. While in the days of the Messiah, Israel will be independent and free from enslavement to foreign powers, the world order will remain otherwise unchanged."[71] The Orthodox tradition enables the conception of the Land of Israel in not only sacred but also workaday temporal terms without veering into outright secularization.

The softening of the messianic dimensions of the return to the Land of Israel has a tempering effect on emotional attachments to it. As a noun, "temper" refers to a disposition, a matrix that sets boundaries on one's affective reactions to external stimuli. As a verbal noun, "tempering" metal maintains its hardness while rendering it more ductile. And indeed Orthodox Jewish sensibilities about Israel can be both harder and more flexible than those of their more secular counterparts. I am not attributing to Jewish Orthodoxy moderate views regarding the Israel–Palestine conflict and the question of territorial compromise. As we will see in chapter 6, the opposite is often the case. I am limiting my observations to the emotional response that Israel elicits in Orthodox Zionists, a response that may be politically extreme in its territorial maximalism and disregard for Palestinian rights but also affectively moderate. It is rooted in confidence more than insecurity, entitlement rather than guilt, and it is free of the moral discomfort, if not outright shame, felt by some Jewish critics of Israel. In short it is an emotional state anchored in fulfillment rather than unmet needs. One need not be Orthodox to have such feelings, nor did all Orthodox Jews share them. But in the early twenty-first century, most American Orthodox Jews embody an unapologetic ethnic and territorial nationalism that falls more within the rubric of Judaic than Sacral Zionism.

In the Name of Love: Criticism and Self-Censorship

Apart from Orthodox Jews, whose support for Israel was typically unqualified and uncomplicated, the organized American Jewish community found its relationship with Israel to be more problematic. Spokespeople for the community had long faced challenges of reconciling an attachment to Israel with its morally troublesome acts dating back to the expulsions of Palestinians in 1948 and 1967 and the military rule over Palestinian citizens of Israel until 1966. During Israel's first decades, the state's newspaper editors, cooperating with government officials, practiced collective self-censorship about security matters. American Jewish journalists did the same, although there was no force from above requiring them to do so.

From the time of its establishment, Israel had appealed to Jews as a beacon of democracy in the Middle East. When Israel did not conform to that image, American Jewish elites kept quiet. Shortly after the country's declaration of statehood in 1948, the American Jewish press waxed enthusiastic about Israel's forthcoming constitution, which would guarantee individual rights and provide the basis for a liberal political and economic order. When plans for a constitution fell through, the newspapers said nothing. In 1970 Boris Smolar urged the historian Yehuda Bauer to censor his forthcoming history of the American Jewish Joint Distribution Committee, which had since World War I provided financial support for Jews in Eastern Europe and the Middle East. Smolar was upset that Bauer intended to describe the opposition to Jewish statehood in 1937 expressed by Felix Warburg, a banker and leader of the "non-Zionist" faction of American Jewish philanthropists. "If these views were made public by Dr. Bauer, the Arabs could capitalize [on] them [in] their propaganda by saying that even American Jewish leaders wanted Arabs to remain a majority," Smolar wrote.[72] In 1984 Smolar praised the Detroit-based journalist Philip Slomowitz who was "discrete in dealing with Jewish leaders" and "consider[ed] it his responsibility to the Jewish people to impose self-censorship on news which, in his judgment, harms Jewish interests when published."[73] Love of the Jewish people and the state of Israel demanded that the truth not always be told.

In an effort to tell the truth and to be heeded, during the 1970s the pioneering American Jewish peace organization Breira (Hebrew for "choice") protested the oppression of Palestinians in the name of love for Israel. In their interactions with the mainstream community, Breira activists professed their love of Israel as a sign that their criticism was constructive and that their sympathy for the Palestinians did not diminish their attachment to the Jewish people. Critics of Breira, however, denied that its members truly loved Israel. They accused Breira members of lacking deep bonds to the country and its language, claiming that a genuine love of Israel had to be unconditional and rooted in absolute loyalty.[74]

Similar professions of love accompanied the establishment in 2007 of J Street, a dovish alternative to the American Israel Public Affairs Committee (AIPAC). Founded in 1963 AIPAC rose to prominence in the 1980s thanks to the strongly pro-Israel orientation of the Reagan administration and the increasing political power of evangelical Christians, for whom the Jewish state represented a fulfillment of prophecy and a necessary precondition for the Second Coming of Christ. Like Israeli Jews who supported a Palestinian state alongside Israel, J Street claimed that only a two-state solution could preserve Israel's character as a Jewish and democratic state. It claimed to act out of a love for Israel and a commitment to the vision of political and social justice embodied in the country's founding principles.[75]

Whereas Breira disappeared a few years after its founding, J Street survived into the 2020s. This was but one sign that in the early twenty-first century the "feeling rules" governing Jewish public speech on Israel were beginning to change. The most acceptable topic for criticism was the State of Israel's discrimination against non-Orthodox Jews. Complaints about nonrecognition of Reform and Conservative conversions to Judaism performed in Israel, or the denial of gender-egalitarian prayer space at the Western Wall, were fierce but familial. Finding fault with Israel's treatment of Palestinians was a more delicate matter. Although advocating for concrete measures such as boycotts or lobbying for US governmental pressure on Israel to end the occupation was forbidden, expressions of mild negative emotions such as unease, disappointment, and frustration could be tolerated.

In 2013 the Israeli journalist Ari Shavit published a highly personal history of the Zionist project, *My Promised Land*, which became a best-seller among American Jews. The book was an act of both homage and critique, and its appeal lay in its presentation of the dark sides of Israel's history as the tragic but necessary counterpart to Zionism's bright and heroic dimensions.[76] By portraying the expulsion of Palestinians in 1948 as both horrific and unavoidable, and the discrimination against Middle Eastern Jewish immigrants as lamentable but surmountable, Shavit communicated a love so deep that it endures despite recognition of the beloved's flaws. (Moreover, the fact that he is Israeli lent his work an authority it would have lacked had the book been penned by an American.) In the same year, Eric Fingerhut, then the president of Hillel International, stated that critique of Israel would be allowed "within the context of a love of Israel, an unequivocal support of Israel."[77] In practice, according to the guidelines drawn up in 2010, there was no place at Hillel for those Jewish students—no matter how religiously observant or otherwise committed to Jewish life—who "deny the right of Israel to exist as a Jewish and democratic state with secure and recognized borders"; "delegitimize, demonize, or apply a double standard to Israel"; or "support boycott of, divestment from, or sanctions against the State of Israel."[78]

As Sarah Anne Minkin observes in her study of the Bay Area Jewish community during the 2010s, local Jewish institutions structured an emotional regime centered around "familial love, collective fantasy, and vulnerability and empowerment."[79] The love was familial because it was predicated on the assumption that American Jews and Israel were bound into a single unit. The bond was mutually protective and attributed to each party the power to shore up the other's vulnerabilities. Israel lived under constant threat, and American Jews had the financial and political means to support it. In turn Israel provided a haven for victims of anti-Jewish hatred and a prophylactic against assimilation. According to Minkin, the underlying fantasy was of Israel as a democratic and socially progressive state, when in fact it privileged Jews over non-Jews in virtually all aspects of life and half the individuals under Israeli sovereignty were either disenfranchised Palestinians living under de facto military occupation or Arab citizens subject to structural and systematic discrimination. Tellingly, foundational documents such as the 2004 Jerusalem Program of the WZO and the 2018 Statement of Principles of the

American Zionist Movement avoided this contradiction by making no mention of non-Jews.[80]

Flouting the Feeling Rules

Since Israel's establishment, some American Jews have refused to marginalize the Palestinians. On the contrary, refugees from the 1948 war and the post-1967 occupation have been at the center of their engagement with Israel. These attachments have not necessarily meant a rejection of Zionism. After World War II the prominent American journalist I. F. Stone sympathized with Holocaust survivors and urged the establishment of a Jewish state, but in 1967 he became, and thereafter remained, deeply critical of Israel for its unyielding stance regarding the Palestinian refugees and what he saw as Israel's unjustified wars of aggression.[81] Similarly, before embarking on an academic career, the political theorist Hannah Arendt worked in Jewish institutions and supported many of Zionism's aims, although she called for a federated binational state in Palestine and rejected militant Israeli nationalism, as she did with nationalisms in general.[82] In 1963 Arendt's critique of Israel's conduct of the trial of Nazi war criminal Adolf Eichmann and of Jewish cooperation with Nazis in occupied Europe during the war infuriated many Jews. In a famous epistolary exchange between Arendt and Gershom Scholem, the scholar of Jewish mysticism whom we encountered in the previous chapter, Scholem accused Arendt of lacking *ahavat Yisra'el*, attachment to and compassion for the Jewish people.[83] Arendt did not reject Israel, but she violated the hegemonic feeling rules by which Jews signaled to each other their affiliation within a Zionist emotional community.

Critical stances toward Zionism are just as varied and just as amenable to interpretation through an affective lens as are supportive ones. As we saw in chapter 1, before 1948, far more Jews worldwide opposed Zionism than supported it. Jews who preferred global socialist revolution or the complete integration of Jews into their homelands considered Zionism to be parochial, aggressive, a waste of time and resources, and a political threat. After 1948 both leftist and assimilationist anti-Zionism went into decline but never disappeared. The traditional anti-Zionism of Reform Judaism, resting on a twin belief in Jewish acculturation and a mission to model ethical behavior for the Gentile world, continued in a secularized version as intellectuals like George Steiner celebrated the Jews' cosmopolitan, globalized existence. Such an approach rejected Jewish nationalism in general and territorially based Zionism in particular.

Despite the American Far Left's growing hostility to Israel during the late 1960s and 1970s, most Jewish leftists maintained Zionist feelings. Toward the end of the twentieth century, however, Jewish anti-Zionism attained a visible, albeit not critical, mass. In 1996 a knot of people in the San Francisco Bay area founded Jewish Voice for Peace (JVP); by 2021 it claimed some 10,000 financial contributors. Supported by academic celebrities such as Judith Butler, Noam Chomsky, and Naomi Klein, JVP stated that it "unequivocally oppose[s] Zionism":

> We know that opposing Zionism, or even discussing it, can be painful, can strike at the deepest trauma and greatest fears of many of us. . . . Through study and action, through deep relationship with Palestinians fighting for their own liberation, and through our own understanding of Jewish safety and self-determination, we have come to see that Zionism was a false and failed answer to the desperately real question many of our ancestors faced of how to protect Jewish lives from murderous antisemitism in Europe. While it had many strains historically, the Zionism that took hold and stands today is a settler-colonial movement, establishing an apartheid state where Jews have more rights than others. Our own history teaches us how dangerous this can be.[84]

JVP did not speak of love for either Israel or Jews but rather of solidarity with Palestinians. Its website quoted the late feminist and lesbian activist Melanie Kaye/Kantrowitz's aphorism that "solidarity is the political version of love." Yet the tone of the JVP's statements on Zionism was purposeful and unemotional—deliberately so—because it accused Israel and Zionists in general of manipulating feelings of Jewish victimhood to mask the reality of Israeli domination.

Zionist criticism of Jewish anti-Zionists often focused as much on affect as fact. The mainstream Anti-Defamation League granted that JVP's intentions were "sincere" but claimed that they lacked the compassion and empathy that would lead them to appreciate Israel's security dilemmas and bind them to the Jewish state.[85] A less charitable approach toward Jewish anti-Zionists came from the British novelist Howard Jacobson, whose darkly comic 2010 novel, *The Finkler Question*, presented them as riddled with shame, guilt, and self-hatred.[86] (Coined after World War I by a Viennese Jewish journalist, the concept of "Jewish self-hatred" was popularized in the 1930s by the German Jewish writer Theodor Lessing to refer to Jews whose longings for acceptance in Gentile society led them to internalize antisemitism and strive desperately to be freed from recognizably Jewish traits.[87]) Similar attacks against American Jewish anti-Zionists claimed that they felt obliged to condemn Israel, along with their Jewishness, to keep in step with social justice movements' association of Jews with white supremacy and Israel with the subjugation of an Indigenous people.[88]

Conclusion

The polemics examined here are more useful for understanding the sensibilities of the accuser than those of the accused. Determining affective motivation depends on a rigorous and open-minded analysis of both words and deeds. Most early twenty-first-century American Jews were not overwhelmed by guilt, shame, disappointment, or embarrassment about Israel. They were, if not fervently Zionist, "Zionish," as my college-age daughter once described her own feelings about Israel. A majority were uneasy with the hawkishness of Israel's government, the expansion of Jewish settlements in the West Bank, the increasing political power of

Orthodoxy, and discrimination against non-Orthodox denominations of Judaism in Israel. The Israeli elections of 2022, which brought to power the most right-wing government in the country's history, promised to intensify this discomfort that so far has been compensated for by the mixture of adhesive positive and negative emotions that characterized the American Zionist romance since 1948.

American Jewish activists who champion robust attachments to Israel acknowledged the need to exchange naive idealism for a new realism, a "mature love" different from the erotic Zionist ardor that had surged through the Jewish community from the 1960s until the turn of the millennium.[89] Most American Jews did not have the opportunity to express such sentiments in public forums, but their ongoing connections with Israel were concretely expressed in donations, travel to and consumption of news about Israel, and the intertwining of Israel into synagogues' religious, educational, and social activities. This attachment lost much of its earlier romantic mood, but it retained a romantic mode in which Zionism remained an unfinished project, both tragic and joyful.

5   *Zionism and the International Community*

GRATITUDE AND BETRAYAL

In November 2012 an escalation in tension between Israel and Hamas led to the IDF's Pillar of Defense operation, an eight-day incursion into Gaza that killed some one hundred Palestinian civilians. Sharon Brous, a rabbi in Los Angeles, responded to the crisis with professions of love for Israel and condemnation of Hamas, alongside empathy for suffering Palestinians and a recognition of their right to live in security in dignity. Daniel Gordis, an American rabbi who had moved to Israel in 1998, responded angrily in the *Times of Israel*:

> On weeks like this, with hundreds of thousands of Israelis sleeping in bomb shelters and many millions more unspeakably frightened, it's become clear that this universalized Judaism has rendered not only platitudinous Jews, but something worse. It bequeaths us a new Jew truly incapable of feeling loyalty. The need for balance is so pervasive that even an expression of gut-level love for Israelis more than for their enemies is impossible. Balance has now bequeathed betrayal.[1]

What did Gordis mean by "betrayal"? Betrayal, according to the sociologist Nachman Ben-Yehuda, is a "violation of trust and loyalty." Trust, in turn, is a relationship based on "confidence" and "predictability," and loyalty assumes fidelity and devotion. Loyalty and trust are feelings whose public display cements interpersonal bonds. Betrayal, however, is an action that is performed by an individual who appears to be loyal and trustworthy but is not. Betrayal is the act of someone "who pretends to be honest and interested, but is in fact manipulative, uninterested, and dishonest." In political life, betrayal "breaches . . . symbolic moral boundaries . . . hierarchies and priorities." The victim of betrayal is overwhelmed by feelings of anger, distress, fear, and disappointment. The strength of these feelings is proportional to the level of trust and loyalty the betrayed party had previously felt toward its betrayer. In domestic politics, this breaching of boundaries is called treason.[2]

Gordis did not explicitly call Brous or people who think like her traitors, but he did associate her and her ilk with betrayal. The links between one who betrays and a traitor are conceptually and etymologically entangled. Gordis implies that Brous and like-minded Jews claim to be loyal to Israel, but they are not. Their profession of love is false or, at best, misguided.

Scaling up from intragroup politics to international affairs, states or state-seeking actors can perform a politics of betrayal, accusing another polity in which they had placed their trust (and perhaps loyalty) of abandoning them for selfish or otherwise impure motives. Accusations of betrayal are particularly bitter when made by weaker groups against stronger ones, by dependents against protectors. Betrayal is not the act of an indifferent power but rather of one in whom members of another collective had placed trust, and the closer the affective bonds between the two parties, the greater the feeling of betrayal once the bonds are broken.

For a weaker party dependent on a stronger one, deployment of the rhetoric of betrayal can follow previous professions of gratitude, an acknowledgment by the weak of services rendered by the strong. In religious discourse, gratitude is incorporated into the act of thanksgiving, a recognition that frail and ephemeral humans are utterly dependent on the eternal and omnipotent God. In politics equals can express mutual gratitude, but in the relations between state-seeking actors to a state or to international bodies, the invocation of gratitude is tied closely to relations of dependence and need.

This chapter considers the language of gratitude and betrayal, and the emotional underpinnings of that language, in the Zionist movement and the State of Israel from the era of Theodor Herzl to the early twenty-first century. Like the previous chapter, this one focuses on the United States but also pays attention to Britain, because without the support of both these countries the State of Israel would neither have been created nor attained its current form. The ubiquity and intensity of the Zionist rhetoric of gratitude toward these and other Great Powers from the 1890s through 1930s were matched by an equally prevalent rhetoric of betrayal from the 1930s until 1948. Invocations of betrayal in Zionist discourse against the international community indicated dependence and a yearning for recognition. After 1948 such professions of Zionist gratitude for the international community declined precipitously. The discourse of betrayal became less prevalent as well, not because of benevolent feelings toward the international community so much as a loss of faith in that community and its member states, as well as a growing sense of independence and self-reliance.

This chapter differs somewhat from its predecessors in both content and form. Whereas the previous chapters were about an internal Zionist discourse, this one focuses on emotional rhetoric regarding the non-Jewish world. Moreover, the previous chapters not only presented primary sources but also synthesized and reframed a substantial body of secondary literature. Because the subject of this chapter has received relatively little scholarly attention, there is considerably more emphasis on primary sources. I pay particular attention to the speeches and writings of Zionist activists and the reporting of Jewish journalists. These sources allow for an expansion of emotional rhetoric from the Zionist and Israeli political elite to a larger segment of the Jewish population. I do not claim that these individuals represent the spectrum or intensity of feelings of millions of individuals. These sources are useful, however, in providing an indication of the kinds of emotional language that were considered acceptable or desirable within public Jewish life. By focusing on community publications that were not explicitly Zionist in orientation, we can also observe the alacrity with which not only solidarity with Israel but also a willingness to take its side in disputes with one's own country became prevalent.

Gratitude as a Strategic Display

Political Zionism straddles a line between cautious and optimistic appraisals of the goodwill of the international community. Lev Pinsker admitted that a territorial solution to the Jewish problem demanded the support of the international community, but he was silent on how that support could be garnered. Theodor Herzl, in contrast, assumed that state governments would foster the creation of a Jewish homeland out of self-interest. As he wrote in *The Jewish State*, once removed from their current homelands, the Jews would no longer present an economic threat, and their property would benefit those who purchased it. "Honest anti-Semites," he wrote, "whilst preserving their independence, will combine with our officials in controlling the transfer of our estates."[3] Antisemites would even buy shares in the joint-stock company that would set up the Jewish state. The Zionists, Herzl continued, would help the Christian purchasers of Jewish property settle into their new homes and businesses. Before departing, Jews would scrupulously pay off any outstanding debts to Gentiles without demanding reciprocity: "we shall act purely for the sake of our own honor."[4]

Herzl's program brimmed with psychological dependence on Gentile opinion of the Jews that matched its political dependence on imperial authority. "We should as a neutral state," he wrote, "remain in contact with all Europe, which would have to guarantee our existence."[5] Once the Jewish state was created it would benefit Europe by protecting the holiest sites in the Christian world and serving as a "wall of defense for Europe in Asia, an outpost of civilization against barbarism."[6] Although he tried to hide it, Herzl was awestruck in the presence of European heads of state, especially the German emperor. Herzl saw Wilhelm II as a personal hero and Germany as a source of inspiration and guidance for the Jewish people: "to live under the protection of this strong, great, moral, splendidly governed, rightly organized Germany," Herzl wrote, "can only have the most salutary effect on the Jewish national character."[7] In contrast Herzl despised the Ottoman sultan Abdulhamid II, to whom he applied a raft of Orientalist stereotypes. Nonetheless Herzl believed that a Jewish state, being small and of no military consequence, would present no threat to any other power, including the Ottoman Empire. At the turn of the nineteenth century, Herzl simultaneously offered Palestine to Germany as an informal protectorate and proposed to the Ottoman Empire that the province become autonomous, a political arrangement in which the Zionists would loyally serve the sultan by paying off the empire's bloated foreign debt and providing military service.

Herzl's boasts of massive Zionist financial capacity were empty. His diplomacy failed because in international relations, actors get what they want primarily by bargaining and threatening, and Herzl had little to offer and even less with which to threaten. There is, however, a third mechanism by which international actors can accomplish their goals, what the political scientist Todd Hall calls "emotional diplomacy."[8] International actors signal intentions to each other through displays of official emotion, which may or may not be genuinely felt but that can indicate and justify major changes in foreign policy.

Herzl never mastered emotional diplomacy; the political theorist and intellectual historian Isaiah Berlin once remarked, "Like many visionaries Herzl understood issues but not human beings."[9] His appeals to the Great Powers were grounded in imperial self-interest, and he was too cold and proud to engage with his interlocutors on an emotional level. Unlike Herzl, the next great figure in the history of Zionist leadership, Chaim Weizmann, possessed great empathy and a capacity to elicit sympathy. A decade after Herzl's death, the outbreak of World War I—and the state of war between the Entente Powers and the Ottoman Empire— placed the Zionist movement and Weizmann in a new geopolitical situation. Weizmann, who had lived in Britain since 1904, now not only had something with which to bargain and threaten but also a basis for emotional diplomacy with the world's greatest imperial power.

Weizmann was sensitive in both meanings of the term: he was easily hurt but also affectively bound up with his interlocutors. A product of traditional Eastern European Jewish society, Weizmann evinced a confident and unreflective Zionism from childhood onward.[10] In his conversations with British government figures, Weizmann communicated as much via emotional signals as by direct references to state interest. He consistently invoked the historic wrongs committed against the Jews, which evoked pity and compassion, alongside their antiquity, morality, and contributions to civilization, which elicited admiration and respect. When he met the British foreign secretary Arthur James Balfour in December 1914, Weizmann presented an elegy on the Jews' legacy of suffering, which, according to Weizmann's account of the encounter, moved the foreign secretary "to *tears*." Weizmann continued, "And he took me by the hand and said I had illuminated for him the road followed by a great suffering nation. . . . He saw me out into the street, holding my hand in silence, and bidding me farewell said very warmly, 'Mind to come again to see me, I am deeply moved and interested, it is not a dream, it is a great cause and I understand it.'"[11]

What practical value can one assign to such expressions of emotion? Most of the vast body of literature on Britain's motives for issuing the Balfour Declaration subordinates compassion to raison d'état, although exactly what the British state was pursuing remains a matter of disagreement.[12] Weizmann offered international Jewish support for the British war effort and played on antisemitic overestimations of Jewish unity and influence. Nor did he hide the fact that the Zionists were pursuing the support of other Great Powers. In other words, he both bargained and threatened. A focus only on the pragmatic components of the negotiations, however, leaves unexplained why the emotional displays occurred in the first place. Emotional signals are means of indicating sincerity and trustworthiness, which in turn foster agreement between political actors. The signals must appear sincere and communicate a willingness to make significant commitments or sacrifices.[13] The Balfour Declaration represented such a commitment, in return for which Weizmann and his Zionist partners were called on to be of equally substantive service.

Weizmann combined Herzl's diplomacy of imperial service with a diplomacy of eliciting sympathy. (This latter kind of diplomacy is an inverted version of Hall's model of a diplomacy of sympathy, in which one state expresses sympathy for another.) Moreover, no sooner had the Balfour Declaration been issued then there emerged another form of emotional display rooted in Weizmann's, and by extension the Zionist movement's, dependence on Britain. I call this a *diplomacy of gratitude.*

Weizmann acknowledged Zionism's dependence on Britain when he said at the outset of the 1919 Paris Peace Conference that "Great Britain was chosen by the Zionists as a protector because of her great experience in dealing with small nations in the East."[14] Weizmann's assertion that the Zionists had the power to choose their protector was in fact an admission of the need for protection. Despite his dignified bearing, Weizmann's relationship with the British ruling class was that of a supplicant, a master of the vertical alliance between Jews and royal authority that had been a key political strategy for Jewish survival since the Middle Ages.[15] Weizmann referred to himself as a *"schnorrer"* (a Yiddish word that connotes begging, mooching, and wheedling) on behalf of the Zionist movement.[16]

Weizmann gained access to the British governing elites in part because of his prewar chemical experiments, which he intensified during the war, on the fermentation of grain sugars to synthesize acetone, an ingredient in smokeless gunpowder. His scientific accomplishments quickly assumed the qualities of legend among Jews throughout the world. According to a Chicago Jewish newspaper, a fortnight after the issuance of the Balfour

Declaration, "As a chemist, [Weizmann] is the inventor of the high explosive now in use by British forces on the western front. He declined to take any reward for this contribution to the success of the war, asking in exchange nothing more than that the British government should listen to the appeal of the Zionists and approve their ambitions."[17] Setting aside its exaggeration—Weizmann did not invent the explosive but rather increased the availability of one of its components—we have a folktale narrative of a loyal servant of the crown who wins royal favor, thereby gaining privileges for his people. The story harkens to tales of the biblical Joseph and Mordechai (in the books of Genesis and Esther, respectively), Sephardic courtiers in medieval Spain, and, in the early modern period, Jews whose wealth or mastery of medical or alchemical knowledge gained favor from Gentile lords.[18]

Celebrations in the Jewish world of the Balfour Declaration's promulgation coded the Zionists' state of dependence on Britain in the diplomacy of gratitude. In late 1917 and early 1918, Zionist meetings routinely expressed gratitude toward Britain. The Zionist leader Nahum Sokolow said that "the word 'gratitude' is too poor to express their [the Jewish people's] sentiment and to define how immeasurably the Jewish people was indebted to the man [Balfour] who stood like a lighthouse in these days of storm."[19]

The word "gratitude" does not always connote dependence on a superior; it can function as a synonym for appreciation, thanks, and welcome. But it is linguistically and conceptually connected with grace, an act of beneficence by a greater power. It is in this sense that worshippers offer thanks to the deity and subjects to their king (e.g., American colonists' "deepest testaments of loyalty and gratitude to our most Gracious Sovereign" conveyed to King George III after the repeal of the infamous Stamp Tax in 1766).[20] After World War I, Jewish writings often invoked "gratitude" in this way. The connection between gratitude and grace was made nicely by the Boston *Jewish Advocate*, which described Passover of 1918 as a festival of contemporary liberation because "conquering

England has graciously offered Palestine as a national home for the Jews."[21]

Within the Zionist movement displaying gratitude was a performance, an act of thanksgiving directed from a weaker to a stronger power in return for just and gracious treatment. One cannot know for sure whether this discourse was purely performative. Its volume and intensity suggest, however, that it was not only a political instrument but also a manifestation of deep feeling. The feelings conveyed in expressions of gratitude included joy, relief, and the ebbing of fear. The massive suffering during and immediately after the war that Jews endured in the blood-soaked realm between the Baltic and Black Seas would be redeemed by the new Jewish National Home, where they and, by extension, Jews everywhere would live in a state of bodily and emotional security.

Feelings of gratitude toward Britain were not uniform. In the United States, Yiddish-speaking socialists and highly acculturated Reform Jews both expressed misgivings—the former out of distaste for imperialism and the latter out of discomfort with a distinct Jewish nationalism. In the United Kingdom the Balfour Declaration elicited anxiety from members of the Anglo-Jewish elite who, despite their great efforts to integrate, might henceforth be viewed as members of a separate and foreign nation. These feelings were particularly strong among the leadership of the Anglo-Jewish Association whose president, Claude Montefiore, responded to its issuance with "grave and serious apprehension."[22] Just a week after this statement, however, misgivings gave way to joy for the British conquest of Jerusalem, which London's *Jewish Chronicle* hailed in messianic terms.[23]

In the British dominion of Canada, the rhetoric of Jewish gratitude for the Balfour Declaration was ubiquitous. The views of Canadian Jews on Zionism were unlike those of Jewry in Eastern Europe, where masses of Orthodox Jews viewed Zionism with suspicion if not outright opposition; or in Western Europe, where assimilationists were no less hostile to

Zionism; or in the United States, where both radical and assimilationist ideologies limited Zionism's appeal. Jewry in Canada came of age in a binational society where, despite ambient xenophobia and racism, minorities faced little resistance to displaying their ethnic identities and establishing unifying institutions. Moreover, although Canada was inching toward full independence, the Anglophone majority remained culturally tied to Britain. In response to the Balfour Declaration, the Canadian Zionist leaders Clarence de Sola and Alexander Sachs expressed loyalty to and trust in Britain. De Sola said, "I have absolute faith in Britain's power, and believe that what she has undertaken she will accomplish." Sachs added, "Israel will offer every year cumulative thanksgiving to this Great Power that in the most critical moment of civilization resets the glory of Zion in the commonwealth of nations."[24] Likewise, the Toronto Jewish community declared, "Jews of this country will continue to feel the deepest devotion and most fervent loyalty to the British flag, which has always been first in flight for human rights the world over."[25]

Canadian Jewish gratitude toward Britain continued long past 1917 and took forms without parallel in the United States. In 1924 the Zionist Organization of Canada's president Archie Freiman spoke of Zionism as a "joint enterprise between the British people and the Jewish people."[26] A few years later, in Toronto, the Schiffer-Hillman Clothing Company commissioned architect Benjamin Brown to design a regal Art Deco structure, whose drawings from the start bore the name Balfour Building. It was opened to great fanfare in 1930.[27]

Just as displays of Jewish gratitude varied across and within countries, so too did the object of gratitude change over time, with the League of Nations and the international community (broadly understood) sharing the billing with Britain as beneficent agents of the fulfillment of Zionist desire. In early 1919 Isaac Goldberg, a polyglot American author and journalist, celebrated the new world order championed by President Woodrow Wilson in his celebrated "Fourteen Points" speech from the previous year. Goldberg analogized from Wilson's call for a prohibition of "private international understandings of any kind" to ending the furtive intercession that had characterized traditional Jewish international politics. Henceforth Jews would enjoy the dignity of a public presence in the halls of diplomacy, which would be increasingly transparent and democratic. The Balfour Declaration would give the Jewish people not only a national home but also a place in the international community.[28] Accordingly the American Jewish press attentively reported on the recognition of Zionism by other states—both the Great Powers that could remake the map of the Middle East and the small ones with which the Zionists could claim affinity.[29]

The fate of Zionism appeared to be linked with that of countries the world over that were experiencing a two-stage liberation process: first by the guns of the Entente's soldiers and then by the pens of the peacemakers in Paris. In October 1918 Itamar Ben-Avi, son of the pioneer Hebraist Eliezer Ben-Yehuda, represented the Zionists at a gathering in Philadelphia's Independence Hall of representatives of stateless European nations who issued a declaration of common aims and their inalienable rights to independence.[30] The *Jewish Advocate* joyously predicted a postwar order in which Armenians would receive Armenia, Syrians would have "northern" Syria, Arabs would have Arabia, and Jews would receive Palestine.[31]

The Jewish claim to Palestine was based not only on the Jews' own historical experience and religious belief but also on a vow to be the Holy Land's stewards for the benefit of humanity. The American Jewish Congress stated in 1918, "The Jews do not go to Palestine to build warships, train armies, found arsenals, invent devilish and murderous machines; but to dwell in peace and cultivate the graces and the learning of civilization. But their continued peaceful existence in their homeland will depend upon the peace of the world."[32]

As the source of Zionists' joy broadened from a Great Power (Britain) to the international community, the diplomacy of gratitude shifted gears from presenting the Balfour Declaration and the Mandate as gifts from benevolent rulers to depicting these political arrangements as the acknowledgment of a right. The 1921 convention of the Canadian Zionist Federation acknowledged "the deepest gratitude and indebtedness of the Jewish people to the British government for the Balfour Declaration written into the public law of nations, which recognizes the right of the Jewish people to a home in Palestine, and which is to make possible the establishment of the Jewish Homeland."[33] More baldly in 1927 the newsletter of the Los Angeles chapter of B'nai B'rith described the declaration as the "first recognition by a modern nation (Great Britain) of the Jewish claim to Palestine as a national homeland."[34] These statements invoked both an inalienable right and dependence on a Great Power to recognize that right and make possible its exercise.

To what, precisely, did Zionists believe they had a right? Although the international Zionist movement did not formally demand statehood in Palestine until 1942, expectations of Jewish statehood were already in the air immediately after the end of World War I. The American Jewish Congress urged that Jews have "complete and unhampered independence in their own land."[35] Its call for a Jewish "commonwealth" (a term widely used at the time as a synonym for a sovereign state) was echoed by the U.S. branch of the Labor Zionist Poalei Tsion, which demanded "an independent, neutral, internationally-guaranteed republic under the protection of the League of Nations in which the Jewish nation is to be an equal member. England, which now possesses Palestine, should help the Jews establish this free Jewish republic."[36] In February 1919, Rabbi Stephen S. Wise, one of the United States' most prominent Jewish leaders, spoke with assurance about a forthcoming "trusteeship on behalf of the Jews of the world over Palestine. . . . Our interests are in the hands of friendly powers, the powers which lead at the peace conference being the friendliest of the people of Israel." Wise directly compared the Zionist cause to that of the "redemption of Belgium and the re-creation of

Serbia"; that is, the creation of sovereign, if small and somewhat fragile, states.[37]

The clarity and frequency with which American Zionists spoke of statehood for Palestine should come as no surprise given the affirmations of Zionism that came from the highest offices of the U.S. government. In December 1918 Congress endorsed a Jewish commonwealth under British trusteeship. (Another bicameral declaration in support of the Balfour Declaration came in May 1922.) In March 1919, President Wilson addressed a delegation of prominent American Jews in Washington, DC, telling them, "I am persuaded that the Allied nations, with the fullest concurrence of our government and people, are agreed that in Palestine shall be laid the foundation of a Jewish Commonwealth."[38] Later that summer, he assured Stephen S. Wise, "Have no fear, Palestine will be yours."[39]

The complex and ambiguous relationship between gratitude and dependence, on the one hand, and the assertion of right and independence, on the other, is further illustrated by the practice of likening the Balfour Declaration to the Magna Carta. On December 7, 1917, the Anglo-Jewish Association called the declaration the "Magna Charta [sic] of the Jewish race."[40] On the occasion of the declaration's fifth anniversary, Charles Untermeyer, a major figure in American Zionist fundraising, saw it "and the Mandate that followed as the new Magna Charta [sic] of the Jewish people the world over. Under the beneficent protection of the Mandate the Jews will be able to return to their native land and there pursue their vocations in peace and prosperity."[41] Both Nahum Sokolow and Chaim Weizmann indulged in the simile. In his testimony before the Peel Commission in 1936, Weizmann vowed that he "could submit to the Commission a series of utterances of responsible statesmen and men in every walk of life in England to show that this declaration was regarded as the Magna Charta [sic] of the Jewish people; it was in a sense comparable with another Declaration made thousands of years before, when Cyrus allowed a remnant of the Jews to return from Babylon and to rebuild the Temple."[42] The comparison with Cyrus repeated one made in 1918 by Elihu Stone, a Massachusetts state legislator, who said, "Surely Great Britain will never be forgotten by the Jewish people and the proclamation of the Government of England declaring Palestine as the homeland of the Jewish people will remain as immortal as the decree of Cyrus."[43]

These invocations are striking. In our own era the Magna Carta is commonly viewed as a concession of aristocratic privileges by an unpopular king to his rebellious barons. In the nineteenth century and the first half of the twentieth century, however, it was widely interpreted as foreshadowing modern notions of individual rights. Nonetheless, even this more generous interpretation of the Magna Carta presents it as a royal charter, bestowed from on high, as opposed to a declaration drafted by a popularly elected body.

Zionists were not the only stateless or colonized people to invoke the Magna Carta; in the late nineteenth and early twentieth centuries, Indian and South African activists did the same. But according to historian Amanda Behm, they did so not to display gratitude to a Great Power for acknowledging their historic rights but to juxtapose current discriminatory British policies with what they believed to be older, binding proclamations of equality and promises of protection by Britain to its colonies. At the end of World War I, anticolonial leaders in countries such as India, Egypt, China, and Korea looked to the international community to recognize their rights to self-determination. They neither wanted nor needed a protector, and they did not express gratitude for colonial rulers' largesse.[44] Zionists found themselves in a fundamentally different position from the colonized world. Movements for independence in the Arab Middle East saw the mandates for Mesopotamia, Syria, and Palestine as an assault on their autonomy and collective rights, even if these mandates were supposed to lead to self-government. The Zionists, in contrast, were dependent on imperial protection, without which the fledgling

Yishuv could not survive, let alone thrive. Only with British help could the Zionists attain their goal, which, in the immediate aftermath of World War I, was clearly one of statehood.[45]

Nor did Zionism's more militant wing develop an alternative to the politics of imperial dependence and the promise of quid pro quo. Vladimir Jabotinsky, who in Zionists' collective memory is considered an ardent champion of Jewish statehood, developed a political program that was entirely dependent on British protection and the incorporation of Jewish Palestine into the British Empire. Throughout the 1920s Jabotinsky suggested that he would be content if the Jewish national home were no more sovereign than an American state or Canadian province.[46] Jabotinsky was the only major Zionist leader to embrace the British politician Josiah Wedgwood's 1928 call for the establishment of Jewish Palestine as a seventh British dominion alongside Canada, Newfoundland, Australia, New Zealand, South Africa, and the Irish Free State. Jabotinsky claimed that even if Palestine became 99 percent Jewish, he would still prefer that Palestine be part of the British Empire than be fully independent.[47] These views had little uptake among British or North American Jewry; whatever gratitude or other positive feelings they had toward Britain, they did not envision a permanent formal relationship. And in the wake of the 1930 Passfield White Paper, which recognized a dual obligation to Jewish and Arab demands in Palestine, Zionist dissatisfaction with Britain began to accelerate.

Righteous Anger and Accusations of Betrayal

Outbursts of intercommunal violence in Palestine in 1920 and 1921 did little to dampen Zionist optimism, but the more destructive August 1929 riots provoked some diaspora Jews to accuse Britain of not doing enough to protect Jewish lives. A demonstration of thirty-five thousand Jews in New York City included Jewish World War I veterans carrying signs that read, "We have fought together with the English army; now they are going against us."[48] In contrast, a mass rally in New York City's Madison

Square Garden passed a resolution "affirming confidence in the honor and good faith of Great Britain."[49] Weizmann continued to speak soothingly of a consonance of British and Zionist interests in Palestine. However, it became increasingly difficult to make this case after March 1930, when the British government's Shaw Commission, appointed to assess the causes of the Arab Revolt, determined that Palestinian Arabs' political and economic interests had been neglected in favor of Zionist ones. In October a follow-up inquiry led by John Hope Simpson recommended limiting Jewish immigration; this recommendation, along with restrictions on Zionist land purchase, were incorporated into an official British policy statement (the Passfield White Paper) later that month.

In response to these policies, Zionist displays of gratitude quickly turned to accusations of betrayal.[50] The Zionist Organization of America's magazine New Palestine called the Hope Simpson inquiry's findings "a concession to criminality."[51] Even well-established British Jews, who had long linked their social status with full-throated support for British policies, got their back up. Leopold Greenberg, a Zionist activist and editor of the Jewish Chronicle, noted that Jews in Palestine, "at the invitation of the Mandatory Power," had done their part by building up the Jewish national home precisely as they were supposed to do under the terms of the Balfour Declaration. The Shaw Commission's report, according to another article in the same paper, had "wounded the feelings of Palestinian Jewry and has hurt—even more than the riots did."[52]

Earlier I proposed a diplomacy of gratitude, which may be official, crafted, and instrumental, or sincere; or some combination of the two. It is more difficult to speak of a diplomacy of betrayal. The expression of anger, frustration, fear, and wounded pride that accompanies feelings of betrayal is unlikely to move the alleged betrayer to change its ways. Public denunciations of Britain may have been intended to shame Britain into altering its policies, but it is more likely that they were sincere expressions of anger, especially because Weizmann, for the most part, did not take part in this chorus of condemnation.

After the publication of the Passfield White Paper in October 1930, bitter rhetoric from Jews accelerated dramatically, with the language of frustration and distress giving way to a most undiplomatic fury. The prominent British Zionist Alfred Mond (Lord Melchett) accused His Majesty's Government of a "grotesque travesty" and betrayal that called into question the sacrifice of British Jews who fought and died for Britain in World War I. Equating the Jewish war effort with Britain's promise to develop a Jewish national home, Mond wrote that the White Paper "is an act of almost unparalleled ingratitude and treachery committed by a government."[53] A week later a protest meeting in Manchester declared the White Paper to be a "betrayal of British honor." An activist from Leeds called every comment in the document "dishonest and hypocritical." Another called it "the greatest act of folly of any Government."[54] However the retraction of the White Paper in February 1931 by Prime Minister Ramsay MacDonald was met by the *Jewish Chronicle* not with thanks but with suspicion and anger. The editor fumed over "palpable betrayal" and called MacDonald's flip-flop "a gilded pill" to which the appropriate reactions were "acute agony," dismay, and disgust.[55] Chaim Weizmann came in for harsh criticism as "contemptuous" toward his supporters for not taking a stronger stand against the government—although it had been Weizmann who had persuaded the prime minister to retract the White Paper. At this point, railed the newspaper, "anything short of a Jewish Commonwealth in Palestine" would be a "surrender."[56]

The 1936–1939 Palestinian-Arab Revolt came as an even greater shock to diaspora Zionists than the 1929 riots because of its scale and duration. As in 1929, Jewish publications attributed the revolt to manipulation of the Palestinian masses by their unscrupulous leaders, but they also blamed Italian fascist and Nazi propaganda. It was psychologically important for Jews in the United States and Palestine alike to believe in the moral righteousness of their cause and to present Arabs of the Land of Israel as docile, perhaps primitive, but rarely savage. One editorial, in Brooklyn's fiery and hawkish *Jewish Examiner*, described Arabs harshly as mangling Jewish children with bombs, shooting Jewish nurses in cold blood, and viciously assaulting aged men and women.[57] Yet even this newspaper did not blame the Arabs, preferring to attribute responsibility to anti-Zionist propaganda by Jewish communists in Palestine and fascists from abroad.[58]

Feelings changed, however, in 1937 when the Peel Commission, which was convened to find a solution to the intracommunal violence in Palestine, issued its recommendations. Its proposal to partition Palestine and to grant the Jews less than one-fifth of its territory was seen by many Jews as a cynical act of British imperialist strategy that would feed both Jewish and Arab extremism. The Philadelphia *Jewish Exponent* described the proposal as "a betrayal of the hopes and aspirations of the Jewish people."[59] Stephen S. Wise called it "deeply violative of British obligations" and "the gravest betrayal of a most sacred trust."[60] He and Jacob de Haas, a veteran journalist and Zionist activist, coauthored a pamphlet on the situation titled *The Great Betrayal*. In London James de Rothschild called the Peel Commission's recommendations a "concession to terrorism" that "tears up the Balfour Declaration."[61] Opponents of partition turned their hopes to the League of Nations and the United States, both of which, under the terms of the Mandate, would be required to approve the proposal. Some American Jews praised partition for recognizing the Jewish claim to statehood and restoring Jewish honor and dignity, but notably, even these upbeat reflections contained no hint of the gratitude toward Britain that had characterized Jewish public discourse in the wake of the issuing of the Balfour Declaration.

Just as the word "gratitude" was on many Jews' lips after World War I, the word "betrayal" was omnipresent in reactions to the May 1939 British White Paper, which abandoned the terms of the Balfour Declaration and proposed in its stead a unitary Arab-Jewish state. There were calls among Jews throughout the United States for protest rallies to express indignation at "the British betrayal." One hundred thousand people flocked to the Palestine Pavilion at the New York City World's Fair to protest and express solidarity. A letter to the *Jewish Advocate* warned that "this betrayal does not arouse in the hearts and breasts of millions of Jews and non-Jews alike only a violent hatred of all things imperialistic, but a desire to do something about it."[62] And an editorial in that paper warned, "Uneasy will the British lion sleep, while the ghosts of Palestine, of Austria, of Czechoslovakia, of Spain, of Ethiopia, and of China return to plague her dreams."[63] According to the Detroit-based *Jewish Chronicle*, Colonial Secretary Malcolm MacDonald "stands as a betrayer of a great trust and as a destroyer of a people's hopes."[64] The *Jewish Exponent* summed up the ambient emotional temperature nicely: "There is only one thing that is worse than being beaten by an enemy, and that is being betrayed by a friend. Too bad that England should have chosen to play this damnable part in one of the darkest periods in all of Jewish history."[65]

Canadian Zionists, who during the early 1920s presented themselves as the most loyal children of the British Empire, now turned against their parent. In early March 1939, nearly three months before the White Paper was issued, the *Canadian Jewish Chronicle* was already seething with anger over what it called an impending "Munich of Zionism," describing the Peel Commission's work as a "white-coated preparation of the victim for the operating table" and suggesting that the British government would be handing over the Jewish people to "the misgovernment of their Arab foes."[66] The newspaper went so far as to reconstruct history, reversing the flow of gratitude from the stronger to the weaker: it claimed that, during the Great War, Prime Minister Lloyd George had expressed gratitude toward "Jewry upon whom they leaned in their hour of need," and that was now being sacrificed "to the Moloch of a misinterpreted political expediency."[67] In the spring of 1939 Canadian Jewish activists harangued Britain for "a colossal betrayal" yet took pains to condemn only certain members of the British government, not the cabinet as a whole and certainly not the British people. There was also a notable and perhaps strategic shift from evoking betrayal and displaying anger to calling for resistance and steely resolve. The Montreal United Palestine Appeal, for example, pivoted away from "conferences, white papers, and commissions" toward "our own efforts, our own sacrifices, our own will!"[68] At last, Canadian Zionist gratitude to Britain had run dry.

What was true for Canadian Zionists was all the more so for their American counterparts. In May 1942, an emergency gathering of Zionist luminaries, including Ben-Gurion, Weizmann, and the leaders of major U.S. Zionist organizations assembled at New York City's Biltmore Hotel. Unaware of the scale of the genocide underway in Europe, the attendees predicted that some two to three million Jews outside the Soviet Union would survive the war, that many of them would be rendered stateless and homeless, and that the entirety of Palestine must become a Jewish "commonwealth" (i.e., sovereign state) to house the refugees. The conference's demand that Britain establish a Jewish state had none of the flattery or offers of a quid pro quo that characterized earlier language about the Balfour Declaration and Mandate.[69]

In the wake of the Holocaust, Jewish feelings of having been betrayed by the world increased exponentially. Fury at the perpetrators of the Holocaust extended to those who kept their distance and did nothing to prevent or mitigate it. Britain was a target for vitriol because of its throttling of Jewish immigration to Palestine, seizure of refugee ships approaching Palestine and detention of their passengers, and crackdown on Zionist anti-British militancy. In public, British Jewry remained conciliatory; on May 14, 1948, the day of the British withdrawal from Palestine, the *Jewish Chronicle* wrote that "profound mistakes have been committed during the period of thirty years' rule, but the overall picture is one on which time will look back with gratitude."[70] American Jews, however, were less circumspect.

Over the course of the fighting in Palestine in 1948, they routinely expressed outrage at the British government for alleged anti-Zionist and pro-Arab sympathies. The radio program *The Eternal Light* devoted two episodes to excoriating the British as supercilious and heartless tyrants who were thwarting the efforts of Holocaust survivors to enter the Promised Land.[71] Balfour Peisner, a Detroit-based lawyer and Jewish activist, was anything but grateful to his namesake's land of origin when he described Palestine under British rule as a "police state" no better than Nazi-occupied Europe.[72] According to a Chicago Jewish newspaper, Palestine in April 1948 was in the position of the Warsaw Ghetto in 1943: Palestine's Jews would either die en masse or "write a new and glorious page in the development of democracy." To the *Jewish Advocate*, the British were a greater enemy to Palestine's Jews than the Arabs.[73]

The U.S. government also came in for savage criticism despite its endorsement of partition in 1947 and recognition of Israel immediately after its establishment in May 1948. The Jewish press railed against the State Department and President Harry Truman for threatening punitive actions against American Jews who fought for Israel, placing an arms embargo against the belligerent parties (which was said to disproportionately harm Israel), and in the winter of 1948 backing away from its initial support for partition to consider a UN Trusteeship. In February the *Jewish Advocate* declaimed that "what is going on in Palestine is the rape of a UN decision which was reached with moral support." The paper castigated the United States for engaging in "treachery, catastrophe, and moral insolvency."[74] A month later the syndicated Jewish journalist Nathan Ziprin wrote of American policy, "The hurt is too deep, the wound too painful, the insult too heavy, the betrayal too unbelievable."[75] By October Boris Smolar, editor-in-chief of the Jewish Telegraphic Agency (JTA) and a widely syndicated columnist, determined that Jews were put off by both the major parties' presidential candidates, Thomas Dewey and Harry Truman, because of their stances on Israel. Henceforth, he wrote, Israel would have to take care of itself, implying that American Jewry would take care of Israel regardless of what the U.S. government wanted.[76]

Expressions of American Jewish gratitude were hard to come by even when the United Nations voted to partition Palestine and create a Jewish state in 1947 and seated Israel as a member of the General Assembly a year and a half later. There was a disconnect between an emotionally agitated American Jewish community and the political vision of the writers of Israel's founding declaration, which emphasized not only the Jewish people's natural right to their homeland but also the crucial role played by the international community in recognizing that right—from the Balfour Declaration to the League of Nations Mandate to the UN vote for partition—and the desire to be part of the new community. The Israeli founding declaration shows no hint of servile gratitude, but it did acknowledge Israel's interdependence on the international community.[77]

Zionist leaders such as Weizmann and Ben-Gurion had counted on that interdependence when, in the spring and summer of 1947, they lobbied the UN Special Committee on Palestine (UNSCOP) to recommend the creation of a Jewish state. The Zionist representatives performed an emotional diplomacy neither of gratitude nor betrayal, but rather of eliciting sympathy and evoking guilt. Zionists who testified before the committee cataloged the destruction of European Jewry and the suffering of hundreds of thousands of Jewish displaced persons (DPs) in camps in Germany and Austria. When members of UNSCOP visited the camps, the Jewish residents spoke with one voice about their desire to live in the Land of Israel.[78] Scholars argue about whether these expressions were spontaneous, encouraged, or coerced, but regardless of their motivations, the DPs enacted an emotional performance with a political aim. Similarly, the Zionist officials who after the war organized illegal Jewish immigration to Palestine knew that most of the ships would be stopped offshore by British authorities, but they continued to operate the transport as a gesture of defiance and a call for attention. The sailing of the SS Exodus, which carried 4,500 Jewish refugees from France to Palestine in July 1947, only to be turned back by the British and returned to Germany, was timed to occur during UNSCOP's deliberations.[79]

In 1947 Zionists' emotional diplomacy vis-à-vis the international community was successful. Although most of the members of UNSCOP cited pragmatic concerns for their support for the partition of Palestine, sympathy for the survivors of the Holocaust and unease that the world had shut its doors to Jewish refugees before the war played a role for delegates such as Jorge Garcia Granados of Guatemala, Paul Mohn of Sweden, and Ivan Rand of Canada. Support for partition from the Soviet Union, Ukraine (which, although part of the USSR, had nominally independent status in the General Assembly), and newly communist states such as Poland and Czechoslovakia stemmed mainly from a desire to weaken Britain's role in the Middle East and promote ethnonationalist homogeneity in the states of East-Central Europe. Nonetheless the Eastern Bloc's support for Israel was couched in the language of redressing Jewish suffering and recognizing the Jews' rights to national self-determination, freedom, and dignity.[80]

Israel, American Jewry, and the Rhetoric of Betrayal, 1948–1975

In 1947, the United Nations endorsed the creation of a Jewish state, and in 1949 Israel was seated as a member of the General Assembly. Over the first twenty-five years of Israel's existence, however, many countries that had been supportive of Israel turned cold, and Israel's supporters came to view the international community with increasing distrust and alarm.

The new State of Israel needed allies, but it had great difficulty finding them. Israel was excluded from the 1955 Bandung Conference of newly independent Asian and African states. In the following year, the invasion by Israel, France, and the United Kingdom of the Sinai Peninsula and Suez Canal zone strengthened perceptions in the formerly colonized world that Israel was an agent of Western imperialism.[81] After the war Israel and France developed a strong military relationship, but it frayed after Israel's victory in 1967, which antagonized Arab states with which France had close economic relations. Britain's painful relationship with Zionism and Palestine, not to mention its own Middle Eastern interests, limited its commitments to Israel. In the 1950s and 1960s Israel benefited from economic assistance and arms sales from the Federal Republic of Germany, but the country was in no position to offer Israel a security guarantee.[82]

Support for Israel from the Soviet Union and Eastern Bloc weakened throughout the 1950s as Israel's ties to the West became clear. Soviet Bloc propaganda did not content itself with condemning Israel as a state but routinely invoked "Zionism" as a shadowy force that united Israel, international Jewry, and U.S. imperialism. During the 1960s the Soviet Union became a leading sponsor of condemnations of Zionism and Israel at the United Nations.

That left Israel with the United States. The Israel–U.S. alliance dated to the Kennedy administration, which, after receiving assurances from Israel in 1962 that it would not be the first party to introduce nuclear weapons into the Middle East, sold Israel antiaircraft missiles. In 1965 and after the 1967 war, Congress authorized the sale of fighter jets to Israel. Richard Nixon, the U.S. president between 1969 and 1974, held decidedly antisemitic views about American Jews but saw Israel as a valuable ally, in part because of Israeli support for his Vietnam strategy and 1972 reelection campaign but mainly for Israel's putative value in the struggle against Soviet encroachment in the Middle East.[83] This view of Israel's utility was popular among the U.S. public, which found in Israel's victories over Soviet-backed Arab states in the wars of 1967 and 1973 psychic compensation for the inability of the U.S. military, bogged down in Vietnam, to vanquish the North Vietnamese Army and the Viet Cong guerrilla forces, other beneficiaries of Soviet support.[84]

Convinced that the United States alone had the will and power to protect Israel and that they had public opinion on their side, American Jews were unnerved on those occasions when their country acted counter to Israel's own stated interests. The American response to Israel's occupation of the Sinai Peninsula and Gaza Strip in 1956 was harsh, as the United States sought to differentiate itself from the "old" imperial powers and did not want to antagonize Arab states. Public voices of American Jewry dealt with the embarrassing situation by barely mentioning British and French involvement, focusing instead on Palestinian guerrillas in the Sinai, the persecution of Egyptian Jews, and the security threat that Gamal Abdel Nasser allegedly presented to Israel and the world. Mainstream American Jewish organizations and publications respected President Dwight Eisenhower but were aghast that his administration might impose sanctions on Israel should it not withdraw from Gaza.

Rather than attack Eisenhower directly, Los Angeles's *B'nai B'rith Messenger* quoted Israeli sources or American critics, such as former secretary of state Dean Acheson or California senator William Knowland.[85] In time, however, the paper took the gloves off, calling Eisenhower an "unhappy desultor" (someone trying to ride two horses at once) who foolishly trusted "Dingo (wild dog) Nasser."[86] Jack Fishbein, editor of the Chicago Jewish paper *The Sentinel*, called for mass protests in Washington: "We must heave out a geshrei ["cry" in Yiddish] that will ring out across the length and breadth of our land. That 'geshrei' must be: 'Let our people go'—into the land of Israel."[87]

In a March 1955 meeting of the Israeli cabinet, Foreign Minister Moshe Sharett pointed out Israel's need to keep the opinion of the United Nations in mind while crafting its military responses to Egypt. After all, he pointed out, the UN had legitimized Israel's creation via the partition resolution just a few years earlier. Ben-Gurion responded, "Not at all! Only the daring of the Jews founded this country, and not some *Oom-Shmoom* [the UN—who cares?] resolution."[88] In the wake of the Suez Crisis, the same tone found its way into American Jewish public rhetoric. In February 1957 the New York Board of Rabbis proclaimed that Israel was "surrounded by nations which have sworn to destroy her, and by the United Nations which refuses to guarantee her existence."[89]

Given this assertiveness toward the United States and the United Nations after the 1956 war, it is striking that on the eve of the 1967 Middle East war, Jewish speech about the international community was mild and measured. There were few strong expressions of disappointment when, in May the United States refused to take military measures to break the blockade Egypt had imposed on the Straits of Tiran, cutting off shipping to and from Israel through the port of Eilat. At the end of May, Stan Rose's editorial in Kansas City's Jewish newspaper advised the Johnson administration that, by breaking the blockade, the United States could score a victory against the Soviet Union and, by implication, improve the U.S. position in Vietnam.[90] But U.S. inaction went without comment, and UN secretary-general U Thant's decision to remove peace-keeping forces from the Sinai was met with expressions of resignation rather than anger. The general mood in American Jewish journalism was that the UN was impotent (a word repeated in two articles in Boston's Jewish paper) and that little should be expected from it.[91] The overall implication was that Israel could not depend on anyone—not the United States and certainly not the UN. Israel had to take care of itself, with American Jews as its closest ally.

With no expectations of a patron, there was little reason to feel betrayed. Jewish reportage after the 1967 war focused on internal matters such as American Jewry's remarkable fundraising accomplishments on behalf of Israel and Israel's rapid return to normal life. Israel's territorial conquests were viewed through the lens of Israeli security, rather than Arab fury or the displacement of hundreds of thousands of Palestinians. In November 1967, the fiftieth anniversary of the Balfour Declaration received only cursory coverage in the American Jewish press. Similarly marginalized was the passing in November of UN Security Council Resolution 242, which both called for Israel to withdraw from recently occupied territories and recognized Israel's right to exist within secure borders.

Whereas 1967 saw the burgeoning of American Jewish love for Israel, as discussed in the previous chapter, the events of 1973 elevated the feeling of anxiety about Israel's precarious position in the world. After Egypt's and Syria's surprise invasion of the Sinai Peninsula and Golan Heights, respectively, on the Jewish Day of Atonement in 1973, feelings of existential fear for Israel, coupled with distrust and disregard for the international community, ran high. The president of the Greater Boston Jewish community called this attack "the worst catastrophe facing the Jewish people since Hitler." Commenting on the president's speech, the Boston paper reflected that the prevalent anxiety among American Jewry stood in marked contrast to the "confidence that had prevailed during the Six-Day War in 1967."[92] Editorials in the paper claimed that Arab states were trying to dismember Israel through both military action and diplomatic support for the "so-called Palestinian refugees." The editorials feared that the United States would adopt a "supine position" toward the Soviet Union to preserve détente.[93] Still there was a sense that the United States was the only surviving heir of the beneficent feelings toward the Jewish people in 1917 and the heady years after the end of World War I.[94]

Intriguingly the Jewish press paid little attention to Operation Nickel Grass, the U.S. airlift of more than 22,000 tons of military equipment to Israel, starting a week into the war and lasting for a month. The airlift was well known in real time and was covered from start to finish in the *New York Times*. Moreover, lead dispatches from the Jewish Telegraphic Agency's daily bulletin, which was distributed to Jewish newspapers throughout the country, publicized it on October 16 and 18:

> The growing American airlift of war materiel to Israel is visible to the public. The most welcome sight these last two days is the huge C-5A Galaxy transports roaring in low from the Mediterranean to land at a military airbase somewhere in the hinterland. . . . The

"Galaxies" have been arriving at increasingly frequent intervals. . . . The daily visitations of the American transports are heartening to the Israelis. They are seen as evidence that Israel has at least one good friend in the world.[95]

But in major U.S. cities, the Jewish press reported very little on it, and when it was mentioned, feelings such as gratitude, thanks, or appreciation were rarely expressed. The Israeli Knesset's resolution of October 17 expressing gratitude toward the United States received little attention. The newspapers took their cue instead from the leaders of major American Jewish organizations. On October 16, a day after the White House confirmed that it would begin "some re-supply" of war materiel to Israel, major Jewish organizations sent President Richard Nixon and Secretary of State Henry Kissinger telegrams expressing "support" for the government's position "in implementing the established policy of maintaining the balance of arms in the Middle East and in supplying Israel with material required to repel Arab aggression and to meet the challenge of the continuing massive Soviet resupply airlift."[96] In mid-November the *Jewish Advocate* noted the Israeli government's thanks to the United States for the "massive airlift of weapons," but the article immediately diluted that gratitude by pointing out the concurrent American assistance to Arab states, which, the author asserted, received more aid from the United States than did Israel.[97]

This understated reporting about the airlift during the war may have been deliberate and even requested by the Nixon administration to avoid the impression of a direct U.S.–Israel alliance. But even if true, this does not explain why the airlift continued to be neglected in Jewish accounts of the 1973 war long after the event, especially because the airlift did crop up occasionally in Jewish journalistic venues, suggesting no coordinated conspiracy of silence. Some American Jewish leaders and writers may have been irked that Kissinger held off implementing the airlift until the war had been going on for a week and Israel had sustained heavy losses.[98]

Continuing patterns dating to 1948, Israel remained dependent on an outside power—but in the Jewish public, the language of gratitude was no longer deemed necessary or appropriate.

In the wake of the 1973 war, almost thirty African countries broke off diplomatic relations with Israel. The Palestinian cause became increasingly popular worldwide, and on November 14, 1974, Palestine Liberation Organization president Yasir Arafat was enthusiastically received by the UN General Assembly. Denunciations of Israel at the United Nations had been made for more than a decade. However, as shown in chapter 2, the pace and intensity of anti-Israel rhetoric picked up markedly after the October 1973 Arab–Israeli war, culminating in UN General Assembly Resolution 3379 that argued, "Zionism is a form of racism and racial discrimination."[99]

The Jewish world was stunned by the resolution. In the debate held before the vote, the Saudi ambassador employed the historical stereotype of Jews as moneychangers, and the Senegalese ambassador claimed that Lord Balfour had Jewish blood.[100] On the day of the vote, the *New York Times* ran a half-page ad by B'nai B'rith directly comparing Resolution 3379 with Nazi persecution of the Jews. Comparisons between Arafat and Hitler were common in the Jewish press and at pro-Israel rallies.[101] Gil Troy sums up the Jewish reaction as follows: "Israelis and Jews felt rejected by the world. . . . The world's abandonment stung. The betrayal was scary."[102]

But who had betrayed Israel, and why was it so upsetting? The UN's moral authority had been called into question, if not dismissed altogether, by vocal American Jews some years before. Moreover, Israel still had many friends at the United Nations. The member states of the European Economic Community and many Caribbean and Latin American states had voted against the resolution. The United States firmly condemned it, as did editorials in more than fifty major American newspapers, moderate student groups, and African American leaders (including the influential columnist Bayard Rustin).[103] In the late 1960s some

American journalists had flirted with a romantic view of Palestinian guerrillas, but the aircraft hijackings of the early 1970s and the kidnapping and killing of Israeli athletes at the 1972 Munich Olympics had driven sympathy with Palestinian revolutionaries to the fringes of public opinion (e.g., the radical edge of the Black Power movement). With the fall of Saigon in April 1975, the long-standing associations among the American public between itself and Israel grew even deeper as Israel could appear to be both a triumphant victor against communist-backed foes on the battlefield and a fellow victim of communist malevolence in the form of Palestinian terrorism. (America's faith in Israel as its surrogate gladiator was reaffirmed on the date of America's bicentennial, July 4, 1976, when Israel responded to the hijacking by Palestinian guerrillas and German leftist extremists of an Israel-bound Air France jet with a daring and successful raid on the Entebbe airport in Uganda.[104])

American Jewry in the mid-1970s was not alone and isolated, but it was anxious. Jews feared that the general public would blame Israel for the Arab states' oil embargo against the United States and other pro-Israel countries that was put in place shortly after the 1973 war. Jews who combined leftism and feminism with sympathy for Israel felt particularly threatened. Since the mid-1960s the American Socialist Workers Party and the Student Nonviolent Coordinating Committee had taken a strongly anti-Zionist line.[105] Letty Cottin Pogrebin, cofounder of *Ms. Magazine*, claimed that at the United Nations and its conferences abroad, "although it was ostensibly the Israelis who had been attacked as racists, I knew the arrow was also meant for me. . . . To feminists who hate Israel I was not a woman."[106] At the UN Women's Conference in Copenhagen in 1980, the feminist magazine *Lilith* reported that "Israel was insulted at every channel" and that the conference's "virulent antisemitism" created a chasm between Jewish and non-Jewish women.[107]

In this atmosphere Rabbi Shlomo Carlebach's stirring tune "Am Yisrael Chai" (The People of Israel Must Live), originally written in 1965, became the Jewish anthem of the era. It was sung at pro-Israel rallies (such as one in New York City on November 11, 1975, that attracted a crowd of some 125,000), and the phrase adorned popular lapel buttons and posters.[108] The 1973 war and 1975 UN resolution created a mood of consternation, solidarity, and resolve. At the same time, the era's identity politics, which revolutionized the self-perceptions of American Blacks, women, Latinos, and Indigenous peoples, also affected Jews, who became more assertive about displaying an ethnonationalist identity tied to Israel.

The Eclipse—and Return—of Gratitude

From the late 1970s American Jewish lobbying for Israel became bolder, as manifested in the rise to prominence during the Reagan administration of the American Israel Public Affairs Committee (AIPAC). As American Jewish voices on behalf of Israel grew more confident, the perceived role of a Gentile leader as Israel's protector steadily diminished in Jewish public discourse. During the negotiations leading up to the Israel–Egypt peace treaty of 1979, positive evaluations of President Jimmy Carter were common but expressed recognition and appreciation between equals, Israel and America, rather than the gratitude of a weaker party toward a stronger one. Shortly after the signing of the peace treaty, Carter received the Mizrahi Women's Organization of America's "America–Israel Friendship" award, citing his "courage, humanity, and vision in bringing together the two neighbor nations, so long at war."[109] The Orthodox newspaper the *Jewish Press* praised Carter for his "persistence and patient tenacity."[110]

However, some American Jews felt entitled to express savage, ad hominem criticism of Carter—also a sign of the perceived equality of power between Israel and the United States. "Carter Just Loves that Sadat," blared a headline in the *Jewish Floridian* in June 1978, referring to the Egyptian president.[111] The newspaper claimed that the Camp David Accords, cooked up in Carter's "fevered little brain," would entail "a series of blood curdling concessions" and would bring "a catastrophe for Israel."[112] Carter was accused of having "mishandled," "misled," and "fumbled" the negotiations; of displaying "childish petulance and surliness"; and, most importantly, of being steadfastly committed to weakening, if not destroying, Israel.[113] These views were shared by Ivan Novick, president of the Zionist Organization of America, who questioned "President Carter's right any longer to decide the future of the State of Israel, or, indeed, of the USA."[114]

Carter's critics revived the rhetoric of betrayal from previous decades, and although they did not make explicit historical comparisons, Israel's foreign minister Moshe Dayan did so in early February 1979:

> During the Holocaust, President Roosevelt saw fit not to open the gates to Jewish refugees. In 1948, while our nation fought for survival against all the Arab states, President Truman—though he recognized Israel—refused to give us even one rifle, not one rifle. In 1956 after the Sinai Campaign, President Eisenhower promised us free navigation in international waters for our unilateral evacuation of the Sinai. But in 1967, when Egypt blockaded the Straits of Tiran, we had to break the blockade ourselves.[115]

Dayan concluded that it was up to Israel, and Israel alone, to ensure that a second Holocaust does not occur: "it will not happen because we will prevent it."

For Israelis and American Jews alike, the only person who could negotiate peace with Egypt while protecting Israel from a second Holocaust was Israel's prime minister Menachem Begin. Begin, not the American president, was the recipient of American Jewish gratitude. After the signing of the Camp David Accords, Theodore Mann, chair of the Conference of Presidents of Major American Jewish Organizations, pledged to Begin the conference's complete and united support, and the chair of the World Zionist Organization promised Begin "the assistance of the entire Jewish people."[116] The *Jewish Press* pledged to Begin "our undying gratitude."[117] At the end of March 1979, 2,700 American Jewish leaders gathered in Avery Fisher Hall in New York City's Lincoln Center to "pay tribute to the man who signed the historic peace treaty."[118] Theodore Mann called the event "a salute to peace in honor of Begin."[119]

Over the following years American Jewish discourse continued to acknowledge Israel's debt to the United States while highlighting the agency of Israel—and, to a lesser extent, of diaspora Jewry. With the waning of the Cold War between 1989 and 1991 and a renewed international push for peace in the Middle East after the Persian Gulf War of 1990–1991, the governments of the United States and Soviet Union called on the UN General Assembly to repeal Resolution 3379. Jewish leaders were acutely aware of the leadership role the United States would need to play in this campaign. "With a strong U.S. commitment, it will happen," said Malcolm Hoenlein, vice chair of the Conference of Presidents.[120] When the repeal did occur in December 1991, however, it was not the work of the United States alone. According to the JTA, some fifty Jewish organizations had been "chomping at the bit to step up their own lobbying activities."[121] Israeli ambassador to the United Nations Yoram Aridor claimed that diaspora Jews, along with the United States and other sympathetic countries, "really mobilized the world, over five continents, to support the repeal."[122] "These are the jobs the World Jewish Congress was created for," said Israel Singer, secretary-general of the organization, which engaged in lobbying in some seventy countries around the world.[123]

The sense of equal partnership between American Jewry, Israel, and the United States remained in place throughout the 1990s and most of the 2000s. During the negotiations leading up to the Israeli–Palestinian accords of 1993 and 1995 (known as Oslo I and Oslo II), the Jewish press depicted President Bill Clinton as a facilitator, rather than a benefactor.[124] Clinton himself justified that perception: at the funeral of the assassinated Prime Minister Yitzhak Rabin in 1995, Clinton eulogized him as "my partner and friend." He ended the eulogy with the words, *"Shalom, haver* (Farewell, friend)."

During the presidency of George W. Bush, the World Trade Center and Pentagon attacks of September 11, 2001, American-led wars in Afghanistan and Iraq, and a broader global "war on terror" further strengthened ties between the United States and Israel. Some American Jews felt that those ties were threatened by Bush's successor Barack Obama, who was more sympathetic than his predecessor to the Palestinian cause and who favored a diplomatic solution to the threat to Israel (and global security more broadly) posed by Iran's nuclear weapons program. The Obama administration clashed with Israeli prime minister Benjamin Netanyahu, who did his utmost to instill fear of Iran into the public both in Israel and throughout the world. Nonetheless over the 2010s Netanyahu's jeremiads against Iran did not throw most American Jews into a panic or induce them to issue angry denunciations of Obama. Israel's relatively stable security situation softened the language of fear and betrayal that had dominated American Jewish public discourse during the 1930s and, mutatis mutandis, the 1970s.

The Jewish world was turned on its head by President Donald Trump's announcement in December 2017 that the United States would recognize Jerusalem as Israel's capital and move its embassy to Jerusalem from Tel Aviv.[125] Given Jerusalem's political sensitivity, many American Jews were ambivalent about this shift, but the Republican Jewish Coalition placed a full-page advertisement in the New York Times thanking Trump for his unwavering support of Israel and "moral clarity" in "standing shoulder to shoulder with the Jewish people" and recognizing Jerusalem as Israel's "eternal capital" (see figure 5).[126] The advertisement presented Trump's act not as a magnanimous or humanitarian gesture but rather as the acknowledgment of what was already the patrimony of the Jewish people by right. Nonetheless, it was dominated by a photograph of a stern-faced Trump alone at the Western Wall, his head bedecked with a yarmulke and his right hand touching the wall's ancient stone. The image conveyed the sense that, although Trump might be answering to a higher power, he was that power's earthly representative. Some

President Trump: You Promised. You Delivered.

Figure 5   Republican Jewish Coalition advertisement in the *New York Times*, December 7, 2017, thanking President Donald Trump for moving the U.S. Embassy in Israel from Tel Aviv to Jerusalem.
Credit: Republican Jewish Coalition and Getty Images.

American evangelical Christians explicitly said as much, and in Israel, an outfit known as the Mikdash Educational Center struck a commemorative medallion featuring Trump in profile with the ancient Persian King Cyrus, who in 538 BCE permitted Jews to return from the Babylonian exile to the Land of Israel.[127]

The Israeli government's dependence on Trump was palpable and was expressed through the language of gratitude. "The Jewish people and the Jewish state will be forever grateful," gushed Netanyahu in a tweet on the day of Trump's announcement.[128] In April 2019 Netanyahu announced plans to name a settlement in the Golan Heights after Trump because of "a need to express our appreciation" for the U.S. president.[129]

In Jerusalem the municipality named a traffic circle in front of the new U.S. Embassy in Trump's honor.[130] Enthusiasm and adoration of Trump penetrated into public opinion in Israel and abroad. Columnists for both the hawkish Israeli news outlet Arutz Sheva and Los Angeles's pluralistic *Jewish Journal* invoked the rabbinic principle of *hakarat hatov* (defined by Arutz Sheva as "gratitude and recognition to the Almighty and to those who have helped us") to offer Trump and his advisers "thanks and gratitude for the good deeds they performed and their gifts to Israel and the Jewish people."[131]

On January 20, 2021, as Trump was about to leave office, Miriam Adelson, the widow of Trump's close ally Sheldon Adelson, wrote a public letter to Trump:

> In the Book of Genesis, when our foremother Leah gives birth to her last son, she says: "This time I will give thanks to the Lord"; therefore, she called his name, Yehuda [from the Hebrew verbal root ה–ד–י for thanksgiving]. It is because of Yehuda that we Jews are named "yehudim" in Hebrew. And it is in the spirit of Yehuda that we give thanks for kinship, for friendship, for courage, for the triumph of truth. US President Donald Trump represents all of these things. And today, as he departs the White House, he deserves our gratitude—as proud Israelis, as proud Americans, and as proud Jews, no matter our politics.[132]

Conclusion

In the early twentieth century the rhetoric of Jewish gratitude was almost entirely secular, linked not only to the beneficence of the British Empire but also the moral justice of self-determination for stateless peoples. In 2017 gratitude was colored by religious and even messianic overtones, and it connoted a unique relationship between the U.S. government and the State of Israel. After World War I enthusiasm for the Balfour Declaration was widespread, but a century later a majority of

American Jews were uneasy about Trump's stridently pro-Israel policies. During the late interwar period and Israel's formative decades, American Jews were quick to accuse the U.S. and British governments, as well as the international community, of betraying Israel, but at the end of the 2010s it was Trump who felt betrayed by American Jews who did not flock to him in appreciation.[133]

Feelings of gratitude and betrayal are manifestations of emotional investment and dependence on an exterior force to achieve the fulfillment of desire. In the twenty-first century American Jews remained emotionally connected with Israel but tended to see U.S. governmental support for Israel as a matter more of right than privilege. Nonetheless American Jews remained sensitive to anti-Zionism as threatening their own well-being and that of the State of Israel. True to the logic that one can only be betrayed by a friend, pro-Zionist Jews were particularly incensed by Jews who distanced themselves from Israel or whose attachments to Israel did not prevent them from being strongly critical of it. It is common among critics of Zionism to liken it to Nazism, but only supporters of Israel compare Jewish critics of the country to *kapos*—the Jews who, during World War II, served as menial functionaries in the concentration and death camps.[134] As we see in our final chapter, Zionism has been both a generator and an object of hatred.

6   *Hating Zionism*

Throughout this book emotions have been linked with desire. Positive emotions respond to the fulfillment of desire or to the anticipation and expectation of its realization. In contrast, negative emotions are generated by the failure to obtain the object of desire or by the anticipation of that object's loss. Like positive emotions, negative ones vary greatly in intensity. They can be, as Sianne Ngai calls them, "ugly feelings," ignoble expressions of pique such as envy or all-consuming fears, jealousies, and outbursts of fury.[1] Hatred is an alloy of negative emotions and, like an alloy, is more durable and enduring than its component parts. It is also qualitatively different, as Eran Halperin highlights: "while anger is focused on the actions of target objects and fear on the consequences of events, hatred is exclusively focused on the object itself."[2] Long-term grievances over perceived wrongdoings, resentments against perceived social inequities, and senses of constant threat feed a desire to separate oneself entirely from an Other, to remove that Other from one's midst, or even to annihilate the Other wherever it may be found. The hated object is perceived as noxious, dangerous, or, in theological terms, evil.

Unlike love, which can either build or break down boundaries, hatred only hardens and preserves them. As a cognitive routine, hate anchors an individual's sense of selfhood and attachment to a community. Daniel Smail has written of medieval French communities in which hatred was a form of social capital, because taking on a preexisting intracommunal hatred integrated individuals into a faction, providing them with an economic and social network.[3] The hater and hated are thus bound together: the former depends on the latter just like a lover on the beloved. "I hate and I love" (*odi et amo*), declaimed the ancient Roman poet Catullus, describing the volatility with which romantic love can turn dark and furious.[4] Two millennia later, the Zionist publicist Nahum Sokolow

noted that the opposite can be the case—that hatred has "a subtle rela-
tion with love. We hate only those with whom we possess affinity. . . .
Human hatred is a passion for physical and spiritual adjustments which,
not knowing how to fulfill itself in love towards its own kind, tries to
break through to success by means of assault, bribery, war."[5]

This chapter traces the interdependence of those who hate and the
objects of hatred in two aspects of Zionism: hatred of Zionism and hatred
in the name of Zionism. We begin by exploring the historic relationship
between antisemitism—an irrational and unjustified negative feeling
about Jews—and Zionism before turning to more recent expressions of
anti-Zionism and the circumstances under which they are and are not
hateful. The second part of the chapter explores forms of Zionist hatred,
particularly hatred of Arabs. I detail the suppression and denial of this
hatred in Zionist public discourse until the early twenty-first century,
when it became socially acceptable and more visible.

The transparency of hatred depends on the prevailing rules of feeling
in a society in any specific time and place. In some settings, hatred, particularly of certain groups, has the status of a respectable, even ennobling emotion. Elsewhere it is disreputable across the board and therefore has to be reframed. In the past, the word "antisemite" was at times
brandished with pride, particularly in German-speaking Europe from
the 1880s through 1945. Since the end of the Second World War, however,
the word has usually elicited opprobrium, so much so that in our own
day it is not uncommon for people who despise Jews to deny that they are
antisemitic. In contrast, the use of the word "Zionist" as a pejorative to
describe Jews as a whole, and to attribute malevolent qualities to them, is
widespread. When employed in political rhetoric in the Arab and Muslim worlds, "Zionism" can refer only to the ideologies and practices of
the state of Israel, but anti-Zionist rhetoric has often spilled over its banks
and unleashed floods of antisemitic hatred.

Other chapters in this book dealt with the recent past, but this chapter is the most engaged with the present. Moreover, although based in

historical narrative and analysis, it also engages in normative evaluation and prescription. The reason for this shift is simple: hatreds of Zionism, or hatreds justified in the name of Zionism, are accelerating, and they are destructive. We are just as obliged to understand the sources of these hatreds as we are for any other feeling; yet unlike love or fear, whose effects are multivalent and can be constructive as well as damaging, hatred can only do harm. Previous chapters invoked emotion to account for the rise, success, and endurance of the Zionist project. This chapter studies an emotion that endangers the well-being of all people who feel or are affected by it, Jewish and Palestinian alike.

Hating Jews, Hating Zionism

There is a passionate controversy whether anti-Zionism is a form of anti-semitism. One can just as well ask whether antisemitism is routinely anti-Zionist. Historically, the answer to this second question has been yes, but there are important exceptions. In Zionism's earliest days, Theodor Herzl had the support of some antisemites, including the Hungarian politician-cum-journalist Ivan von Simonyi and the notorious French journalist Edouard Drumont, who responded enthusiastically to the First Zionist Congress in 1897. For more than a decade Drumont championed Zionism, not only because it would get the Jews out of Europe but also because Zionists were, he believed, men of honor who wanted to construct their own land rather than leech off the wealth of others. By 1913, however, Drumont had soured on Zionism, which had given up the Herzlian goal of a mass transfer of Jews to Palestine via the acquisition of an imperial charter. Drumont blamed this shift on Jewish plutocrats like Maurice de Hirsch, whom he mistakenly thought controlled Zionism along with global banking capital.[6]

In Germany, antisemites opposed Zionism from its inception. Wilhelm Marr, the journalist who has the dubious distinction of coining the word "antisemitism," wrote at the time of the First Zionist Congress that "the entire matter is a foul Jewish swindle, in order to divert the attention of the European peoples from the Jewish Problem."[7] Eugen Dühring—whose corrosive tract of 1881, *The Jewish Question as a Question of Racial Noxiousness for the Existence, Morals, and Culture of Nations*, shook young Herzl to the core—dismissed Jewish mass settlement in any one place as impossible. "Nomadism, he wrote, "is their world-historical condition. Without it and alone among themselves they would eat one another alive."[8] In the last edition of the book, published posthumously in 1930, Dühring switched course and determined that Jews were well on the way to establishing in Palestine a central point from which to plot world conquest. The Jewish snake encircling the globe, he warned, would soon have a head, and the only solution to the problem was to repeat the Roman "clearing action" in Palestine after the Jewish revolts in the first and second centuries CE, "but in an entirely different and far more comprehensive sense."[9] The only effective response to Zionism, Dühring implied, was mass murder.

The geopolitical events that changed Dühring's mind were Germany's defeat in World War I, the Balfour Declaration, and the League of Nations' award to Britain of the Mandate for Palestine. Before World War II, despite the antisemitic elements in French and Italian fascism, both movements adopted an instrumental approach to Zionism; during World War II a senior official in the collaborationist Vichy regime described Zionism as "the only truly effectual solution [to the Jewish Question] that is both completely humane and Christian."[10] But in Germany, the centrality of antisemitism in Nazism and the humiliation engendered by the loss of its overseas empire at the hands of the Western powers left little room for sympathy for Jewish aspirations in the Middle East. The Nazi ideologue Alfred Rosenberg wrote in the early 1920s that Jews had initiated the world war to obtain their state in Palestine. Yet because they were incapable of any of the creative or administrative labor required for statecraft, Rosenberg claimed that what the Jews called a state would really be a power base for their global, nefarious economic operations. In turn, Adolf Hitler wrote in *Mein Kampf* that a Jewish state, "endowed with sovereign rights and removed from intervention of other states," would become "a haven for convicted scoundrels and a university for budding crooks."[11] In this criminal enterprise, Hitler suggested, Jews enlisted the British as willing dupes. For a defeated people, the antisemitic trope of Jewish omnipotence was a discursive correlate to a feeling of German powerlessness.

The most sustained antisemitic treatment of post-Balfour Zionism did not, however, come from defeated Germany but from the victorious United States. Its author, William J. Cameron, served between 1921 and 1927 as editor of the *Dearborn Independent*, a virulently antisemitic newspaper owned by the automobile magnate Henry Ford. Under Cameron's editorship, the newspaper disseminated an English-language paraphrased version of *The Protocols of the Elders of Zion*, a notorious forgery composed in fin de siècle Russia that claimed to record a meeting of an international Jewish conspiracy for global control. There was no daylight between Cameron and Ford, who lunched together regularly in the private dining room of the Ford factory. Ford's hatred of Jews fit well with Cameron's adherence to the British-Israelite movement, which avowed that the ten lost tribes of Israel were the ancestors of the Anglo-Saxons and that the Jews were descended from a mongrel Asiatic race known as Judah. During the 1920s, Cameron met at least twice with the Nazi agent Kurt Ludecke, who had been sent to the United States to mobilize support.[12]

Cameron's anti-Zionism was a natural extension of his antisemitism. Zionists, he wrote, brought about World War I to make the British their puppets in the Middle East and to wrest Palestine out of the wreckage of the Ottoman Empire. The British government in Palestine was clearly "Jewish" because its first high commissioner was the Zionist Sir Herbert Samuel.[13] Zionism served the interests of both Jewish capital and Jewish Bolshevism, which were linked in that the former feared the latter and wanted to be spared their wrath. This obsession with Bolshevism illustrates the extent of the Red Scare in the United States in the immediate postwar era. Cameron's anti-Bolshevism and British-Israelism reinforced each other. If the Red Scare was a manifestation of fear of communism, British-Israelism was an expression of anxiety over the changing ethnic makeup of the United States in the wake of pre-1914 mass immigration and resentment of the economic success of non-WASP Americans. Cameron implored Christians not to be misled by what he called the Jews' honeyed but false claims to be restoring their biblical homeland.

Palestine's Arabs are notably missing from the European and American critiques of Zionism. Cameron's screeds made one stray reference to the purloining of the Palestinians; others did not mention them at all. During the interwar period, the antisemites' critique of Zionism was an extension of fantasies of Jewish conspiracy and criminality. If these critiques had a humanitarian aspect, the driving motivation was not concern for Palestine's Indigenous population so much as for the victimized masses of Christendom who were supposedly hapless objects of Jewish manipulation. More genteel forms of anti-Zionism, however, protested the establishment of a Jewish state in the name of justice for the Arab people and of U.S. foreign policy interests. As Harry Emerson Fosdick, pastor of New York City's Park Avenue Baptist Church said in 1927, "To the Jews Zionism is an idealistic movement, but . . . to the Arabs it is a predatory movement. The Arab cannot compete with the Jew. The Arab knows that, and the Jew knows that. It makes the Jew confident and aggressive, but it makes the Arab angry and resentful."[14] After World War II, the Committee for Justice and Peace in the Holy Land, founded by the distinguished educator Virginia Gildersleeve and the intelligence operative Kermit Roosevelt Jr., led this campaign. Although genteel antisemitism may well have lurked underneath the committee's activities, the American Jewish press took pains to treat its leaders with respect and to avoid accusations of hateful motivations. As the Boston *Jewish Advocate* wrote of Gildersleeve and Roosevelt, anti-Zionism was not necessarily equivalent to antisemitism, but it could keep company with or unwittingly give support to the latter.[15]

Unlike antisemitism in Europe and North America, Arab anti-Zionism placed Arab concerns front and center. Early on, its language was hostile yet not vicious. In the early twentieth century, Palestinians expressed fears of displacement from their lands and country, and Ottoman officials worried about the creation of a new minority problem akin to that presented by the Armenians.[16] In Egypt and Syria, intellectuals combined realistic assessments of Zionism's achievements with exaggerated beliefs in Jewish power. The Muslim reformer Rashid Rida wrote approvingly of Jewish solidarity, scientific knowledge, and wealth. The Jews, he wrote in 1899, "lack nothing but sovereign power in order to become the greatest nation on the face of the earth, an objective they pursue in a normal manner."[17] Later, in 1905, the secular Arab nationalist Najib Azuri described Jews as a people striving purposefully to establish a state, asserting that "on the final outcome of this struggle, between the two peoples representing two opposing principles, will depend the destiny of the entire world."[18] Azuri's comment is intriguing not only for its view that the fate of humanity rests on the outcome of the Zionist–Arab struggle but also for its presentation of both Jews and Arabs as nations. Unlike European antisemitism, which conceived of Jews as unassimilable, Arab anti-Zionism after Azuri would come to claim that Jews did not constitute a people but only a religious community. To argue otherwise might open the way to accepting Zionism's fundamental principles, if not its program.[19]

After World War I, the incorporation of virulent antisemitism into anti-Zionism occurred in response to increased Jewish immigration to Palestine. It is no coincidence that an Arabic translation of *The Protocols of the Elders of Zion* appeared in 1925, during the largest wave of Zionist immigration to date. The translation was made by a Catholic priest in Egypt, but within a year it was available in Palestine, and Jerusalem's Latin Patriarchate urged the faithful to read it to understand what the Zionists had in store for Palestine. During the tense months leading up to Arab riots throughout Palestine in August 1929, the Palestinian leader Mohammed

Amin al-Husseini publicized portions of the *Protocols* in connection with alleged Jewish plots to take possession of the Temple Mount.[20]

After Israel's establishment, the approach of antisemites to Zionism split off into two directions. On one path, antisemitism continued to cleave to anti-Zionism. In the Soviet Union and the Eastern Bloc, communist ideology preserved older tropes of Jewish nomadism and rootlessness under the rubric of "cosmopolitanism." Ironically, this "cosmopolitanism" also implied parochialism and loyalty to the capitalist West and to international Jewry centered in the State of Israel. In the United States, antisemites made the opposite accusation that Zionism was an agent of communism. In 1964, the far-right John Birch Society described Israel as having been established to serve the interests of the Kremlin and of being "50 to 70 per cent under Communist control," run by a clique of socialists clinging to power and imposing catastrophic economic policies.[21] Although most antisemites in the West had the Cold War on their minds, some still harped on the imperial conflict of the early twentieth century. In 1985, the lawyer and writer Robert John published in the *Journal of Historical Review*, a front for Holocaust denial, a lengthy, densely footnoted article accusing Zionists of having pushed the United States into World War I. Maintaining long-standing antisemitic associations of Jews with criminality and sexual depravity, John accused Jews of blackmailing Woodrow Wilson over an adulterous affair and pressuring him to appoint the Zionist Louis Brandeis to the Supreme Court. While Brandeis pressured Wilson to declare war on Germany, Chaim Weizmann threatened to "smash the British Empire as we smashed the Russian Empire," should a declaration of support for Zionism not be forthcoming.[22]

Antisemitic language took on a new dimension at the end of the 1980s. Writers on the Far Right began to use "Zio" as a pejorative for "Jew." At first, it was connected with "Nazi" to form "ZioNazi," a hostile reference to the state of Israel and its supporters. Over the course of the early twenty-first century, however, "Zio" broke away from specific links to Zionism or Israel and became a derogatory term for all Jews. The broader use of the term was popularized by David Duke, a former Grand Wizard of the Knights of the Ku Klux Klan and member of the Louisiana State House of Representatives.[23] "Zio" was frequently linked with a second noun or adjective by way of a hyphen, endowing that word with what are thought to be irradicable and noxious Jewish qualities (e.g., "Zio-Marxists," "Zio-economics," "Zio-media," "Zio-feminists"). In 2015, a Canadian antisemitic monthly newspaper, commenting on then-prime minister Stephen Harper's support for Israel, bemoaned that he had been "co-opted by Canadian ZioFascists with their eyes set on turning Canada into a ZioMarxist vassal state."[24]

The same Canadian monthly also accused Israel of plotting the destruction of the World Trade Center on 9/11 and claimed that a "rich Zionist Jew Larry Silverstein had just bought the World Trade Center and took out a massive insurance policy" shortly before the attacks.[25] Such statements, alongside the paper's frequent invocations of financial conspiracies cooked up by the Rothschilds and George Soros, demonstrate continuities between early twentieth-century forms of antisemitism and its latest incarnations. Antisemites incorporated Zionism into their fulminations against Jews, yet the core of their beliefs was not affected. They presented Israel as just another example of Jewish malevolence. In that vein, the Canadian antisemitic newspaper describes Israelis as "Christ-hating Jewish Talmudic terrorists" and "bloodthirsty Talmudic Zionist Jews."[26]

The other path taken by antisemitism since 1948 has been to embrace Israel while expressing ambivalence, if not hostility, toward diaspora Jews. In the 2010s and early 2020s, increasingly authoritarian regimes in Hungary and Poland produced whitewashed histories of their persecutions of Jews in World War II. Public figures accused Jews of collaboration with the postwar communist regimes and of not being true members of the nation, and traditional Catholic antisemitism continued to be expressed in Poland. Yet the regimes admired Israel for its commitment to ethnonationalism, its reluctance to admit immigrants alien to the dominant nationality, and its military strength.[27] A similar trend was visible in the United States, where the "White Nationalist" (i.e., white supremacist) activist Richard Spencer supported Israel's 2018 Nation-State Law, calling it a "path forward for Europeans."[28] President Trump flirted with antisemitism in public remarks about American Jews, but as we saw at the end of the last chapter, he lent Israel's right-wing government unshakable support. He did so largely to please evangelical Christians, whose proclaimed love for the Jewish people could conceal exasperation with Jews for not supporting Israel sufficiently and, more importantly, for continuing to deny Jesus's divinity.

In the most fervent forms of early twenty-first-century evangelical Christianity, Catullus's phrase "I hate and I love" could not be more apt. In the aftermath of Israel's 2021 elections, evangelical leader Mike Evans, enraged that Benjamin Netanyahu might be ousted from the premiership, harangued Netanyahu's opponents: "If they keep up this pathetic, political strip-tease act, this theater of the absurd, I'll spend the rest of my life fighting them all, mobilizing millions of evangelicals to join me in the fight. I understand how the Holocaust happened. German Jews were busy insulting each other, drunk on the wine of pride. They did not see the smoke of Auschwitz rising because they were more German than they were Jews." Directly comparing Netanyahu's adversaries to the killers of Jesus, Evans added, "These would-be pretend strip-tease actors . . . are screaming at the top of their lungs, 'Crucify Him, crucify him!' It is sick and shameful to see such a group running like rabid dogs possessed with power and revenge." Finally, furious over what he saw as a lack of gratitude for the U.S. diplomatic decisions for which Evans claimed credit, he asked, "What appreciation do you show us? You shit right on our face. How dare you!"[29] The boundary between love and hatred is fine indeed.

Hating Zionism, Hating Jews?

Thus far we have followed vectors projecting from antisemitism to anti-Zionism. They can also go in the opposite direction, but constructing the vector equation depends on the definition of its variables. If you define Zionism as the national liberation movement of the Jewish people and Israel as central to contemporary Jewish life, and if in your view the only legitimate expression of Zionism is Jewish sovereignty and hegemony within the Land of Israel, then someone who opposes Israel as a Jewish state is ipso facto an antisemite. Yet, the act of cementing diaspora Jewry with Israel and arguing that all Jews do or must support the country in its current form open Jews worldwide to accusations that they are responsible for Israel's actions. In fact, as we saw in chapter 4, most American Jews do feel emotionally attached to Israel, but the depth, intensity, and valence of those attachments vary greatly. The same can be said for Jews within Israel itself. Hostility toward Jews founded on assumptions about their bonds with Israel are clearly antisemitic. Violence, harassment, or discrimination against Jews is criminal whether its motives are antisemitic or not.

What of hostile language that solely targets Israel? At what point does criticism become a sign of hatred? And is hatred of Israel always equivalent to hatred of Jews? Since 1948, hostile comments about Zionism and Israel have been commonplace, especially in the Arab and Muslim worlds and in the former Communist Bloc. In leftist (or, in current parlance, progressive) circles in Europe and North America, hostility to Israel intensified in the wake of the Second Intifada in 2000 and violent confrontations in 2008–2009, 2012, 2014, and 2021 between Israel and Hamas in the Gaza Strip.[30] Heightened racial tensions in the United States during the Trump administration and the rise of the Black Lives

Matter movement intensified sympathies with racialized minorities and oppressed Indigenous peoples worldwide—especially Palestinians. During and after the Israel–Gaza violence in May 2021, thousands of academics endorsed harsh critiques of Israel and statements of solidarity with the Palestinians.[31]

Accompanying these statements was growing support for the Boycott, Divestment, and Sanctions (BDS) movement against Israel, which was founded in 2005. The movement presented differing versions of its goals, some extending as far as the dissolution of Israel as a state with a Jewish character. At a minimum the movement demanded that Israel withdraw from the Occupied Territories, dismantle the security barriers and walls it erected in the West Bank and East Jerusalem, recognize the right of Palestinian refugees from 1948 and of their descendants to return to their homes, and grant full equality to Israel's Palestinian citizens.[32] The Israeli government and mainstream Jewish organizations worldwide reacted to the BDS movement with alarm. They, along with major Jewish organizations in the diaspora, saw BDS as the latest chapter in an unrelenting quest by Israel's enemies to destroy the state of Israel.

Although its achievements were meager, the BDS movement so unnerved the Israeli government that in 2017 it enacted legislation denying entry into the country of boycott activists, including those who advocated a limited boycott of goods and services produced or provided by the settlements in the West Bank. In July 2021, when Ben & Jerry's ice cream announced it would no longer sell its products in the West Bank, the Israeli president Isaac Herzog called the act one of "economic terrorism," and Yair Lapid, the foreign minister and head of the largest party in Israel's governing coalition, called it "a shameful surrender to antisemitism."[33] In the United States, reactions from Jewish organizations were more measured, with the Anti-Defamation League saying it was "disappointed" because such actions feed "into dangerous campaigns that seek to undermine Israel."[34]

Such responses assumed that any speech or action that attempts to compel the government of Israel to alter its policies, let alone its character, is tantamount to an effort to destroy the country and is therefore antisemitic. This assumption blurs the distinction between rational and irrational sources of hostility. Antisemitism is irrational in that it prejudges Jews to be members of a coherent body possessed of common character traits and exercising unwholesome influence. Such an entity does not exist. There can, however, be a rational base to negative feelings about a state, which does exist and which, according to Max Weber's famous phrase, "is the only human community that within a specific territory . . . claims a monopoly on the legitimate use of physical force."[35] A state's actions can wreak havoc on people's lives—or end them. The hatred that victims of a state feel toward their victimizers may be all-consuming and destructive, but it is not necessarily irrational.

In chapter 2 we examined Moshe Dayan's 1956 eulogy for Ro'i Rotberg, who had been killed by Arab guerrillas at a kibbutz on the Gaza border. The eulogy took Arab hatred for granted and found it neither irrational nor misplaced: "Let us not hurl blame at the murderers. Why should we complain of their hatred for us? Eight years have they sat in the refugee camps of Gaza, and seen, with their own eyes, how we have made a homeland of the soil and the villages where they and their forebears once dwelt."[36] Dayan's putative empathy was, in fact, a form of condescension, because it made blanket assumptions about an essentialized enemy. But he did not accuse that enemy of being antisemitic.

This leads to a further problem with automatically conflating anti-Zionism with antisemitism. Anti-Zionism can stem from deep-seated, unquenchable hatred, but it can also stem from a more transitory emotion such as anger. Anger is an expression of unmet needs and is directed at the source blocking the satisfaction of those needs. Hatred, in contrast, attributes not only wrongdoing but also inveterate malevolence to the hated party. It feeds desires to be rid of them altogether. Anger over the oppression of the Palestinians and the denial of their rights of self-determination, security, and dignity can indeed be bound up with a hatred of Israel that assumes destructive and violent dimensions. Anger toward Israel can, however, also be free of the expression or promotion of hatred, even if that anger is passionate and disturbing to people who sympathize with Israel.

What stands out about the Palestinian cause is not the emotions of those at its center but the intensity of feeling of outside observers. People who know and care little about oppressed peoples throughout the world have passionate feelings about Israel/Palestine. Even the language used to describe the Israeli-Palestinian struggle is unique. For example, in English and German, the phrase "right to exist" (*Existenzrecht*) enjoyed some currency in the nineteenth century and after World War I in connection with stateless European peoples' aspirations for independence. Its usage spiked, however, from the 1970s through early 2000s, and it was employed almost exclusively with reference to the cases of Israel and a future Palestinian state. (Of the top 178 items returned under a Google search for "right to exist," more than 90 percent refer to Israel/Palestine.[37])

The reasons for this intensity of awareness and passion are manifold. Israel's Jewish character is one of them. Other reasons are the legacy of colonialism, as discussed in chapter 2, and Israel's location in a territory venerated by Christians and Muslims, who comprise more than 40 percent of humanity. If Israel had been founded as a Christian state by Protestant enthusiasts as a latter-day Crusader Kingdom and the same fate had befallen the Palestinian Arabs, hostility toward this Christian Zionism would be no less fierce than it is today. A Christian state in Palestine would, in fact, likely be hated more widely because its connection with Western colonialism would be more direct and it could not appeal to the conscience of humanity as the vehicle of a phoenix-like rebirth of a people consumed in the fires of the Holocaust.[38]

This affective complexity—the need to distinguish anger from hatred and to disentangle hostility to Jews from other sources of negative attention toward Israel—is disregarded in the most widely accepted definition of antisemitism in the international community, which was issued by the European Union's Monitoring Center on Racism and Xenophobia in 2005 and endorsed in 2016 by the International Holocaust Remembrance Alliance. The definition considers it antisemitic to consider Israel "a racist endeavor." There are certainly antisemites who call Israel racist. Yet, given Zionism's claims, enshrined in the Nation-State Law of 2018, that only Jews have the right of self-determination in Israel, as well as the subordinate or subaltern status of Arabs within Israel and the Occupied Territories, it is not necessarily hateful to see in Israel, as per the *Oxford English Dictionary* definition of racism, the presence of "prejudice, discrimination, or antagonism directed against a person or people on the basis of their membership in a particular racial or ethnic group."

In sum, there is abundant evidence of negative conceptions of Israel that catalyze or are catalyzed by anti-Jewish hatred. A negative view of Israel can, however, stem from emotions such as disappointment and anger—feelings that, if blended with sympathy, could stimulate meliorative actions directed not at destroying Israel so much as reforming it.

When Zionism Began to Hate

To those who feel oppressed, victimized, or threatened, hatred is a noble emotion. It anchors personal identity by defining the self in terms of its not being an Other. A person living in a state of economic or political insecurity may be nonetheless ontologically secure, practicing cognitive routines in which the enemy, being ever present, is a source of psychic strength.[39] Hatred provides a sense of purpose, and it compensates for perceived wrongs by instilling a yearning for revenge. Hatred elevates the humiliated and dignifies the dishonored.

Veins of hatred run through Jewish civilization. In the Hebrew Bible, the pagan peoples of ancient Palestine, who tempt the Israelites to abandon their God, are abominable. God commands the Israelites to annihilate the Amalekites, the Israelites' inveterate enemies. In medieval and early modern Europe, where Jews lived as a small and often persecuted minority, Jewish culture was steeped in fantasies (and, occasionally, acts) of vengeance against Christians.[40]

In the wake of the Kishinev Pogrom of 1903, Hayim Nahman Bialik wrote poems brimming with anger and despair, and his condemnation of revenge against the Jews' tormentors revealed how tempted he and his readers were to embrace it.[41] The Holocaust wiped away inhibitions to frank expressions of hatred, as in Uri Tzvi Greenberg's sulfurous poem "We Were Not Likened to Dogs among the Gentiles":

> We were not led like sheep to the slaughter in the boxcars
> For like leprous sheep they led us to extinction
> Over all the beautiful landscapes of Europe . . .
> The Gentiles did not handle their sheep as they handled our bodies
> Before the slaughter they did not pull out the teeth of their sheep
> They did not strip the wool from their bodies as they did to us
> They did not push the sheep into the fire to make ash of the living
> And to scatter the ashes over streams and sewers.[42]

Another poet, Abba Kovner, did more than declaim hatred for Gentiles. A partisan and one of the leaders of the Vilna Ghetto resistance during World War II, Kovner spent the later years of the war hunting down German soldiers and local collaborators. After the war, Kovner planned to kill six million Germans by poisoning the water supply of major German cities. Although that scheme came to naught, he and his confederates did lace arsenic into bread supplied to a German POW camp. (Many were sickened, but none died.[43])

Both Greenberg and Kovner were Zionists—Greenberg on the Right, Kovner on the Left. During the 1948 war, Kovner directed his hatred of Gentiles onto Arabs and he wrote propaganda pamphlets, whose savagery and bloodlust were off-putting even to hardened commanders.[44] Zionist attitudes toward Arabs were usually more complex than Kovner's unhinged fury, reflecting the colonial and national aspects of the Zionist-Palestinian conflict. In a colonial setting, there is room in the mind of the newcomer for paternalism, admiration, and respect for the native, as well as fear, disregard, and contempt. In a national conflict, the range of feelings between the groups is different, moving from friendship, comity, and conviviality to rivalry, resentment, and hatred based on shifting legal and socioeconomic statuses.[45] In Palestine before 1948, the two models mingled together, but after Israel's establishment the latter became dominant.

Pre-1948 Zionist rhetoric about Arabs could be hostile without being hateful. In the early twentieth century, the death of Jewish settlers at the hands of Arabs was a cause for anger and public mourning but not for calls for wholesale vengeance.[46] Vladimir Jabotinsky's iconic essay from 1923, "On the Iron Wall," urged an uncompromising militance in the face of Arab opposition to Zionism, but he saw that opposition as rational and commanding of respect.[47] In his final book, *The Jewish War Front* (1940), Jabotinsky maintained that once Arabs had given up their dreams of an Arab Palestine, they would enjoy complete equality in the Jewish state—so much so that "in every Cabinet where the Prime Minister is a Jew, the vice-premiership shall be offered to an Arab, and vice-versa. Proportional sharing by Jews and Arabs both in the charges and in the benefits of the State shall be the rule with regard to Parliamentary elections, civil and military service, and budgetary grants."[48]

Menachem Begin, who claimed Jabotinsky's mantle as the leader of Revisionist Zionism, had very different views. To recall the terminology used in chapter 1, Jabotinsky was a cosmopolitan Statist Zionist, but Begin was a visceral Judaic Zionist. Begin was also different affectively. Jabotinsky's persona was forceful and passionate, but he rarely displayed the fears, resentments, and hatreds common among the oppressed. Begin, in contrast, was both buffeted and formed by hatred—of the Nazis, who killed his family along with 90 percent of the Jews in his native Poland, and of Stalinism, whose antisemitism and anti-Polish hatreds he felt firsthand between 1940 and 1942 when he was imprisoned in a Soviet jail and labor camp. Unlike Kovner, however, Begin did not immediately transfer his hatred of the Jews' European oppressors to Arabs. In 1944, he became the leader of an underground militia in Palestine, the Irgun Tzva'I Le'umi, that attacked Arabs and British alike. In his memoir *The Revolt*, published only three years after Israel's establishment, Begin expressed hatred not of Arabs nor of his political rivals within the Yishuv (whom he accused of baselessly hating him) but, of all his opponents, only Britain.

At the start of the book Begin asks if there was "hate in our actions . . . and is that emotion expressed in this book? To such a question the sincere answer is 'Yes.'" He continues,

> It is axiomatic that those who fight have to hate—something or somebody. And we fought. We had to hate first and foremost, the horrifying, age old, inexcusable utter *defenselessness* of our Jewish people, wandering through millennia, through a cruel world to the majority of whose inhabitants the defenselessness of the Jews was a standing invitation to massacre them. We had to hate the humiliating disgrace of the homelessness of our people. We had to hate—as any nation worthy of the name must and always will hate—the rule of the foreigner, rule, unjust and unjustifiable per se, foreign rule in the land of our ancestors, in our own country. We had to hate the barring of the gates of our country to our own brethren, trampled and bleeding and crying out for help in a world morally deaf.

The hatred of Britain was justified because that country "frustrated [the Zionists'] efforts for national independence, and ruthlessly withstood their attempts to regain their national honor and restore their self-respect."[49] Begin goes on to elevate hatred to "a manifestation of that highest human feeling, love": "For if you love Freedom, you must hate Slavery; if you love your people, you cannot but hate the enemies that compass their destruction; if you love your country, you cannot but hate those who seek to annex it. Simply put, if you love your mother, would you not hate the man who sought to kill her; would you not hate him and fight him at the cost, if need be, of your own life?"[50] For Begin and even more militant right-wing radicals such as Avraham Stern, Abba Achimeir, and Yehoshua Heschel Yeivin, hating Britain and struggling to remove the British from Palestine were honorable and placed Zionists in the company of the freedom fighters of the world.[51]

These feelings of ennobling hatred have little to do with the fury that overtook Jews and Arabs alike during outbursts of intercommunal violence in Mandate Palestine. As Hillel Cohen has shown, the riots of 1929, which from a Zionist perspective were directed entirely by Arabs against Jews, in fact involved killing on both sides that was motivated by mutual hatred.[52] The widespread killing of civilians, expulsions, and massacres during the 1948 war fed off reservoirs of fear, hatred, and utter disregard for the humanity of the enemy. In any war, close combat engenders rage, which is less an emotion than a state of consciousness in which the structured self dissolves and the articulation of feeling is drowned in a sea of adrenaline.[53] (In the Middle Ages in Europe, displays of royal rage were a means of communicating the sovereign's power, but by modern times rage had become disreputable, indicative of a lack of self-discipline.[54]) Thus the IDF encouraged recruits to feel a "rational hatred" toward the enemy, a feeling that would both propel them into battle and restrain them from committing atrocities.[55]

Both hatred and rage have political value. The first, like controlled fission in a nuclear plant, is a source of political power, but the second, more akin to a thermonuclear explosion, can destroy the regime that deploys it. Over the past century, many regimes have cultivated hatred and tolerated—even stoked—rage. After World War II, however, multinational states that had been the sites of internecine killing became more circumspect about fomenting political hatred of internal enemies. In post-1945 Yugoslavia, the mutual slaughter during the war of both Serbs and Croats, and of Bosnian Muslims by Serbs, was covered up under the slogan "Brotherhood and Unity."[56] In Israel, although thousands of Israeli Jews bore the knowledge of what they had done during the 1948 war, the instruments of official memory—the state, the educational system, and the means of mass communication—presented a sanitized version, denying not only the violence wrought by Jews against Palestinians but also the presence of hatred and rage behind it.

As Fatma Müge Göçek writes in her study of Turkish violence against Armenians, all states are founded in episodes of collective violence, but denial of that violence is no less central, and the closer the acts are to the state's founding moment, the more intense the denial.[57] For Göçek, Turkish denial of the Armenian genocide is indicative of fears that the state is isolated, struggling for survival in a hostile world, with the response to that insecurity being to deny or minimize the violence, blame the enemy, or claim it was unavoidable and commonplace. (I would summarize this approach as "It didn't happen, but if it did happen it wasn't that bad, and if it was bad we had no choice, and even if we had a choice everyone else was doing it.") These observations apply as well to Israel's denial of the Nakba. Israeli governmental estimates reduce the size of the Palestinian exodus in 1948 from more than 700,000–750,000 (the most widely accepted figures in scholarship and the international community) to 550,000–600,000. In Israeli official memory, the Palestinians fled of their own accord or were compelled by Arab commanders to leave their homes. When evidence of expulsion is irrefutable, as in the towns of Lydda and Ramle in July 1948, it is presented as a regrettable, isolated, and justified act of military necessity.[58] This apologetic rhetoric can also include references to the prevalence worldwide of war and population displacement at the time of Israel's creation.

The denial of hatred accompanies the denial of violence. By the mid-twentieth century, it had become ignoble in global political rhetoric for a dominant majority to hate a minority. It happened frequently enough, but regimes that conceived of themselves or wished to be perceived as

liberal needed to deny that such feelings existed. In the young state of
Israel, there was palpable fear and hostility toward Arab states (especially
Egypt), Palestinian transborder infiltrators (most of whom were unarmed
peasants trying to return to Israel or at least recover their possessions,
though some were armed militants), and Arab citizens of Israel. (During
the 1956 war, nearly fifty Arabs who had unknowingly violated a military
curfew were murdered by Israeli border police outside the village of Kafr
Kassem.[59]) Nonetheless, hatred of the country's Arab minority was not
expressed in school textbooks, the newspapers, or the radio.[60] The media
and schoolbooks acknowledged the absence of most of Palestine's Arabs
using neutral terms such as "Arab refugees" and "abandoned Arab villages." They spoke of the Arabs within Israel as "the Arab minority" or
"the Arab sector," which remained largely invisible because of the stric-
tures of military rule and its concentration in specific parts of the country.[61] According to Israeli public discourse, Jews and Arabs did not hate
each other.[62] As in postwar Yugoslavia, there was little to be gained by
promoting such hostility, even if the power and demographic imbalances
between Israeli Jews and Arabs, as well as the policy of separating Arabs
from Jews, were radically different from Yugoslavia's vision of "Brotherhood and Unity."

As we saw with Begin, love of one's own community can justify
hatred of its enemies. But as the cultural theorist Sara Ahmed has argued,
declarations of love make it possible to deny hatred altogether. Acts of
self-preservation may require the use of intimidation or force, which is
presented as the inevitable consequence of love and as unaccompanied
by hatred.[63] The American Orthodox rabbi Meir Kahane, who advocated
removing Arabs from the state of Israel, was fond of saying, "I don't hate
Arabs; I love Jews." In fact, however, the denial of hatred in the name of
love is a ruse, as we see in the theologically justified hatred that was central to Kahane's thought. During the late 1960s and early 1970s, the radicalism of American ethnic politics inspired him to establish the Jewish
Defense League, whose foundational principles were "love of Jewry" and

"dignity and pride," followed by "iron" (the ability and courage to wage violence against one's enemies), discipline, and faith.[64]

After Kahane moved to Israel in 1971, his thought became darker, apocalyptic, and even more militant. He saw the sacred duty to establish a kingdom of God in the Land of Israel being violated by secular Jews not only by their non-observance but also by their endorsement of democracy, which gave political rights to non-Jews. As much as Kahane hated secular Jews, however, he hated Gentiles more, associating the non-Jewish world as a whole with the Holocaust. Kahane's advocacy for complete Jewish separation from the Gentile world, physically in the land of Israel and politically via a Torah state, exemplifies hatred's desire to flee—or destroy—a source of existential threat.[65]

By the end of the 1970s, Kahane's hatred of Gentiles had focused on Arabs, whose removal from Israel he considered a political and theological necessity. In 1980, while serving a jail sentence for planning to attack Palestinians, he wrote a book titled *They Must Go!* in which he attempted to justify the mass transfer of Arabs. The book constantly invokes Arab hatred of Israel and the Jews. In its early chapters, Kahane pretends to respect Arabs, using language similar to that of Jabotinsky and arguing that they will never give up their land and cannot be bought off by honeyed promises of material benefit or political inclusion. His accusation against liberal Zionists of contempt for Arab steadfastness, however, is hypocritical. As the book progresses, Kahane writes about Arabs in increasingly hostile and racist language, calling them prone to "cynicism and duplicity," crime, violence, sexual perversion, and licentiousness.[66] He is particularly concerned about the sexual threat posed by Arab men to Jewish women:

> There is no doubt that the sexual crimes committed by Arabs against Jewish women are derived from both the usual sickness and what one might call the [Black Panther leader] "Eldridge Cleaver" phenomenon (as expressed in *Soul on Ice*) of wishing to attack and

degrade the enemy. The more the Arabs multiply and reach Jewish areas, the greater will be the number of general crimes, and sexual ones in particular, committed against the Jews.[67]

The connection with American racist fears of miscegenation between Blacks and Whites is obvious. Kahane places that fear, which he elaborates in pornographic detail, into the biblical context that "Esau hates Jacob" and that "the Arabs of Israel represent Hillul Hashem [desecration of the name of God] in its starkest form."[68]

It took thirteen years after Kahane's move to Israel for his political party Kakh (Thus) to win enough votes to send him to the Knesset. Kahane sat in parliament for only two years before his party was banned for inciting racism, and he was assassinated by an Egyptian American in New York in 1990. Nonetheless, since the 1980s his racist religiosity, at times blended with homegrown Israeli messianic Zionism, has struck roots in segments of Israel's Jewish population.[69]

The identification of Arabs with *chillul hashem* justified attacks against Palestinians in the early 1980s by a Jewish settler underground. These attacks were accompanied by a foiled plot to blow up the Dome of the Rock on Jerusalem's Temple Mount to hasten the advent of the messianic age. The American physician and West Bank settler Baruch Goldstein fired on Muslim worshippers in Hebron's Cave of the Patriarchs in 1994, killing twenty-nine before he himself was killed by the survivors. (The massacre occurred on the Jewish holiday of Purim, which celebrates the Jews' salvation from annihilation in ancient Persia, and which, according to the biblical book of Esther, ended with Jews slaughtering their would-be killers.) In the early twenty-first century, right-wing activists in Israel advocated for the transfer of Arabs from Israel and against the presence of African asylum seekers in the country. The organization Lahava (Flame), founded in 2005, campaigned against social or intimate interactions between Jews and non-Jews in Israel. In 2021, a neo-Kahanist party, Otzmah Yehudit (Jewish Power), sat in the

Knesset with a single representative. In elections in the following
November, a Religious Zionist joint list including Otzmah Yehudit won
14 seats in the 120-seat Knesset and appeared poised to exert considerable influence over settlement and security policy.

The roots of Kahanism's increased popularity lay in a series of events
over the twenty-first century's first two decades. The Second Intifada
of 2000–2005, during which some one thousand Israelis were killed,
strengthened Israeli anti-Arab feeling, and in the following years rocket
attacks on Israel from Hamas and Islamic Jihad militants in the Gaza
Strip raised anti-Arab passion to a boil. This passion blurred distinctions
between Palestinians in the Occupied Territories and those who were
citizens of Israel. On Election Day in 2015, the reelection campaign of
Israeli prime Minister Benjamin Netanyahu sent potential supporters
text messages that "turnout is three times higher in the Arab sector."
Netanyahu himself posted a video on his Facebook page in which he
warned that "the right is in danger of losing power, the Arab voters are
moving in droves to the polling stations. We only have you. Go to vote.
Bring your friends and relatives. Vote Likud to close the gap between us
and Labor. And with your help, and God's help, we will form a national
government that will protect the state of Israel."[70]

In the 2010s and since then, calls of "Death to Arabs" have been heard
at Israeli political demonstrations and soccer games involving Arab teams,
Arab players, or players with Arab-sounding names. Far-right fans of the
Beitar Jerusalem team sang demeaning or threatening chants, such as
"We will burn down your village! Shuafat[71] will go up in flames!" As one
fan put it crisply, "*Gizanut—zo arakhim* (racism is a value)."[72]

Hateful speech accompanied or encouraged violent acts. Throughout
the 2010s there was an uptick in attacks by Israeli Jews against Palestinians, and settler violence in the West Bank spiked in 2022. The use of
lethal force against Palestinians by the Israeli army and border police
was common and widely condoned. In Hebron in 2016, an Israeli soldier
shot dead a Palestinian assailant who had already been incapacitated by

military forces and was lying, without moving, on the ground. More than half of Israelis opposed the soldier's arrest, and 40 percent thought his action was appropriate.[73]

Survey data from the twenty-first century's first two decades suggest that anti-Arab sentiment is widespread among Israeli Jews. In 1999, a scholarly study of xenophobia in Israel referred to a recent survey in which 77 percent of Israeli Jews opposed sexual relations between Arabs and Jews, and 56 percent opposed granting Arabs equal social rights. The degree of religious observance was strongly correlated with the level of hatred toward Arabs.[74] Subsequent surveys confirmed the strong correlation between religiosity and intolerance, as well as increasing levels of anti-Arab animosity over time. Surveys from 2003–2009 showed that about one-third of Israeli Jews did not feel "ready" to have an Arab friend and half did not want an Arab neighbor. Between 60 and 70 percent perceived Israel's Arabs as a "demographic threat," even though only 15 to 20 percent of Jews had been personally insulted, threatened, or otherwise harmed by an Arab. Only two-thirds of Jews felt Arabs should be allowed to vote for the Knesset, and just one-third felt Arabs should be allowed to purchase land where they wished.[75] By 2016, almost half of Israeli Jews agreed that "Arabs should be expelled or transferred from Israel," with support for expulsion rising to 59 percent among ultra-Orthodox Jews and 71 percent among national religious Jews.[76] In 2018, 90 percent of Jewish survey respondents objected to their daughter befriending an Arab boy, and almost as many objected to a friendship between their son and an Arab girl.[77] More than one-third were bothered by the fact that half of Israel's pharmacists are Arab. A survey of Israeli teenagers, publicized in February 2021, found that 24, 42, and 66 percent of secular, religious, and ultra-Orthodox Jews, respectively, expressed fear or hatred of Arabs. Forty-nine percent of Religious Zionist youth and half as many of their secular peers supported denying Arabs the right to vote.[78]

Surveys also revealed Arab hostility to Jews that was at least as intense as Jewish animosity toward Arabs.[79] According to the early 2021 survey, Arab teens held negative attitudes about secular, Religious Zionist, and ultra-Orthodox Jews, with the strongest hatred directed against the ultra-Orthodox.[80] The timing of this survey overlapped with growing numbers of clashes between Jewish and Arab youths in downtown West Jerusalem and Jerusalem's Old City. The Israel–Hamas hostilities in May 2021 sparked violent altercations between Jews and Arabs in mixed communities throughout Israel. There were considerably more acts of Arab violence against Jews or destruction of Jewish property (e.g., synagogues, cars) than the other way around.

The government's response was telling. It conflated Arab violence against Jews within Israel with the thousands of rockets fired by Hamas at Israeli cities. It failed to acknowledge the structural reasons behind Israeli Arabs' fury, such as long-standing social and economic discrimination, lack of access to land for housing, inadequate social services, and a weak governmental response to skyrocketing violent crime in Arab communities. Although the government condemned Jewish violence against Arabs, it emphasized Jewish victimhood. Israel's president Reuven Rivlin referred to the burning of synagogues in Lod as a "pogrom" committed by "a bloodthirsty Arab mob." The mayor of Lod compared the arson to Kristallnacht, the massive Nazi-organized pogrom throughout Germany on the night of November 9, 1938. The prime minister said that the destruction "reminds us of scenes from our people's past," and the justice minister made the same point even more clearly: "There were times when Jews were defenseless and powerless against their attackers. Thank God those times have passed."[81]

Israel's citizens had understandable reasons to be terrified by rockets falling all around them while intercommunal violence raged in the country's cities. But fear and self-pity in the face of violence committed against Israel made possible the minimization, rationalization, and transfer of responsibility for Israel's own acts; the blurring of lines between aggression and self-defense; and the denial of widespread anti-Arab hatred.

Such bundling of negative emotions and attribution of blame to the Other are common in deeply divided societies.

How widely are these feelings shared among members of those societies' diasporas, observed from a distance? We do not have survey data documenting diaspora Jews' feelings about Arabs. American Jews, however, are known to be consistently more dovish than Israelis regarding possibilities for Israeli-Palestinian peace. According to a 2020 Pew survey, the vast majority of non-Orthodox American Jews believed that an enduring two-state option was possible, and only a minority of the non-Orthodox thought that Israel was doing enough to pursue peace with the Palestinians.[82] These figures suggest a certain level of trust toward and respect for Palestinians, feelings that are unlikely to coexist with hatred.

That American Orthodox Jews are considerably less likely to share such optimism or to criticize the Israeli government's hardline policies is consistent with our analysis in chapter 4 of a confident, firm Orthodox emotional attachment to Israel that is undiminished by, and often supportive of, Israel's treatment of Palestinians both within Israel and in the Occupied Territories. To the extent that neo-Kahanist hatred of Arabs exists within the American Jewish community, it is most common among the Orthodox. That said, in Israel and the Occupied Territories, Orthodox Jews demonstrate a range of feelings toward Arabs, from hateful contempt to a humanitarian though hierarchical paternalism, and even (for some) to unalloyed sympathy and respect.[83] Such a spectrum is likely to exist throughout the Jewish world.

Conclusion

Hatred can penetrate all forms of Jewish self-ascription. The affective pathogens—the fears, frustrated desires, and accumulated memories of past wrongs—that are responsible for antisemitism's most virulent variants also produce violent Arabophobia and Islamophobia. The difference between Zionism and antisemitism is not that one is free from hatred and the other is synonymous with it. All nationalisms can be cruel and exclusionary, and Zionism is no exception. But national identifications can also be inspirational and inculcate a yearning for achievement and solidarity. Antisemitism, too, provides a sense of emotional satisfaction in that it accounts for personal failures and limitations, but its therapeutic powers are feeble unless it is stoked to a frenzy, the consequences of which have all too often been disastrous.

Hate has a sociobiological rationale to the extent that it promotes in-group solidarity, inhibits exogamy, and justifies violence against proven or potential enemies of the community. Like the body's immune system, however, the emotional culture of a society can become hyperactive, weakening the body politic by attacking its own members or external elements that, in fact, present no substantive threat. In an asymmetrical conflict the stronger party's hatreds do greater harm to the weaker party than the other way around, but the stronger party also damages itself. At the time of writing, the majority of Israeli Jews and of those who speak for diaspora Jewry have not accepted this lesson.

Conclusion

The conflation of the word "Zionism" with a nationalist movement, a nation-state, and diverse ethnoreligious communities throughout the world makes it challenging to study Zionism as a uniform historical phenomenon. Despite the vast differences between the State of Israel and diaspora Jewries, however, significant continuities have characterized Jewish feelings about Israel worldwide. Those continuities demonstrate the value of conceiving of Zionism as a series of emotional clusters that develop independently yet display similar characteristics across locations or can be transmitted globally via the print and electronic media, as well as personal interaction. Although after 1948 the initial point of the Zionist emotional vector was and continues to be the State of Israel, both before and after that Zionist emotional discourse was and continues to be generated and disseminated worldwide.

This book is about the articulation of feeling, which takes two forms. A person uses language to express the relationship between desire and its fulfillment, and between one's cognitive and somatic state. It can also be an instrumental discourse designed to elicit emotion, and hence certain actions, from others. In the realm of political emotion, the focus of this book, the instrumental articulation of feeling motivates people to donate money, join organizations, support political causes, and fight in wars. Although these forms are conceptually distinct, in practice they are blurred. Elite actors may sincerely believe in their emotionally compelling language, and for ordinary people the explication of feeling can be inseparable from performative gestures that, in a feedback loop, solidify and enhance the emotions they are trying to express.

There is an important distinction between the instrumental articulation of feeling and manipulation. The latter implies passivity and a lack of creative agency on the part of the objects of politically emotional language. This book presents a more dialogic relationship between elite and popular discourse. The emotional language of political leaders is not duplicated so much as refracted by the media, clergy, and educators. This fragmentation of political emotion occurs even within the institutional structures of a state, especially a liberal democracy. This is even more the case among ethnoreligious groups with which identification is voluntary and that lack central governing and educational institutions. (In a free society, one cannot choose to be of Jewish origin, but one may choose whether and how to identify as Jewish.) When emotional language meets with a positive response, it does so because it resonates with people's preexisting wants, needs, and values.

The articulation of feeling is entangled with the expression of ideas. This is particularly the case with political emotion, the feelings that tie one's well-being to that of a broader community. Criteria for belonging to the community, responsibilities of membership, levels of equity and inequity within and between communities, and threats to the community's safety are shaped by the presence of positive emotions such as love, pride, and solidarity and negative ones such as fear, resentment, anger, and hatred. Political emotion is therefore an inherent and essential component of collective sensibility.

There is a vast difference, however, between collective sensibility and political theory or doctrine. Few Zionists have read Herzl's *The Jewish State* in its entirety or the writings of any of Zionism's founding figures, but exposure to snippets from their works, compelling images (such as Herzl at the Zionist Congresses or young people working on a kibbutz), and formative experiences (such as the Birthright program) form powerful emotional bonds with Zionism as a project and with others who take part in it.

This book's structure affirms the inextricability of Zionism and emotion. Its three sections—on taxonomies of Zionism, Zionism's relations with colonialism, and the variety and intensity of Zionist emotional expression—are mutually reinforcing. Most forms of Zionism embraced hierarchical and Orientalizing views of Arabs (including Arab Jews), but

Statist Zionism was particularly keen to forge alliances with colonial powers. Any emotion could exist within the varieties of Zionism set forth in chapter 1. For example, fear for the physical security of the Jewish people characterized Statist Zionism, but Hebraic Zionism could be no less fearful, whether in the form of anxiety over Jewish cultural assimilation or Gershom Scholem's trepidation regarding the catastrophic messianic energy embedded within the Hebrew language. Some forms of Zionism were more likely to feature certain emotions (e.g., honor and dignity in Statist and Transformative Zionism, respectively; solidarity in Philanthropic Zionism; and hatred in Judaic Zionism). Love in all its varieties was prominent across the Zionist taxonomic system, but its familial, erotic, and spiritual forms were particularly apparent in Ethnic, Transformative, and Sacral Zionism, respectively.

As we saw in chapters 3–6, Zionism's emotional palette changed over time. The erotic elements submerged in the fin de siècle's sentimental love of Zion became increasingly dominant in the twentieth century before waning from the 1970s onward. The public display of gratitude to the international community, so prominent in the Zionism of the post-Balfour era, all but disappeared in the later interwar and postwar periods, despite the Zionist project's ongoing dependence on Great Power patronage. In Israel, the socially licit expression of hatred toward Palestinian Arabs was a product of tensions surrounding the Oslo peace process and the fear that gripped Israeli society during the Second Intifada. The emotional spectrum found within diaspora Jewish communities and Israel also varied: post-1948 diaspora Zionist identity centered around anxiety for Israel's safety, whereas Israeli identity—although hardly free from fear—was anchored in the features of a nation-state such as territory, language, and vernacular culture.

Hope was a central emotion to the early Zionist movement, for the obvious reasons that it had accomplished so little and Jewish needs were so great. But the ongoing salience of this emotion in Zionism is notable. As shown in Imber's poem "Tikvateinu," discussed in chapter 3, hope is fundamentally a passive emotion emerging from thwarted desire and obstructed agency. The original biblical meaning of *tikvah* in Joshua 2:17–18 is a cord—literally, something to hold onto—and in Zechariah 9:12 it appears in the phrase "prisoners of hope," suggesting that hope was a means of combating despair. Hosea 2:15's famous reference to a "gateway of hope" (*petakh tikvah*) evokes the expectation of divine redemption and trust in its eventual arrival, a combination nicely featured in Habakkuk's admonition, "Though it tarry, wait for it, it shall surely come" (2:3–4). Echoes of biblical associations of hope with patient and passive yearning are prominent in Imber's poem and in its revised version that became the Zionist and Israeli national anthem.

From the time of Herzl onward, however, the Zionist movement was dynamic, not passive, and the emotional underpinnings of its achievements were galvanizing, action-oriented feelings like eros, joy, solidarity, resolve, consternation, and anger, rather than quietist hope. Insight into why Zionism has continued to pay homage to hope comes from Hannah Arendt, who, following the eighteenth-century philosopher Gotthold Ephraim Lessing, considered hope, as well as fear, to be politically dangerous emotions because they encourage paralysis rather than action and distort the understanding of reality. (Hope "overleaps" reality, whereas fear "shrinks back from it."[1]) During World War II, Arendt wrote of hope and fear as "the two archenemies of Jewish politics" because hope that deportation to the East would be benign and fear of massive Nazi retaliation dissuaded Jews from resisting their Nazi tormenters.[2] Fear and hope, Arendt claimed, lead to states of "despair and unconcern"— unconcern being an enervating compound of optimism and fatalism.[3]

In the Zionist context, hope and fear play different but reinforcing roles, and each can be immobilizing. Justifiable fear within a particular moment—of a persecuting regime, an angry mob, a suicide bombing, or a threatening state—can harden into inveterate suspicion and distrust that are impervious to changing circumstances. At first glance, hope has the opposite valence. "Lift your eyes with hope, not through the rifle's sights," implores the "Song for Peace," composed by Yaakov Rotblit and Yair Rosenblum in 1969 and first performed by an Israeli military troupe. It later became the anthem of the 1990s peace movement, and on November 4, 1995, Prime Minister Yitzhak Rabin joined in singing it at a public rally moments before his assassination by a right-wing extremist. In the following year, the singer-songwriter Aviv Gefen, who was present at the rally, paid tribute to Rabin in an earnest "Song of Hope" in the style of John Lennon's "Imagine."[4] Hope can indeed inspire the taking of risks for peace or assume goodwill from one's putative enemy. But it can also encourage temporizing—playing for time, assuming a future strategic or material advantage, and betting that grave problems of the moment will resolve themselves without intervention.

Israel is not the only country whose national anthem expresses hope for its own establishment. It shares much in common with Poland, which, on its reconstitution as an independent state after World War I, adopted as its anthem a poem written in 1797, two years after the dissolution of the Kingdom of Poland, averring that "Poland is not yet lost." In both Poland and Israel, the singing of an anthem yearning for unattained statehood heightens the glory of the now existing state. Far more than Polish nationalism, however, Zionism has been and continues to be a global project with multiple goals. These goals are as disparate as enduring peace and security for the state of Israel, the advent of the messiah, strengthening Jewish ethnic consciousness and warding off assimilation in the diaspora, and the transformation of Jews into authentic, harmonious, and productive beings imbued with military prowess and civic virtue. Not only do these goals remain unattained despite the achievement of Jewish statehood, there is also no foreseeable point at which they could be attained. Zionism remains, therefore, a permanent revolution and as salient in the twenty-first century as it was at the end of the nineteenth. Greater than the sum of Israeli or diaspora Jewish institutional structures, Zionism is part of the emotional substrate of Jews throughout the world.

Further Reading

(This list is limited to English-language books that are widely available and would be of interest to students and general readers. Please consult the Notes for references to more specialized sources.)

Almog, Oz. *The Sabra: The Creation of the New Jew*. Berkeley: University of California Press, 2000.

Alroey, Gur. *An Unpromising Land: Jewish Migration to Palestine in the Early Twentieth Century*. Stanford: Stanford University Press, 2014.

Avineri, Shlomo. *The Making of Modern Zionism: The Intellectual Origins of the Jewish State*, rev. ed. New York: Basic Books, 2017.

Barnett, Michael. *The Star and the Stripes: A History of the Foreign Policies of American Jews*. Princeton, NJ: Princeton University Press, 2016.

Beinart, Peter. *The Crisis of Zionism*. New York: Picador, 2012.

Ben-Dror, Elad. *UNSCOP and the Arab-Israeli Conflict: The Road to Partition*. London: Routledge, 2022.

Bergamin, Peter. *The Making of the Israeli Far-Right: Abba Ahimeir and Zionist Ideology*. London: I. B. Tauris, 2021.

Berkowitz, Michael. *Zionist Culture and West European Jewry before the First World War*. New York: Oxford University Press, 1993.

Berman, Aaron. *Nazism, the Jews, and American Zionism 1933–1948*. Detroit: Wayne State University Press, 1990.

Chetrit, Sami Shalom. *Intra-Jewish Conflict in Israel: White Jews, Black Jews*. London: Routledge, 2009.

Cohen, Hillel. *Year Zero of the Arab-Israeli Conflict: 1929*. Waltham, MA: Brandeis University Press, 2015.

Diamond, James. *Homeland or Holy Land? The "Canaanite" Critique of Israel*. Bloomington: Indiana University Press, 1986.

Elon, Amos. *The Israelis: Founders and Sons*. New York: Penguin, 1981.

Engel, David. *Zionism*. London: Routledge, 2009.

Feige, Michael. *Settling in the Hearts: Jewish Fundamentalism in the Occupied Territories*. Detroit: Wayne State University Press, 2009.

Gans, Chaim. *A Just Zionism: On the Morality of the Jewish State*. New York: Oxford University Press, 2008.

Goldman, Samuel. *God's Country: Christian Zionism in America*. Philadelphia: University of Pennsylvania Press, 2018.

Gribetz, Jonathan Marc. *Defining Neighbors: Religion, Race, and the Early Zionist-Arab Encounter*. Princeton, NJ: Princeton University Press, 2014.

Hacohen, Dvora. *To Repair a Broken World: The Life of Henrietta Szold, Founder of Hadassah*. Cambridge, MA: Harvard University Press, 2021.

Halamish, Aviva. *Kibbutz: Utopia and Politics. The Life and Times of Meir Yaari, 1897–1987*. Boston: Academic Studies Press, 2017.

Halperin, Liora. *Babel in Zion: Jews, Nationalism, and Language Diversity in Palestine, 1920–1948*. New Haven, CT: Yale University Press, 2015.

Halperin, Liora. *The Oldest Guard: Forging the Zionist Settler Past*. Stanford: Stanford University Press, 2021.

Hazkani, Shay. *Dear Palestine: A Social History of the 1948 War*. Stanford: Stanford University Press, 2021.

Heller, Daniel. *Jabotinsky's Children: Polish Jews and the Rise of Right-Wing Zionism*. Princeton, NJ: Princeton University Press, 2017.

Herf, Jeffrey. *Israel's Moment: International Support for and Opposition to Establishing the Jewish State, 1945–1949*. New York: Cambridge University Press, 2021.

Hertzberg, Arthur. *The Zionist Idea*. New York: Harper & Row, 1959.

Hirschhorn, Sara Yael. *City on a Hilltop: American Jews and the Israeli Settler Movement*. Cambridge, MA: Harvard University Press, 2017.

Jacobson, Abigail, and Moshe Naor. *Oriental Neighbors: Middle Eastern Jews and Arabs in Mandatory Palestine*. Waltham, MA: Brandeis University Press, 2016.

Kabalo, Paula. *Israel Community Action: Living through the War of Independence*. Bloomington: Indiana University Press, 2020.

Kaplan, Amy. *Our American Israel: The Story of an Entangled Alliance*. Cambridge, MA: Harvard University Press, 2018.

Kaplan, Eran. *The Jewish Radical Right: Revisionist Zionism and Its Ideological Legacy*. Madison: University of Wisconsin Press, 1995.

Kaplan, Eran, and Derek Penslar, eds. *The Origins of Israel, 1882–1948: A Documentary History*. Madison: University of Wisconsin Press, 2011.

Karsh, Efraim. *Palestine Betrayed*. New Haven, CT: Yale University Press, 2010.

Katz, Emily Alice. *Bringing Zion Home: Israel in American Jewish Culture, 1948–1967*. Albany: State University of New York Press, 2015.

Kedar, Nir. *Law and Identity in Palestine: A Century of Debate*. New York: Cambridge University Press, 2019.

Kelner, Shaul. *Tours that Bind: Diaspora, Pilgrimage, and Israeli Birthright Tourism*. New York: New York University Press, 2012.

Khalidi, Rashid. *The Hundred Years' War on Palestine: A History of Settler Colonialism and Resistance, 1917–2017*. New York: Macmillan, 2020.

Kimmerling, Baruch. *Zionism and Territory: The Socio-Territorial Dimensions of Zionist Politics*. Berkeley: Institute of International Studies, University of California, 1983.

Klein, Menachem. *Lives in Common: Arabs and Jews in Jerusalem, Jaffa, and Hebron*. New York: Oxford University Press, 2014.

Krämer, Gudrun. *A History of Palestine: From the Ottoman Conquest to the Founding of the State of Israel*. Princeton, NJ: Princeton University Press, 2008.

Lainer-Vos, Dan. *Sinews of the Nation: Constructing Irish and Zionist Bonds in the United States*. New York: Polity, 2013.

Laqueur, Walter, *A History of Zionism*. New York: Shocken, 1975.

Levine, Mark. *Overthrowing Geography: Jaffa, Tel Aviv, and the Struggle for Palestine, 1880–1948*. Berkeley: University of California Press, 2005.

Linfield, Susie. *The Lion's Den: Zionism and the Left from Hannah Arendt to Noam Chomsky*. New Haven, CT: Yale University Press, 2020.

Lockman, Zachary. *Comrades and Enemies: Arab and Jewish Workers in Palestine, 1906–1948*. Berkeley: University of California Press, 1996.

Loeffler, James. *Rooted Cosmopolitans: Jews and Human Rights in the Twentieth Century*. New Haven, CT: Yale University Press, 2018.

Luz, Ehud. *Parallels Meet: Religion and Nationalism in the Early Zionist Movement*. Philadelphia: Jewish Publication Society, 1988.

Magid, Shaul. *Meir Kahane: The Public Life and Political Thought of an American Jewish Radical*. Princeton, NJ: Princeton University Press, 2021.

Mahla, Daniel. *Orthodox Judaism and the Politics of Religion: From Prewar Europe to the State of Israel*. Cambridge: Cambridge University Press, 2020.

Mirsky, Yehudah. *Rav Kook: Mystic in a Time of Revolution*. New Haven, CT: Yale University Press, 2014.

Mitelpunkt, Shaul. *Israel in the American Mind: The Cultural Politics of U.S.-Israeli Relations, 1958–1988*. New York: Cambridge University Press, 2018.

Morris, Benny. *The Birth of the Palestinian Refugee Problem Revisited*. New York: Cambridge University Press, 2004.

Morris, Benny. *1948: The First Arab-Israeli War*. New Haven, CT: Yale University Press, 2008.

Moss, Kenneth. *An Unchosen People: Jewish Political Reckoning in Interwar Poland*. Cambridge, MA: Harvard University Press, 2021.

Myers, David. *Re-Inventing the Jewish Past: European Jewish Intellectuals and the Zionist Return to History*. New York: Oxford University Press, 1995.

Nelson, Cary. *Israel Denial: Anti-Zionism, Anti-Semitism, and the Faculty Campaign against the Jewish State*. Bloomington: Indiana University Press, 2019.

Neumann, Boaz. *Land and Desire in Early Zionism*. Waltham, MA: Brandeis University Press, 2011.

Nur, Ofer. *Eros and Tragedy: Jewish Male Fantasies and the Masculine Revolution of Zionism*. Boston: Academic Studies Press, 2014.

Patt, Avinoam. *Home and Homeland: Jewish Youth and Zionism in the Aftermath of the Holocaust*. Detroit: Wayne State University Press, 2009.

Pedahzur, Ami. *The Triumph of Israel's Radical Right*. New York: Oxford University Press, 2012.

Penslar, Derek. *Israel in History: The Jewish State in Comparative Perspective*. London: Routledge, 2006.

Penslar, Derek. *Jews and the Military*. Princeton, NJ: Princeton University Press, 2013.

Penslar, Derek. *Theodor Herzl: The Charismatic Leader*. New Haven, CT: Yale University Press, 2020.

Pianko, Noam. *Jewish Peoplehood: An American Innovation*. New Brunswick, NJ: Rutgers University Press, 2011.

Piterberg, Gabriel. *The Returns of Zionism: Myths, Politics and Scholarship in Israel*. London: Verso, 2008.

Porat, Dina. *The Blue and the Yellow Stars of David: The Zionist Leadership in Palestine and the Holocaust, 1939–1945*. Cambridge, MA: Harvard University Press, 1990.

Rabinovitch, Simon, ed. *Defining Israel: The Jewish State, Democracy, and the Law*. Cincinnati: Hebrew Union College Press, 2018.

Raider, Mark A., and Miriam B. Raider-Roth, eds. *The Plough Woman: Records of the Pioneer Women of Palestine—A Critical Edition.* Lebanon, NH: Brandeis University Press, 2002.

Ravitzky, Aviezer. *Messianism, Zionism, and Jewish Religious Radicalism.* Chicago: University of Chicago Press, 1996.

Reimer, Michael. *The First Zionist Congress: An Annotated Translation of the Proceedings.* Albany: State University of New York Press, 2019.

Reinharz, Jehuda. *Chaim Weizmann: The Making of a Zionist Leader.* New York: Oxford University Press, 1985.

Reinharz, Jehuda. *Chaim Weizmann: The Making of a Zionist Statesman.* New York: Oxford University Press, 1993.

Rhett, Maryanne. *The Global History of the Balfour Declaration: Declared Nation.* London: Routledge, 2016.

Robinson, Shira. *Citizen Strangers: Palestinians and the Birth of Israel's Liberal Settler State.* Stanford: Stanford University Press, 2013.

Roby, Bryan. *The Mizrahi Era of Rebellion: Israel's Forgotten Civil Rights Struggle 1948–1966.* Syracuse, NY: Syracuse University Press, 2015.

Rodinson, Maxime. *Israel: A Colonial-Settler State?* Atlanta: Pathfinder Press, 1973.

Ross, Dennis. *Doomed to Succeed: The U.S.–Israel Relationship from Truman to Obama.* New York: Farrar, Straus, and Giroux, 2016..

Rozin, Orit. *The Rise of the Individual in 1950s Israel: A Challenge to Collectivism.* Waltham, MA: Brandeis University Press, 2011.

Saposnik, Arieh. *Becoming Hebrew: The Creation of a Jewish National Culture Babel in Zion.* New York: Oxford University Press, 2008.

Sasson, Theodore. *The New American Zionism.* New York: NYU Press, 2014.

Schneer, Jonathan. *The Balfour Declaration.* New York: Random House, 2012.

Schoeps, Julius. *Pioneers of Zionism: Hess, Pinsker, Rülf.* Berlin: De Gruyter, 2013.

Segev, Tom. *The Seventh Million.* New York: Hill and Wang, 1993.

Segev, Tom. *A State at Any Price: The Life of David Ben-Gurion.* New York: Farrar, Straus, and Giroux, 2019.

Shafir, Gershon. *Land, Labor and the Origins of the Israeli-Palestinian Conflict, 1882–1914.* Cambridge: Cambridge University Press, 1989.

Shapira, Anita. *Berl: The Biography of a Socialist Zionist: Berl Katznelson, 1887–1944.* Cambridge: Cambridge University Press, 1984.

Shapira, Anita. *Land and Power: The Zionist Resort to Force, 1882–1948.* New York: Oxford University Press, 1992.

Shapira, Anita. *Yigal Allon, Native Son: A Biography.* Philadelphia: University of Pennsylvania Press, 2012.

Shavit, Ari. *My Promised Land.* New York: Spiegel and Grau, 2013.

Shavit, Yaacov. *Jabotinsky and the Revisionist Movement, 1925–1948.* London: Routledge, 1988.

Shenhav, Yehouda. *The Arab Jews: A Postcolonial Reading of Nationalism, Religion, and Ethnicity.* Stanford: Stanford University Press, 2005.

Shilo, Margalit. *Princess or Prisoner? Jewish Women in Jerusalem, 1840–1914.* Waltham, MA: Brandeis University Press, 2002.

Shindler, Colin. *The Rise of the Israeli Right.* Cambridge: Cambridge University Press, 2015.

Shoham, Hizky. *Carnival in Tel Aviv: Purim and the Celebration of Urban Zionism.* Boston: Academic Studies Press, 2014.

Shumsky, Dmitry. *Beyond the Nation-State: The Zionist Political Imagination from Pinsker to Ben-Gurion.* New Haven, CT: Yale University Press, 2018.

Simmons, Erica. *Hadassah and the Zionist Project.* Lanham, MD: Rowman & Littlefield, 2006.

Stanislawski, Michael. *Zionism: A Very Short Introduction.* New York: Oxford University Press, 2017.

Troy, Gil. *Moynihan's Moment: America's Fight against Zionism as Racism.* New York: Oxford University Press, 2013.

Troy, Gil, ed. *The Zionist Ideas: Visions for the Jewish Homeland: Then, Now, Tomorrow.* Philadelphia: Jewish Publication Society, 2018.

Veracini, Lorenzo. *Israel and Settler Society.* London: Pluto Press, 2006.

Vital, David. *The Origins of Zionism.* Oxford: Oxford University Press, 1975.

Vital, David. *Zionism: The Formative Years.* Oxford: Oxford University Press, 1982.

Vital, David. *Zionism: The Crucial Years.* Oxford: Oxford University Press, 1987.

Waxman, Dov. *Trouble in the Tribe: The American Jewish Conflict over Israel.* Princeton, NJ: Princeton University Press, 2016.

Yadgar, Yaacov. *Israel's Jewish Identity Crisis: State and Politics in the Middle East.* Cambridge: Cambridge University Press, 2020.

Zakim, Eric. *To Build and Be Built: Landscape, Literature, and the Construction of Zionist Identity.* Philadelphia: University of Pennsylvania Press, 2006.

Zertal, Idith. *From Catastrophe to Power: The Holocaust Survivors and the Emergence of Israel.* Berkeley: University of California Press, 1998.

Zerubavel, Yael. *Recovered Roots: Collective Memory and the Making of Israeli National Tradition.* Chicago: University of Chicago Press, 1995.

Acknowledgments

I owe this book to the High Table at St. Anne's College, Oxford. At Oxford I taught in the Department of Politics and International Relations, and in 2014 a lunchtime conversation with my colleague Todd Hall, who works on emotions in International Relations, piqued my interest. I started reading in the field of the history of emotions and added a unit on emotions to my courses on nationalism and nationalist movements. I had already been asked to contribute a volume on Zionism for Rutgers University Press's Key Words in Jewish Studies series, and after I moved to Harvard in 2016 and began regularly teaching courses on the history of emotions, I decided to combine my interests and produce a history of Zionism through the lens of emotion.

Throughout this book's long gestation, Deborah Dash Moore and Jonathan Boyarin have been unfailing sources of support, wise counsel, and constructive critique. It is an honor to publish this book in the Key Words series and to join the ranks of those who have already contributed to it. The production team at Rutgers University Press has been a pleasure to work with, and I am especially grateful to Christopher Rios-Sueverkruebbe for his careful attention to the manuscript.

Jonathan Gribetz, Tsiona Lida, Shaul Magid, and Kenneth Stern read the entire manuscript with a keen eye and generosity of spirit. Liat Radcliffe Ross's editing was exceptionally helpful. I am also grateful to the many colleagues who commented on portions of the manuscript and drafts of articles that preceded it: Bashir Bashir, Johannes Becke, Lila Corwin Berman, Hasia Diner Arie Dubnov, Leila Farsakh, Ethan Katz, Rebecca Kobrin, Helaina Kravitz, Pnina Lahav, Geoffrey Levin, Lisa Leff, Maud Mandel, Gavriel Rosenfeld, Orit Rozin, Anita Shapira, and Steven Zipperstein. For illuminating conversations, which led me down exciting paths of inquiry and saved me from embarrassing errors, I thank Seth Anziska, David Armitage, Omer Bartov, Michael Berkowitz, Omri Boehm, Michael Brenner, Alon Confino, Faisal Devji, John Efron, David Feldman, Ute Frevert, Sylvia Fuks Fried, Peter Gordon, Abigail Green, Karen Grumberg, Liora Halperin, Ruth Harris, Susannah Heschel, Adriana Jacobs, Eran Kaplan, Alexander Kaye, James Loeffler, Sara Lipton, Olga Litvak, Zachary Lockman, Erez Manela, Yehudah Mirsky, Kenneth Moss, Paul Nahme, Kalypso Nikolaïdis, Yaron Peleg, David Rechter, Arie Saposnik, Stephanie Schüler-Springorum, Joshua Shanes, Eugene Sheppard, Dan Smail, Joshua Teplitsky, Harold Troper, Stefan Vogt, Dov Waxman, Yaacov Yadgar, Yael Zerubavel, and Ron Zweig.

Daniel Brickman and Ariella Kahan provided indispensable research assistance. The staffs of the Central Zionist Archive, National Library of Israel, Israel State Archive, and Center for Jewish History in New York City were unfailingly helpful, even during the worst of the pandemic. I owe a special debt of gratitude to Charles Berlin, Violet Radnofsky, and Elizabeth Vernon of Widener Library's Judaica Division, which was an essential source of research material for this book.

I thank the publishers of the following journal articles and book chapters, portions of which appear in this book: "What if a Christian State Had Been Established in Modern Palestine?" in *What Ifs? Of Jewish History from Abraham to Zionism*, ed. Gavriel Rosenfeld (Cambridge: Cambridge University Press, 2016), 142–164; "What We Talk about When We Talk about Colonialism," in *Colonialism and the Jews*, ed. Maud Mandel, Ethan Katz, and Lisa Leff (Bloomington: Indiana University Press, 2017), 327–340; "Declarations of (In)Dependence: Tensions within Zionist Statecraft, 1896–1948," *Journal of Levantine Studies* 8, no. 1 (Van Leer Institute, 2018): 13–34; "What's Love Got to Do with It? The Emotional Language of Early Zionism," *Journal of Israeli History* 38, no. 1 (2020): 25–52; "Towards a Field of Israel/Palestine Studies," in *Between the "Jewish Question" and the "Arab Question": Contemporary Entanglements and Juxtapositions*, ed. Bashir Bashir and Leila Farsakh (New York: Columbia University Press, 2020), 173–197; and "Solidarity as an Emotion: American Jewry and the 1948 Palestine War," *Modern American History* 5, no. 1 (2022): 27–52.

Given that this is a book about emotion, it is fitting to close the acknowledgments with my wife Robin, our children Joshua and Talia, their spouses Marisa and Tom, and our grandchildren Selma, Bruno, and Maximilian. They are sources and objects of the most psychically rewarding emotions: unconditional love, generosity, and sympathy. They are a constant reminder that political emotions—how people feel about communities, movements, and countries—are abstractions of the interpersonal emotions that form the core of our being. My family's love has sustained me, and I hope that my love has anchored them as well.

Cambridge and Toronto
November 2022

Notes

INTRODUCTION

1. The book was first published in 1976. For the latest edition see Raymond Williams, *Keywords: A Vocabulary of Culture and Society* (Oxford: Oxford University Press, 2014).

2. "BBC Poll: Germany Most Popular Country in the World," May 23, 2013, https://www.bbc.com/news/world-europe-22624104.

3. Nahum Sokolow, *History of Zionism, 1600–1918*, 2 vols. (New York: Longmans, Green and Co, 1919), and *Hibbat Zion* (Jerusalem: Rubin Mass, 1941); Adolf Boehm, *Die Zionistische Bewegung*, 2 vols. (Berlin: Jüdischer Verlag, 1935–1937).

4. Since the late 1970s, Anita Shapira has produced a stream of pioneering scholarship that blends the social, political, and cultural history of Zionism within Palestine's pre-1948 Jewish community, the Yishuv. Much of it is in the form of articles collected in Hebrew volumes but whose English versions remain scattered. Many of her core ideas, however, are contained within her monograph *Land and Power: The Zionist Resort to Force, 1882–1948* (New York: Oxford University Press, 1992). For other important work on the social and cultural history of Zionism in pre-1948 Palestine, see Yael Zerubavel, *Recovered Roots: Collective Memory and the Making of Israeli National Tradition* (Chicago: University of Chicago Press, 1995); Oz Almog, *The Sabra: The Creation of the New Jew* (Berkeley: University of California Press, 2000); Arieh Saposnik, *Becoming Hebrew: The Creation of a Jewish National Culture Babel in Zion* (New York: Oxford University Press, 2008); and Liora Halperin, *Babel in Zion: Jews, Nationalism, and Language Diversity in Palestine, 1920–1948* (New Haven, CT: Yale University Press, 2015). Recent literature exploring the multiple meanings of Zionism in the diaspora before World War II includes Joshua Shanes, *Diaspora Nationalism and Jewish Identity in Habsburg Galicia* (New York: Cambridge University Press, 2012); Tatjana Lichtenstein, *Zionists in Interwar Czechoslovakia: Minority Nationalism and the Politics of Belonging* (Bloomington: Indiana University Press, 2016); and Daniel Heller, *Jabotinsky's Children: Polish Jews and the Rise of Right-Wing Zionism* (Princeton, NJ: Princeton University Press, 2017).

5. There are three important exceptions: Boaz Neumann, *Land and Desire in Early Zionism* (Waltham, MA: Brandeis University Press, 2011); Nitzan Lebovic, *Zionism and Melancholy: The Short Life of Israel Zarchi* (Bloomington: Indiana University

Press, 2019); and Orit Rozin's ongoing work on emotion in the young State of Israel, such as "Infiltration and the Making of Israel's Emotional Regime in the State's Early Years," *Middle Eastern Studies* 52, no. 3 (2016): 448–472, and "Pahad be-tsel tota-heihah shel suriyah: kibutsei ha-sfar u-mishtar ha-regashot hayisre'eli [*In the Shadow of Syria's Artillery: Frontier Kibbutzim and the Israeli Emotional Regime*]," *Iyunim Bitekumat Yisra'el* 26 (2016): 109–181.

6. In his monumental and meandering history of France from 1848 to 1945, originally published in two volumes in 1973 and republished in five, Theodore Zeldin provided what he called "a history of French passions," loosely organized into categories such as ambition, love, anger, pride, taste, and anxiety. Another early exploration of the history of the passions, also massive and unstructured, is Peter Gay's five-volume series, *The Bourgeois Experience: Victoria to Freud* (1984–1998).

7. For example, Thomas Laquer, "Bodies, Details and the Humanitarian Narrative," in *The New Cultural History,* ed. Lynn Hunt (Berkeley: University of California Press, 1989), 176–204; Lynn Hunt, *Inventing Human Rights* (New York: Norton, 2007), 35–69; Nicole Eustace, *Passion Is the Gale: Emotion, Power, and the Coming of the American Revolution* (Chapel Hill: University of North Carolina Press, 2008), and *1812: War and the Passions of Patriotism* (Philadelphia: University of Pennsylvania Press, 2012).

8. Rogers Brubaker, "Ethnicity without Groups," *European Journal of Sociology / Archives Européennes de Sociologie / Europäisches Archiv für Soziologie* 43, no. 2 (2003): 163–189.

9. Affect theory, produced mainly by scholars of cultural studies, devotes much attention to fear; see Sara Ahmed, *The Cultural Politics of Emotion* (London: Routedge, 2004), 62–81; and Brian Massumi, "The Future Birth of the Affective Fact: The Political Ontology of Threat," in *The Affect Theory Reader,* ed. Melissa Gregg and Gregory J. Seigworth (Durham, NC: Duke University Press, 2010), 52–70. The relative lack of historical attention to positive emotions was noted by Darrin McMahon in "Finding Joy in the History of Emotions," in *Doing Emotions History,* ed. Susan J. Matt and Peter N. Stearns (Champaign: University of Illinois Press, 2014), 103–119. For full-bodied explorations of the diversity of human emotion see Ute Frevert, *Emotions in History—Lost and Found* (Budapest: Central European University Press, 2011), and *Mächtige Gefühle: Von A wie Angst bis Z wie Zuneigung—Deutsche Geschichte seit 1900* (Frankfurt a.M.: Fischer Verlag, 2020).

10. Benedict Anderson, *Imagined Communities: Reflections on the Origin and Spread of Nationalism,* rev. ed. (London: Verso, 1984), 141.

11. William Reddy, *The Navigation of Feeling: A Framework for the History of Emotions* (Cambridge: Cambridge University Press, 2001), 129.

12. William Reddy, "Against Constructionism: The Historical Ethnography of Emotions," *Current Anthropology* 38 (1997): 335.

13. William Reddy, *The Making of Romantic Love: Longing and Sexuality in Europe, South Asia, and Japan, 900–1200* (Chicago: University of Chicago Press, 2012).

14. Barbara Rosenwein proposes this concept in the introductions to her monographs *Emotional Communities in the Early Middle Ages* (Ithaca, NY: Cornell University Press, 2006) and *Generations of Feeling: A History of Emotions, 600–1700* (Cambridge: Cambridge University Press, 2016).

15. For example, Lisa Feldman Barrett, *How Emotions Are Made: The Secret Life of the Brain* (New York: Houghton Mifflin Harcourt, 2017)

16. Peter N. Stearns and Carol Z. Stearns, "Emotionology: Clarifying the History of Emotions and Emotional Standards," *American Historical Review* 90, no. 4 (1985): 813–836.

17. Roger Petersen, *Understanding Ethnic Violence. Fear, Hatred, and Resentment in Twentieth-Century Eastern Europe* (Cambridge: Cambridge University Press, 2012), 3.

18. Rosenwein, *Generations of Feeling,* 150–151.

19. Theodore Kemper, *A Social Interactional Theory of Emotions* (New York: Wiley, 1978), 47.

20. Paul Hoggett and Simon Thompson, eds., *Politics and the Emotions. The Affective Turn in Contemporary Political Studies* (London: Bloomsbury, 2012), 2–3.

21. Lauren Berlant, *Cruel Optimism* (Durham, NC: Duke University Press, 2011).

22. On political emotion, see Corey Robin, "The Language of Fear: Security and Modern Politics," in *Fear across the Disciplines*, ed. Jan Plamper and Benjamin Lazier (Pittsburgh: University of Pittsburgh Press, 2012), 118–131; Mark Steinberg, "Emotions History in Eastern Europe" and Nicole Eustace, "Emotions and Political Change," *Doing Emotions History*, 74–99 and 163–183; and John Protevi, "Political Emotion," in Christian von Scheve and Mikko Salmela, eds., *Collective Emotions* (Oxford: Oxford University Press, 2014), 326–340.

23. An emphasis on the collective and the stimulus for heroic measures on its behalf separate political emotion from what the literary scholar Sianne Ngai calls "minor and unprestigious" feelings such as envy and irritation, which are limited to the interpersonal realm and attest to "obstructed agency" rather than

the capacity to act. Sianne Ngai, *Ugly Feelings* (Cambridge, MA: Harvard University Press, 2005), 3, 6.

24. Corey Robin, *Fear: The History of a Political Idea* (New York: Oxford University Press, 2004).

25. Joanna Bourke, *Fear: A Cultural History* (London: Virago, 2005).

26. A rare sustained treatment of love as a political emotion is Martha C. Nussbaum, *Political Emotions: Why Love Matters for Justice* (Cambridge, MA: Harvard University Press, 2013).

27. Frevert, *Emotions in History*, 40–85.

28. Rosenwein, *Generations of Feeling*, 8.

29. Brian Porter, *When Nationalism Began to Hate: Imagining Modern Politics in Nineteenth Century Poland* (New York: Oxford University Press, 2002).

30. Zachary Foster, "The Invention of Palestine" (PhD diss., Princeton University, 2017).

CHAPTER 1 — STAGING ZIONISM

1. Trump's use and defense of the term were widely reported in the U.S. media in October 2018. See, for example, the *Washington Post* on October 23, 2018, https://www.washingtonpost.com/politics/trump-im-a-nationalist-and-im-proud-of-it/2018/10/23/d9adaae6-d711-11e8-a10f-b51546b10756_story.html.

2. Amos Oz, *Be-or ha-tekhelet ha-'azah* (Tel Aviv: Sifriat Po'alim, 1979), 148.

3. Anthony Smith, "Zionism and Diaspora Nationalism," *Israel Affairs* 2, no. 2 (1995): 1–19.

4. Azar Gat and Alexander Yakobson, *Nations: The Long History and Deep Roots of Political Ethnicity and Nationalism* (Cambridge: Cambridge University Press, 2012).

5. Adam Teller, *Rescue the Surviving Souls: The Great Jewish Refugee Crisis of the Seventeenth Century* (Princeton, NJ: Princeton University Press, 2020), 158–159, 294.

6. In 1869, the chief rabbi of Vienna, Adolf Jellinek, published a book titled *Der jüdische Stamm*. For a discussion of *Stamm* as a form of collective identity in the writings of Jellinek and his contemporaries, see Derek J. Penslar, *Shylock's Children: Economics and Jewish Identity in Modern Europe* (Berkeley: University of California Press, 2001), 135–137.

7. "Le Vainqueur," *L'Univers Israélite* 1871, 49.

8. The term *klal yisrael* has early modern origins but gained currency in nineteenth-century Hasidic writings. Many thanks to Shaul Magid for this information.

9. Aviezer Ravitzky, *Messianism, Zionism, and Jewish Religious Radicalism* (Chicago: University of Chicago Press, 1996), 211–234. There is, however, a contrary rabbinic view (Ketubot 110b–111a) that "one should always live in the Land of Israel, even in a town most of whose inhabitants are idolaters, but let no one live outside the land, even in a town most of whose inhabitants are Israelites, for whoever lives in the Land of Israel may be considered to have a God, but whoever lives outside the land the Land may be regarded as one who has no God. For it is said in Scripture, *'To give you the land of Canaan, to be your God'* (Leviticus 25:38)." Many thanks to Jonathan Gribetz for this reference.

10. Gur Alroey, *An Unpromising Land: Jewish Migration to Palestine in the Early Twentieth Century* (Stanford: Stanford University Press, 2014).

11. Margalit Shilo, *Princess or Prisoner? Jewish Women in Jerusalem, 1840–1914* (Waltham, MA: Brandeis University Press, 2002).

12. Jacob Katz, "The Forerunners of Zionism," in *Essential Papers on Zionism*, ed. Jehuda Reinharz and Anita Shapira (New York: NYU Press, 1996), 33–45. Michael Stanislawski has argued that, in the early twentieth century, Orthodox rabbis sympathetic to Zionism and instrumental in founding the Mizrachi Orthodox Zionist movement invented the concept of rabbinic forerunners as a means of self-legitimization. Michael Stanislawski, *Zionism: A Very Short Introduction* (New York: Oxford University Press, 2017), 12.

13. Cited in Samuel Goldman, *God's Country: Christian Zionism in America* (Philadelphia: University of Pennsylvania Press, 2018), 85.

14. William Henry Johnstone, *Israel in the World, or, the Mission of the Hebrews to the Great Military Monarchies* (London: John Farquhar Shaw, 1854).

15. Nahum Sokolow, *History of Zionism, 1600–1918* (London: Longmans, Green and Co, 1919), I: 198–201. For the document, see II: 259–261.

16. Michael Reimer, *The First Zionist Congress: An Annotated Translation of the Proceedings* (Albany: SUNY Press, 2019), 305 (Herzl's speech), 384–385 (Reimer's commentary on Dunant).

17. Reproduced in Sokolow, *History of Zionism*, I: 124.

18. Goldman, *God's Country*, 67. See also his discussion of the memorial on pp. 65–69, 92–96.

19. The year 1840 was 5600 in the Jewish calendar.

20. Michael K. Silber, "The Emergence of Ultra-Orthodoxy: The Invention of a Tradition," in *The Uses of Tradition: Jewish Continuity in the Modern Era*, ed. Jack Wertheimer (New York: Jewish Theological Seminary of America, 1992), 23–84.

21. Cited in Shlomo Avineri, *The Making of Modern Zionism: The Intellectual Origins of the Jewish State*, rev. ed. (New York: Basic Books, 2017), 54.

22. "Schlesinger, Akiva Yosef," and "Natonek, Yosef," *YIVO Encyclopedia of Jews in Eastern Europe*, https://yivoencyclopedia.org/article.aspx/Schlesinger_Akiva_Yosef; https://yivoencyclopedia.org/article.aspx/Natonek_Yosef (accessed December 30, 2021).

23. David Sorkin, *The Transformation of German Jewry, 1780–1840* (Oxford: Oxford University Press, 1987), 41–78; Shmuel Feiner, *The Jewish Enlightenment* (Philadelphia: University of Pennsylvania Press, 2002); Olga Litvak, *Haskalah: The Romantic Movement in Judaism* (New Brunswick, NJ: Rutgers University Press, 2012).

24. For this reason, Michael Stanislawski dates Zionism's beginnings to 1872; *Zionism: A Very Short Introduction*, 15–16.

25. Quoted in Eliyahu Stern, *Jewish Materialism: The Intellectual Revolution of the 1870s* (New Haven, CT: Yale University Press, 2018), 180–181.

26. Derek J. Penslar, *Zionism and Technocracy: The Engineering of Jewish Settlement in Palestine, 1870–1918* (Bloomington: Indiana University Press, 1991), 16–18.

27. Zecharias Frankel, "Die gegenwärtige Lage der Juden in Palästina," *Monatschrift für die Geschichte und Wissesnschaft des Judentums* 3 (1854): 291.

28. Frankel, "Die gegenwärtige Lage der Juden in Palästina," 157–159.

29. Frankel, "Die gegenwärtige Lage der Juden in Palästina," 227.

30. Heinrich Graetz, *Volkstümliche Geschichte der Juden* (Berlin: Benjamin Harz, 1923), I: 1. The 1890 Hebrew version of Graetz's full-length *History* begins with a paraphrase of this paragraph but then goes back to the original order of the text, with the rest of the geographical information about ancient Palestine coming several pages in. Tzvi Graetz, *Divrei yemei yisra'el*, tr. Shaul Pinchas Rabinowitz (Jerusalem: Makor, 1972), v. I, p. 3. (Graetz wrote a brief forward, dated 5648 [1888], for this version.)

31. In the twentieth century, these concepts from ancient and medieval Jewish civilization would become a staple of Religious Zionist thought. See Netta Cohen, "Jews and Climate Science in Palestine" (DPhil. thesis, University of Oxford, 2019), 15, 138.

32. Graetz, *Volkstümliche Geschichte der Juden*, 8.

33. Graetz, *Volkstümliche Geschichte der Juden*, 11.

34. In this sense he was unlike his celebrated compatriot Heinrich Heine, whose iconic 1827 poem "Ein Fichtenbaum steht einsam" (A Pine Tree Stands Alone) tells of a frigid, dormant northern pine dreaming of a lonely palm tree in the sun-baked Orient. On the significance of Heine's poem in modern European and Hebrew literature, see Adriana X. Jacobs, *Strange Cocktail: Translation and the Making of Modern Hebrew Poetry* (Ann Arbor: University of Michigan Press, 2018), 112.

35. Graetz to Pinsker, 30 January 1885, in Heinrich Graetz, *Tagebuch und Briefe* (Tübingen: Mohr, 1977), 403.

36. Heinrich Graetz, *The Structure of Jewish History and Other Essays,* ed. Ismar Schorsch (New York: Jewish Theological Seminary, 1975), 124.

37. Although most historians give short shrift to the activity of Hibat Tsion, shortly before his death the Zionist publicist and leader Nahum Sokolow (1859–1936) completed a volume titled *Hibbat Zion* (Jerusalem: Rubin Mass, 1941). Sokolow conceived of Hibat Zion as a deep-seated love of both the Jewish nation and Land of Israel. For him, the activities of the Hovevei Tsion constituted the final chapter of an ancient bond, and he sharply differentiated it from Zionism, which he associated with the organizational and diplomatic activity of Theodor Herzl.

38. Alex Bein, "The Origin of the Term and Concept 'Zionism,'" in *Herzl Year Book: Essays in Zionist History and Thought* (New York: Herzl Press, 1959), 2:1–27.

39. Tal Becker, "Beyond Survival: Jewish Values and Aspirational Zionism," *Havruta* (Summer 2011): 56–63.

40. Chaim Gans, *A Just Zionism: On the Morality of the Jewish State* (New York: Oxford University Press, 2008).

41. A Google Ngram shows that usage of the term "Liberal Zionism" in English-language books increased more than tenfold between 2000 and 2019. https://books.google.com/ngrams/graph?content=Liberal+Zionism&year_start =1948&year_end=2019&corpus=26&smoothing=3&direct_url=t1%3B%2CLib-eral%20Zionism%3B%2Cco#t1%3B%2CLiberal%20Zionism%3B%2Cco (accessed June 11, 2022).

42. Gil Troy, ed., *The Zionist Ideas: Visions for the Jewish Homeland: Then, Now, Tomorrow* (Philadelphia: Jewish Publication Society, 2018).

43. Franz Oppenheimer, "Stammesbewusstsein und Volksbewusstsein," *Die Welt*, February 18, 1910, 143. The most recent and detailed intellectual biography

of Oppenheimer is Dekel Peretz, "'Zionism and Cosmopolitanism:' Franz Oppenheimer and the Dream of a Jewish Future in Germany and Palestine" (PhD diss., University of Potsdam, 2020).

44. See the table quantifying memberships in American Zionist organizations throughout the interwar period and World War II in Samuel Halperin, *The Political World of American Zionism* (Detroit: Wayne State University Press, 1961). For a brief and insightful history of Hadassah, see Deborah Dash Moore's and Mira Katzburg-Yungman's entry in the *Encyclopedia of Jewish Women* (https://jwa .org/encyclopedia/article/hadassah-in-united-states). For a monographic treatment, see Erica Simmons, *Hadassah and the Zionist Project* (Lanham, MD: Rowman & Littlefield, 2006).

45. Noam Pianko, *Jewish Peoplehood: An American Innovation* (New Brunswick, NJ: Rutgers University Press, 2011).

46. Shlomo Avineri's *The Making of Modern Zionism* provides biographical sketches of Lilienblum, Ben-Yehuda, and Ahad Ha-Am. For a detailed study of Ahad Ha-Am, see Steven Zipperstein, *Elusive Prophet: Ahad Ha-Am and the Origins of Zionism* (Berkeley: University of California Press, 1993).

47. Abigail Jacobson and Moshe Naor, *Oriental Neighbors: Middle Eastern Jews and Arabs in Mandatory Palestine* (Waltham, MA: Brandeis University Press, 2016), 99–100.

48. Anita Shapira, "My Heart Is in the East and I Am in the West," in *From Europe's East to the Middle East: Israel's Russian and Polish Lineages*, ed. Kenneth Moss, Benjamin Nathans, and Taro Tsurumi (Philadelphia: University of Pennsylvania Press, 2022), 70–86.

49. See David Ellenson, "Reform Zionism Today: A Consideration of First Principles," in Troy, *The Zionist Ideas*, 437.

50. Holly Williams, "Mind Your (Minority) Language: Welsh, Gaelic, Irish and Cornish Are Staging a Comeback," *The Independent*, January 19, 2013, https:// www.independent.co.uk/news/education/schools/mind-your-minority -language-welsh-gaelic-irish-and-cornish-are-staging-comeback-8454456.html (accessed December 30, 2021).

51. *The Jewish Chronicle*, June 19, 1863, 5. On Montefiore, see Abigail Green, *Moses Montefiore: Jewish Liberator, Imperial Hero* (Cambridge, MA: Belknap Press, 2010).

52. Pinsker's 1882 pamphlet *Auto-Emancipation* is conventionally described as the first Political Zionist text, but Lilienblum's 1881 essay "On Israel and Its Land" distinguished between the emotional appeal of the national idea and the

necessity of a state in Eretz Israel to provide for the Jews' security and material needs. Stern, *Jewish Materialism*, 170–171, 175–176.

53. Dmitry Shumsky, *Beyond the Nation-State: The Zionist Political Imagination from Pinsker to Ben-Gurion* (New Haven, CT: Yale University Press, 2018).

54. Telegram from Walter Henry Shoals, United States Consul-General in Basel, to Secretary of State James Byrnes, 30 December 1946, in *Foreign Relations of the United States, 1946: The Near East and Africa, v. VII*, https://history.state.gov /historicaldocuments/frus1946v07/d570 (accessed November 8, 2022).

55. Nir Kedar, *David Ben-Gurion and the Foundation of Israeli Democracy* (Bloomington: Indiana University Press, 2021).

56. Nir Kedar traces the development of the concept of Israel as a "Jewish and democratic state" in *Law and Identity in Palestine: A Century of Debate* (New York: Cambridge University Press, 2019). See also Ruth Gavison, "Reflections on the Meaning and Justification of the Term 'Jewish' in the Expression, 'Jewish and Democratic State,'" in *The Israeli Nation-State: Political, Constitutional, and Cultural Challenges*, ed. Fania Oz-Salzberger and Yedidia Stern (Boston: Academic Studies Press, 2014), 135–163.

57. Pew Foundation, "Israel's Religiously Divided Society," 2016, https://www .pewforum.org/2016/03/08/israels-religiously-divided-society (accessed December 30, 2021).

58. Kenneth Moss, "From Zionism as Ideology to the Yishuv as Fact: Polish Jewish Relations to Palestine on the Cusp of the 1930s," in *From Europe's East to the Middle East*, 271–304; and *An Unchosen People: Jewish Political Reckoning in Interwar Poland* (Cambridge, MA: Harvard University Press, 2021).

59. Yaacov Shavit, *Ha-mitologiyah shel ha-yemin* (Kfar Saba: Beit Berl, 1986).

60. "Israel's Netanyahu Urges 'Mass Immigration' of Jews after Denmark Shooting," *Slate*, February 15, 2015, https://slate.com/news-and-politics/2015/02/benjamin -netanyahu-urges-mass-immigration-of-jews-to-israel-after-denmark-attacks.html (accessed July 4, 2022); "'Come home!' Israeli Minister Urges French Jews amid Terror Wave," *Times of Israel*, June 26, 2015, https://www.timesofisrael.com/come-home -israeli-minister-urges-french-jews-amid-terror-wave/ (accessed July 4, 2022).

61. Zionists often accepted the prevalent yet inaccurate notion that Jews lacked a military tradition or shirked military service in the diaspora. A more charitable Zionist critique of diaspora Jewish military performance was that Jews had indeed fought bravely in "foreign" armies (i.e., in the Jews' lands of residence), but that their heroic sacrifices did nothing to diminish antisemitism. Derek Penslar, *Jews and the Military* (Princeton: Princeton University Press, 2013), 7.

62. Hizky Shoham, "From 'Great History' to 'Small History': The Genesis of the Zionist Periodization," *Israel Studies* 18, no. 1 (2013): 31–55; Liora Halperin, *The Oldest Guard: Forging the Zionist Settler Past* (Stanford: Stanford University Press, 2021).

63. Joshua Shanes, *Diaspora Nationalism and Jewish Identity in Habsburg Galicia* (New York: Cambridge University Press, 2012).

64. Aron Rodrigue, "From *Millet* to Minority: Turkish Jewry," in *Paths of Emancipation: Jews, States, and Citizenship*, ed. Pierre Birnbaum and Ira Katznelson (Princeton: Princeton University Press, 1995), 254; Julia Phillips Cohen, *Becoming Ottomans: Sephardi Jews and Imperial Citizenship in the Modern Era* (New York: Oxford University Press, 2014), 103–131.

65. Tatjana Lichtenstein, *Zionists in Interwar Czechoslovakia: Minority Nationalism and the Politics of Belonging* (Bloomington: Indiana University Press, 2016)

66. Raphaella Bilski Ben-Hur, *Every Individual a King: The Social and Political Thought of Ze'ev Vladimir Jabotinsky* (Washington, DC: B'nai B'rith, 1993); Daniel Heller, *Jabotinsky's Children: Polish Jews and the Rise of Right-Wing Zionism* (Princeton, NJ: Princeton University Press, 2017).

67. Allon Gal, *Brandeis of Boston* (Cambridge, MA: Harvard University Press, 1980); Jonathan D. Sarna, "A Projection of America as It Ought to Be: Zion in the Mind's Eye of American Jews," and Michael Brown, "Henriette Szold's Progressive American Vision of the Yishuv," in *Envisioning Israel: The Changing Ideals and Images of American Jews*, ed. Allon Gal (Detroit: Wayne State University Press, 1996), 41–59, 60–80.

68. On Birthright, see Shaul Kelner, *Tours that Bind: Diaspora, Pilgrimage, and Israeli Birthright Tourism* (New York: NYU Press, 2012). On the origins of American Jewry's embrace of Israeli material culture, see Emily Alice Katz, *Bringing Zion Home: Israel in American Jewish Culture, 1948–1967* (Albany: SUNY Press, 2015).

69. Sarah Bunin Benor, Jonathan Krasner, and Sharon Avni, *Hebrew Infusion. Language and Community at American Jewish Summer Camps* (New Brunswick: NJ: Rutgers University Press, 2020).

70. Pew Foundation, "Israel's Religiously Divided Society."

71. Reproduced in Troy, *The Zionist Ideas*, xii.

72. Theodor Herzl, *Complete Diaries* (New York: Herzl Press, 1960), 151, 155, 171, 196, 287; and *Zionist Writings: Essays and Addresses* (New York: Herzl Press, 1973–1975), I: 151.

73. Ehud Luz, *Parallels Meet: Religion and Nationalism in the Early Zionist Movement* (Philadelphia: Jewish Publication Society, 1988).

74. In *Orthodox Judaism and the Politics of Religion: From Prewar Europe to the State of Israel* (Cambridge: Cambridge University Press, 2020), Daniel Mahla demonstrates that the Mizrahi (later the National Religious Party) and the non-Zionist Agudat Yisrael struggled for the spotlight as guardians of Torah in the Yishuv and early state of Israel.

75. Eran Kaplan and Derek Penslar, eds., *The Origins of Israel, 1882–1948: A Documentary History* (Madison: University of Wisconsin Press, 2011), 368–372.

76. For a succinct and insightful introduction to Rabbi Kook's thought, see Yehudah Mirsky, *Rav Kook: Mystic in a Time of Revolution* (New Haven, CT: Yale University Press, 2014).

77. There is a sizable literature on the settlement movement in the Occupied Territories. For a particularly valuable analysis of settler thought, see Michael Feige, *Settling in the Hearts: Jewish Fundamentalism in the Occupied Territories* (Detroit: Wayne State University Press, 2009).

78. The concept of Judaic Zionism is similar to that of "neo-Zionism," which was popularized by the Israeli sociologist Uri Ram; for example, "Post-Zionist Studies of Israel: The First Decade," *Israel Studies Forum* 20, no. 2 (2005): 22–45. The term "neo-Zionism" has been widely used by critics of Zionism with particular reference to the post-1967 settlement enterprise in the Occupied Palestinian Territories. But as Amal Jamal has pointed out, many aspects of neo-Zionism in fact predate 1967. Amal Jamal, "Neo-Zionism and Palestine: The Unveiling of Settler-Colonial Practices in Mainstream Zionism," *Journal of Holy Land and Palestine Studies* 16, no. 1 (2017): 47–78. I see no reason to attach the prefix "neo" to something that is not new and, in fact, is entangled with forms of Zionism dating to the interwar period.

79. Cited in Yona Hadari-Ramage, "War and Religiosity: The Sinai Campaign in Public Thought," in *Israel: The First Decade of Independence* ed. S. Ilan Troen and Noah Lucas (Albany: SUNY Press, 1995), 364.

80. Yosef Ber Soloveitchik, "Kol Dodi Dofek" (1956), https://www.sefaria.org/Kol_Dodi_Dofek?lang=bi (accessed December 6, 2021).

81. Norman Lamm, "Our Dependence upon Israel's Independence" (1966), archives.yu.edu/gsdi/collect/lammserm/index/assoc/HASHcade/dir-doc.pdf (accessed December 6, 2021).

82. Yaacov Shavit, *The New Hebrew Nation: A Study in Israeli Heresy and Fantasy* (London: Frank Cass, 1987); James Diamond, *Homeland or Holy Land? The 'Canaanite' Critique of Israel* (Bloomington: Indiana University Press, 1986); Roman Vater, "'A Hebrew from Samaria, Not a Jew from Yavneh': Adya Gur

Horon (1907–1972) and the Articulation of Hebrew Nationalism" (PhD diss., University of Manchester, 2015).

83. Peter Bergson, "Post-Zionism" (Letter to the Editor), *New York Herald Tribune*, December 10, 1947; Eri Jabotinsky, "Israel and Zionism: Why Israel Has No Constitution," in *The Levant: Behind the Arab Curtain* (New York: Levant Press, 1952), 44.

84. "Ultra-Orthodox Are Proud Israelis Who Don't Feel Oppressed, Survey Shows," *Haaretz*, July 17, 2020. Levels of ultra-Orthodox identification with Israel vary by gender, ethnic origin, and sectarian affiliation. Among women, 77 percent feel "pride" in being Israeli; among men the figure is 64 percent. Ultra-Orthodox Jews of Middle Eastern and North African origin are more likely to feel at home in Israel than are Jews of Eastern European origin. Among the latter, Hasidim, adherents of a mass mystical movement originating in the eighteenth century, are more strongly attached to Israel than anti-Hasidic "Lithuanian" ultra-Orthodox Jews.

85. Sara Yael Hirschhorn, *City on a Hilltop: American Jews and the Israeli Settler Movement* (Cambridge, MA: Harvard University Press, 2017), 173–175.

CHAPTER 2 — ZIONISM AS COLONIALISM

1. Yoram Hazony, *The Virtue of Nationalism* (New York: Basic Books, 2018).

2. Fayez Sayegh, *Zionist Colonialism in Palestine* (Beirut: Palestine Liberation Organization Research Center, 1965), https://www.freedomarchives.org/Documents/Finder/DOC12_scans/12.zionist.colonialism.palestine.1965.pdf. Quotation is from page 5.

3. For UN General Assembly Resolution 3151, see p. 33, https://digitallibrary.un.org/record/642340?ln=en; and for Resolution 3379, see p. 84, https://documents-dds-ny.un.org/doc/RESOLUTION/GEN/NR0/000/92/IMG/NR000092.pdf?OpenElement (accessed June 12, 2022). For the 1975 *Report of the World Conference of the International Women's Year* see p. 3. https://documents-dds-ny.un.org/doc/UNDOC/GEN/N76/353/95/PDF/N7635395.pdf?OpenElement (accessed June 12, 2022).

4. Maxime Rodinson, *Israel: A Colonial-Settler State?* (Atlanta: Pathfinder Press, 1973); Edward W. Said, "Zionism from the Standpoint of Its Victims," *Social Text* 1 (1979): 7–58.

5. Said, "Zionism from the Standpoint of Its Victims," 28–29.

6. Lorenzo Veracini, *Settler Colonialism: A Theoretical Overview* (Basingstoke, UK: Palgrave Macmillan, 2010), 17–52.

7. Lorenzo Veracini, *Israel and Settler Society* (London: Pluto Press, 2006); Baruch Kimmerling, *Zionism and Territory: The Socio-Territorial Dimensions of Zionist Politics* (Berkeley: Institute of International Studies, University of California, 1983); Gershon Shafir, *Land, Labor and the Origins of the Israeli-Palestinian Conflict, 1882–1914* (Cambridge: Cambridge University Press, 1989); and Gabriel Piterberg, *The Returns of Zionism: Myths, Politics and Scholarship in Israel* (London: Verso, 2008).

8. See, for example, Omar Jabary, Mezna Qato, Kareem Rabie, and Sobhi Samour, "Past is Present: Settler Colonialism in Palestine," *Settler Colonial Studies* 2, no. 1 (2012).

9. See, for example, Leila Farsakh, "Palestinian Economic Development: Paradigm Shifts since the First Intifada," *Journal of Palestine Studies* 45, no. 2 (2016): 55–71; Adam Hanieh, "Development as Struggle: Confronting the Reality of Power in Palestine," *Journal of Palestine Studies* 45, no. 4 (2016): 32–47; Nadim Rouhana and Areej Sabbagh-Khoury, "Memory and the Return of History in a Settler-Colonial Context," in *Israel and Its Palestinian Citizens,* ed. Nadim Rouhana and Sahar Huneidi (Cambridge: Cambridge University Press, 2017), 393–432; and Rashid Khalidi, *The Hundred Years' War on Palestine: A History of Settler Colonialism and Resistance, 1917–2017* (New York: Macmillan, 2020).

10. Hermann Giliomee, *The Afrikaners: Biography of a People* (London: Hurt & Co., 2011), xiii–xiv.

11. Nicole Eustace, *Passion Is the Gale: Emotion, Power, and the Coming of the American Revolution* (Chapel Hill, NC: University of North Carolina Press, 2008), and *1812: War and the Passions of Patriotism* (Philadelphia: University of Pennsylvania Press, 2012).

12. Alexander Schölch, *Palästina im Umbruch 1856–1882: Untersuchungen zur wirtschaftlichen und sozio-politischen Entwicklung* (Stuttgart: Steiner, 1986); Gudrun Krämer, *A History of Palestine: From the Ottoman Conquest to the Founding of the State of Israel* (Princeton, NJ: Princeton University Press, 2008), 71–100.

13. Moshe Leib Lilienblum, "'Al tihiyat yisrael 'al adamat avotav," *Kol Kitvei Moshe Leib Lilienblum* (Odesa: Tseitlin Press, 1912–13), v. IV, 31, 60. See also his essay "Ha-regesh ve-ha-mitzvah be-'inyan ha-yishuv," in the same volume, 207–227.

14. Quotations are taken from the English translation in Julius Schoeps, *Pioneers of Zionism: Hess, Pinsker, Rülf* (Berlin: De Gruyter, 2013), 122–125.

15. Reproduced in Ben-Tsion Dinur, chief ed., *Sefer toledot ha-haganah* (Jerusalem: Ha-sifriyah ha-tsiyonit, 1954), I: 4–5.

16. Simmons, *Hadassah and the Zionist Project* (Lanham, MD: Rowman & Littlefield), 2006; Ariella Kahan, "Friends or Foes? Palestinian Arabs in the Eyes of

American Women Zionists, 1929–1948" (Cambridge, MA: Harvard Library, 2020).

17. Areej Sabbagh-Khoury, "Colonization Practices and Interactions at the Frontier: Ha-Shomer Ha-Tzair Kibbutzim and the Surrounding Arab Villages at the Margins of the Valley of Jezreel/Marj Ibn 'Amer, 1936–1956" (PhD diss., Tel Aviv University, 2015).

18. Scott Atran, "The Surrogate Colonization of Palestine, 1917–1939," *American Ethnologist* 16, no. 4 (1989): 719–744.

19. Derek Penslar, "Rebels without a Patron State: How Israel Financed the 1948 War," in *Purchasing Power: The Economic Dimensions of Modern Jewish Life*, ed. Rebecca Kobrin and Adam Teller (Philadelphia: University of Pennsylvania Press, 2015), 171–192.

20. Deborah A. Starr and Sasson Somekh, eds., *Mongrels or Marvels: The Levantine Writings of Jacqueline Shohet Kahanoff* (Stanford, CA: Stanford University Press, 2011), 180.

21. Theodor Herzl, *The Jewish State* (New York: American Zionist Emergency Council, 1946), 15, and *The Complete Diaries of Theodor Herzl* (New York: Herzl Press, 1960), 69, 210.

22. Derek Penslar, *Zionism and Technocracy: The Engineering of Jewish Settlement in Palestine, 1870–1918* (Bloomington: Indiana University Press, 1991), 19.

23. Mark Levine, *Overthrowing Geography: Jaffa, Tel Aviv, and the Struggle for Palestine, 1880–1948* (Berkeley: University of California Press, 2005); Eric Zakim, *To Build and Be Built: Landscape, Literature, and the Construction of Zionist Identity* (Philadelphia: University of Pennsylvania Press, 2006); Liora Halperin, *Babel in Zion: Jews, Nationalism, and Language Diversity in Palestine, 1920–1948* (New Haven, CT: Yale University Press, 2014).

24. Menachem Klein, *Lives in Common: Arabs and Jews in Jerusalem, Jaffa, and Hebron* (New York: Oxford University Press, 2014).

25. Tami Razi, "'Yehudiyot-Araviyot?' Etniyut, le'umiyut u-migdar be-tel-aviv ha-mandatorit," *Teoriyah u-Vikoret* 38–39 (2011): 137–160.

26. Yehouda Shenhav, *The Arab Jews: A Postcolonial Reading of Nationalism, Religion, and Ethnicity* (Stanford, CA: Stanford University Press, 2005).

27. Abigail Jacobson and Moshe Naor, *Oriental Neighbors: Middle Eastern Jews and Arabs in Mandatory Palestine* (Waltham, MA: Brandeis University Press, 2016), 188–189.

28. Yuval Evri and Hagar Kotef, "When Does a Native Become a Settler? (With Apologies to Zreik and Mamdani)," *Constellations* 29, no. 1 (2022), 3–18. See also Caroline Kahlenberg, "How Locals Became Settlers: Mizrahi Jews and

Bodily Capital in Palestine, 1908–1948" (PhD diss., Harvard University, 2021); and the short but pithy intervention by Jonathan Gribetz, "'To the Arab Hebrew': On Possibilities and Impossibilities," *International Journal of Middle East Studies* 46, no. 3 (2014): 589–592.

29. John Efron, "From Mitteleuropa to the Middle East: Orientalism through a Jewish Lens," *Jewish Quarterly Review* 94 (2004): 490–520; Susannah Heschel, "Orientalist Triangulations: Jewish Scholarship on Islam as a Response to Christian Europe," in *The Muslim Reception of European Orientalism: Reversing the Gaze*, ed. Susannah Heschel and Umar Ryad (London: Routledge, 2019), 147–167.

30. Gil Eyal, *The Disenchantment of the Orient: Expertise in Arab Affairs and the Israeli State* (Stanford, CA: Stanford University Press, 2008), 62–93.

31. Yael Zerubavel, "Memory, the Rebirth of the Native, and the 'Hebrew Bedouin' Identity," *Social Research* 75, no. 1 (2008): 320–321.

32. Liora Halperin, *The Oldest Guard: Forging the Zionist Settler Past* (Stanford, CA: Stanford University Press, 2021).

33. Hillel Cohen, *Year Zero of the Arab-Israeli Conflict: 1929* (Waltham, MA: Brandeis University Press, 2015).

34. Caroline Kahlenberg, "The Tarbush Transformation: Oriental Jewish Men and the Significance of Headgear in Ottoman and British Mandate Palestine," *Journal of Social History* 52, no. 4 (2019): 1212–1249.

35. See Mitch Ginsburg's definitive translation in "When Moshe Dayan Delivered the Defining Speech of Zionism," *Times of Israel*, April 28, 2016, https://www.timesof israel.com/when-moshe-dayan-delivered-the-defining-speech-of-zionism/.

36. Yael Zerubavel, *Desert in the Promised Land* (Stanford, CA: Stanford University Press, 2019). Barak's speech is available at https://mfa.gov.il/mfa/mfa-archive /1996/pages/fm%20barak-%20address%20to%20njcrac%20-%20feb%2011-%20 1996.aspx (accessed December 30, 2021).

37. Derek Penslar, "Herzl and the Palestinian Arabs: Between Myth and Counter-Myth," *Journal of Israeli History* 24 (2004): 65–77.

38. Constantin Zureiq's short book *Mana't al-Nakba* (The Meaning of Disaster), published in Arabic in 1948 and eight years later in English translation (Beirut: Khayat, 1956), used the word "Nakba" to describe the failure of the Arab world to defend Palestine. But over time the more specific meaning of the Palestinian exodus gained currency.

39. In South Africa, apartheid became official policy in 1948, but its origins may be traced to the segregationist Land Act of 1913. The Land Act was abolished in 1991.

40. Marc Bloch, "A Contribution towards a Comparative History of European Societies," in *Land and Work in Medieval Society* (Berkeley: University of California Press, 1967), 58; George M. Frederickson, *The Comparative Imagination* (Berkeley: University of California Press, 2000), 7–13.

41. Johannes Becke, "Towards a De-Occidentalist Perspective on Israel: The Case of the Occupation," *Journal of Israeli History* 33 (2014): 1–23. See also *Settlers in Contested Lands: Territorial Dispute and Ethnic Conflicts*, ed. Oded Haklai and Noephytos Loizides (Stanford, CA: Stanford University Press, 2015); Awet Tewelde Weldemichael, *Third World Colonialism and Strategies of Liberation: Eritrea and East Timor Compared* (Cambridge: Cambridge University Press, 2013).

42. Kate Brown, *A Biography of No Place: From Ethnic Borderland to Soviet Heartland* (Cambridge, MA: Harvard University Press, 2004), chap. 7.

43. Lorenzo Veracini, "The Other Shift: Settler Colonialism, Israel, and the Occupation," *Journal of Palestine Studies* 42, no. 3 (2013), 26–42; Becke, "Towards a De-Occidentalist Perspective."

44. On the interplay between cultural and environmental forces behind the creation of the "new Hebrew," see sympathetic accounts in Oz Almog, *The Sabra: The Creation of the New Jew* (Berkeley: University of California Press, 2000); Anita Shapira, "The Bible and Israeli Identity," *Association for Jewish Studies Review* 28, no. 1 (2004): 11–41; Shapira, *Yigal Allon, Native Son: A Biography* (Philadelphia: University of Pennsylvania Press, 2012), 1–34; along with the critical perspective of Piterberg, *Returns of Zionism*.

45. Zali Gurevitch and Gideon Aran, "Al ha-makom: anthropologya yisre'elit," *Alpayim* 4 (1991): 9–44.

46. John Canup, *Out of the Wilderness: The Emergence of an American Identity in Colonial New England* (Middleton, CT: Wesleyan University Press, 1990), 12–13.

47. Boaz Neumann, *Land and Desire in Early Zionism* (Waltham, MA: Brandeis University Press, 2011).

48. Reproduced in Canup, *Out of the Wilderness*, 82.

49. Hermann Giliomee and Lawrence Schlemmer, *From Apartheid to Nation-Building* (Oxford: Oxford University Press, 1990), 3–4; Frederickson, *Comparative Imagination*, 54–55.

50. The Hebrew literary scholar Yaron Peleg has portrayed Zionist writers in late Ottoman Palestine as mostly incurious about Arabs. As Peleg relates, however, there was an important exception: Moshe Smilansky's collection of stories *B'nei 'Arav*, published in 1911 under the pseudonym Khawaja Musa (*Orientalism*

and the Hebrew Imagination [Ithaca, NY: Cornell University Press, 2005], 76). Moreover, only one story in the collection, "Latifa," portrays a male Jew expressing interest in a female Arab. In this story, the female is a fourteen-year-old girl, described primarily in terms of the beauty of her eyes, and the Jewish narrator's interests in her appear to be more fraternal and protective than erotic. An English translation of the story was published in Moshe Smilansky, *Palestine Caravan* (London: Methuen & Co, 1935), 265–269.

51. Yaron Peleg, "Heroic Conduct: Homoeroticism and the Creation of Modern, Jewish Masculinities," *Jewish Social Studies* 13, no. 1 (2006): 31–58.

52. Canup, *Out of the Wilderness*, 219.

53. Canup, *Out of the Wilderness*, 219.

54. Giliomee and Schlemmer, *From Apartheid to Nation-Building*, 20; Saul Dubow, *Racial Segregation and the Origins of Apartheid in South Africa, 1919–1936.* (Oxford: Macmillan/St Antony's College, 1989), 4.

55. Giliomee and Schlemmer, *From Apartheid to Nation-Building*, 50. Giliomee, *Afrikaners*, 404, 470, 474.

56. Frederickson, *Comparative Imagination*, 39, 44–46.

57. Even with the Negev desert, which takes up the southern half of the area, in the late nineteenth century Palestine's population density was almost four times that of North or South America; without the Negev, it was similar to that of Lebanon.

58. Leonard Thompson, *A History of South Africa* (New Haven, CT: Yale University Press, 2000), 160.

59. Sami Shalom Chetrit, *Intra-Jewish Conflict in Israel: White Jews, Black Jews* (London: Routledge, 2009); Bryan Roby, *The Mizrahi Era of Rebellion: Israel's Forgotten Civil Rights Struggle 1948–1966* (Syracuse, NY: Syracuse University Press, 2015).

60. Excerpt from a 1981 documentary about the Israeli elections of that year, "Begin Speech 1981," https://www.youtube.com/watch?v=u-OhAJyyubQ (accessed December 30, 2021).

61. Ella Shohat, "Sephardim in Israel: Zionism from the Standpoint of Its Jewish Victims," *Social Text* 19/20 (1988): 1–35.

62. David Prochaska, *Making Algeria French: Colonialism in Bône, 1870–1920* (Cambridge: Cambridge University Press, 1990); Patricia M. E. Lorcin, "Rome and France in Africa: Recovering Colonial Algeria's Latin Past," *French Historical Studies* 25, no. 2 (2002): 295–329.

63. David Carroll, "Camus's Algeria: Birthrights, Colonial Injustice, and the Fiction of a French-Algerian People," *MLN* 112, no. 4, (1997): 517.

64. Carroll, "Camus's Algeria," 571.

65. Compare Kimmerling, *Zionism and Territory*, with Frederickson, *Comparative Imagination*, 55–56.

66. Thompson, *History of South Africa,* 144–145, 155–167; Giliomee and Schlemmer, *From Apartheid to Nation-Building*, 9–21, 31.

67. Neumann, *Land and Desire*, 78–115.

68. Giliomee, *Afrikaners*, 215–224, 366, 372, 376–377, 429; Emanuel Sivan, "Colonialism and Popular Culture in Algeria," *Journal of Contemporary History* 14, no. 1 (1979): 21–53; David Prochaska, "History as Literature, Literature as History: Cagayous of Algiers," *American Historical Review* 101, no. 3 (1996): 670–711.

69. Shachar Pinsker, *Literary Passports: The Making of Modernist Hebrew Fiction in Europe* (Stanford, CA: Stanford University Press, 2011), and *A Rich Brew: How Cafés Created Modern Jewish Culture* (New York: New York University Press, 2018).

70. Gurevitch and Aran, "Al ha-makom." In the Hebrew, the authors differentiate between *makom* with "mem gadol" and "mem katan" (M and m).

CHAPTER 3 — ZIONISM TO 1948

1. I cannot provide definitive quantitative evidence of the popularity of these terms, but a Google Ngram of "hibat tsion" and "Hovevei Tsion" in Hebrew texts shows they first appeared in the late 1870s, increased in use until about 1900, and then declined rapidly, only to shoot up exponentially after 1930. During the first peak, I assume that Jewish nationalists identified themselves in these terms, whereas by the time of the second wave of popularity, hibat tsion had become a historical phenomenon and the object of commemorative writing.

2. Naomi Seidman, *The Marriage-Plot, or, How Jews Fell in Love with Love—and with Literature* (Stanford, CA: Stanford University Press, 2016), 32. See also Olga Litvak, *Haskalah: The Romantic Movement in Judaism* (New Brunswick, NJ: Rutgers University Press, 2011), 136–145.

3. Abraham Mapu, *The Love of Zion* (New Milford, CT: Toby Press, 2006), 11–12.

4. Mapu, *Love of Zion*, 27.

5. Mapu, *Love of Zion*, 70.

6. Mapu, *Love of Zion*, 84.

7. Moses Hess, *Rome and Jerusalem: A Study in Jewish Nationalism* (New York: Bloch, 1918), 43.

8. Hess, *Rome and Jerusalem*, 86.

9. Hess, *Rome and Jerusalem*, 125.

10. Hess, *Rome and Jerusalem*, 141.

11. Hess, *Rome and Jerusalem*, 45.

12. Marcus Pyka, *Jüdische Identität bei Heinrich Graetz* (Göttingen: Vandenhoeck & Ruprecht, 2009), 234.

13. Jeffrey Blutinger, "Writing for the Masses: Heinrich Graetz, the Popularization of Jewish History, and the Reception of National Judaism" (PhD diss., University of California at Los Angeles, 2003), 261.

14. Heinrich Graetz, "The Rejuvenation of the Jewish Race," in *The Structure of Jewish History and Other Essays*, ed. Ismar Schorsch (New York: Jewish Theological Seminary, 1975), 148.

15. Heinrich Graetz, *Geschichte der Juden vom Beginne der Mendelssohnschen Zeit 1750 bis in die neueste Zeit 1848* (Leipzig: Leiner, 1870), vi.

16. Heinrich Graetz, *Tagebuch und Briefe* (Tübingen: Mohr, 1977), 322.

17. Heinrich Graetz, *Volkstümliche Geschichte der Juden* (Berlin: Benjamin Harz, 1923), 39.

18. George Eliot, *Daniel Deronda* (New York: Modern Library, 2002), 485.

19. Eliot addressed the restoration of the Jews at greater length in her essay "The Modern Hep! Hep! Hep!=" published in 1879. Eliot justifies the return of Jews to Palestine in terms of contemporary political conditions and the Jews' own possession of "an adequate community of feeling as well as widespread need in the Jewish race." The path to the Jews' "renovated national dignity," writes Eliot, is their own sense of historic bond with their "illustrious prophets," because "the effective bond of human action is feeling, and the worthy child of a people owning the triple name of Hebrew, Israelite, and Jew feels his kinship with the glories and sorrows, the degradation and the possible renovation of his national family," http://www.online-literature.com/george_eliot/theophrastus -such/18/ (accessed March 21, 2019).

20. From a biographical work written by Sokolow in 1889, reproduced in Shmuel Verses, "Daniel Deronda ba-'intonut uva-sifrut ha-ivrit," *Molad* 8, no. 39–40 (1980): 180.

21. Mikhal Dekel, "Who Taught this Foreign Woman about the Ways and Lives of the Jews? George Eliot and the Hebrew Renaissance," *English Literary History* 74, no. 4 (2007): 785.

22. I am quoting from the unpaginated Hebrew text of the introduction and the novel, available at http://benyehuda.org/frischmann/daniel.deronda.html (accessed May 30, 2018).

23. Reproduced in *Die Welt* 3, January 19, 1900, 14. The hymn was adopted by the Zionist society Kadima in Vienna, and in the early twentieth century, a copy of the sheet music was advertised in the Zionist newspaper *Die Welt* as a premium for purchasing annual membership in the Zionist Organization.

24. *Meshorerei hibat tsion: Toldoteihem u-mihvar shireihem shel M. M. Dolitzky, M. Ts., Maneh, K. A. Shapira, N. H. Imber* (Tel Aviv: Drimer, 1949/1950), 9–11. On the hymn's creation and reception, see Eliyahu Hacohen, "'Al harerei tsion: be-hipus ahar hymnon le'umi," in *Lesoheah im ha-'aliyah ha-rishonah*, ed. Yafa Berkowitz and Yossi Land (Tel Aviv: Ha-kibbutz Ha-me'uhad, 2010), 233–242.

25. *Meshorerei hibat tsion*, 6.

26. Cited in Ethel Lithman, *The Man Who Wrote Hatikvah* (London: Cazenove, 1979), 86. The poem "Watch on the Jordan" was consciously modeled after the German nationalist hymn "Die Wacht am Rhein" and was even sung to its melody. The translation made by the Anglo-Jewish writer Israel Zangwill ably captures its militant spirit:

Rest in peace, loved land,
For we rest not, but stand . . .
When the bolts of war rattle,
To shirk not the battle . . .
When our trumpet is blown,
And our standard is flown,
Then we set our watch!

Reproduced in J. Kabako, ed., *Master of Hope: Selected Writings of Naphtali Herz Imber* (London: Herzl Press, 1985), 334–335.

27. The poem is available in Hebrew, Hebrew with Roman alphabetical transliteration, and English translation; see http://www.nationalanthems.info /il_%27.htm (accessed May 17, 2021).

28. "May they grow strong, the hands of our gifted brothers. . . . Don't let your spirits fall, but be joyous, with song. . . . Come, with one voice, shoulder to

shoulder, to the aid of the people." Hayim Nahman Bialik, "Birkat Ha-Am," https://benyehuda.org/bialik/bia010.html (accessed March 30, 2019).

29. Edwin Seroussi, *"Hatikvah*: Conceptions, Receptions, and Reflections," *Yuval Online* 9 (2015): 11, http://www.jewish-music.huji.ac.il. See also Cecil Bloom, "Imber, His Poem, and a National Anthem," *Jewish Historical Studies* 32 (1990–1992): 317–336.

30. No less effective was the stirring, majestic melody of "Hatikvah." The power of Cohen's melody is demonstrated by the fact that another composer in the Jewish agricultural colonies, Leon Igly, had earlier set Imber's poem to music, but it never caught on because its complex melodic structure; Hacohen, "Al harerei tsion," 245–246. On the power of music to move humans into high-intensity emotional states, including the experience of the sublime, see James Loeffler, "When Hermann Cohen Cried: Zionism, Culture and Emotions," *Jewish Social Studies*, forthcoming.

31. The final lines of Mapu's *The Love of Zion* speak of hope—"I have hoped, my love, I have hoped, and your love is dearer to me than life"—but this hope is for the resolution of a personal, not collective, crisis and for the attainment of true love, not the restoration of Zion.

32. The quotations from Bloch's work are reproduced in Richard H. Roberts, "An Introductory Reading of Ernst Bloch's 'The Principle of Hope,'" *Literature and Theology* 1, no. 1 (1987): 89–112.

33. Yosef Hayim Yerushalmi, "Toward a History of Jewish Hope," in *The Faith of Fallen Jews*, ed. David N. Myers and Alexander Kaye (Waltham, MA: Brandeis University Press, 2013), 310, 314.

34. Leon Pinsker, *Auto-Emancipation: An Appeal to His People by a Russian Jew*, n.p., https://www.jewishvirtuallibrary.org/quot-auto-emancipation-quot -leon-pinsker (accessed March 29, 2019).

35. Isaak Rülf, "Aruchas Bas-Ammi: Israels Heilung" (1883), reproduced in Julius H. Schoeps, *Pioneers of Zionism: Hess, Pinsker, Rülf*, ed. Julius H. Schoeps (Berlin: De Gruyter, 2013), 123.

36. I develop these themes in *Theodor Herzl: The Charismatic Leader* (New Haven, CT: Yale University Press, 2020).

37. Nordau to Herzl, February 26, 1896, Central Zionist Archive, Jerusalem, H1\1692-18.

38. Arthur Hertzberg, *The Zionist Idea* (New York: Harper & Row, 1959), 482.

39. Hertzberg, *Zionist Idea*, 499.

40. Hertzberg, *Zionist Idea*, 521.

41. Compare Peter Stearns, *Shame: A Brief History* (Urbana: University of Illinois Press, 2017), with Ute Frevert, *Emotions in History: Lost and Found* (Budapest: Central University Press, 2011), 37–85.

42. Ute Frevert, *The Politics of Humiliation: A Modern History* (New York: Oxford University Press, 2020).

43. Hertzberg, *Zionist Idea*, 265.

44. Anita Shapira, "Herzl, Ahad Ha-Am, and Berdichevsky: Comments on their Nationalist Concepts," *Jewish History* 4, no. 2 (1990): 63–64.

45. Shapira, "Herzl, Ahad Ha-Am, and Berdichevsky," 64.

46. In fact, some men did engage in self-defense, but to no avail. On the creation of the poem, see Steven J. Zipperstein, *Pogrom. Kishinev and the Tilt of History* (New York: Liveright, 2018), 109–143. For a complete English translation of the poem, see H. N. Bialik, "The City of Slaughter," in *Complete Poetic Works of Hayyim Nahman Bialik*, ed. Israel Efros (New York: Histadruth Ivrit of America, 1948), I: 129–43.

47. Jonathan Marc Gribetz, *Defining Neighbors: Religion, Race, and the Early Zionist-Arab Encounter* (Princeton, NJ: Princeton University Press, 2014), 128–130.

48. Nissim Ya'acov Malul, "Our Status in the Country, or the Question of Learning Arabic," in *Modern Middle Eastern Jewish Thought: Writings on Identity, Politics, and Culture, 1893–1958*, ed. Moshe Behar and Zvi Ben-Dor Benite (Waltham, MA: Brandeis University Press, 2013), 67.

49. Malul, "Our Status in the Country," 69.

50. On the origins of modern Hebrew literature prior to and external to Zionism, see Shachar Pinsker, *Literary Passports: The Making of Modernist Hebrew Fiction in Europe* (Stanford, CA: Stanford University Press, 2010). On the role of Hebraism in the fin de siècle Yishuv, see Arieh Saposnik, *Becoming Hebrew: The Creation of a Jewish National Culture Babel in Zion* (New York: Oxford University Press, 2008)

51. See the discussion of Bialik's essay "Concealment and Revealment in Language," in William Cutter, "Ghostly Hebrew, Ghastly Speech: Scholem to Rosenzweig, 1926," *Prooftexts* 10 (1990): 420.

52. Both the German original and English translation are reproduced in full in Cutter, "Ghostly Hebrew, Ghastly Speech." The quotations are taken from the English translation on pages 417–418.

53. The philosopher Jacques Derrida read the letter somewhat differently, claiming that Scholem both dreaded and anticipated Zionism's apocalyptic potential and that Scholem saw Hebrew maintaining its sacrality, even when vulgarized. Annabel Herzog, "'Monolingualism' or the Language of God: Scholem and Derrida on Hebrew and Politics," *Modern Judaism* 29, no. 2 (2009): 226–238.

54. Anita Shapira, *Berl: The Biography of a Socialist Zionist: Berl Katznelson, 1887–1944* (Cambridge: Cambridge University Press, 1984).

55. In 1991, the book was published in English translation under the less revealing title *The Blue Mountain*.

56. Boaz Neumann, *Land and Desire in Early Zionism* (Waltham, MA: Brandeis University Press, 2011), 39.

57. See his 1928 poem "Toil," in *Modern Hebrew Poetry: A Bilingual Anthology*, ed. and trans. Ruth Finer Mitz (Berkeley: University of California Press, 1966), 178–187.

58. Dafna N. Izraeli, "The Zionist Women's Movement in Palestine, 1911–1927: A Sociological Analysis," *Signs* 7, no. 1 (1981): 101.

59. Reproduced in Dror Abend-David, "Gender Benders and Unrequited Offerings: Two Hebrew Poems by Rachel Bluwstein-Sela and Dovid Hofshteyn," *Prooftexts* 31, no. 3 (2011): 210–211.

60. Batya Brenner, *The Plough Woman: Records of the Pioneer Women of Palestine—A Critical Edition*, ed. Mark A. Raider and Miriam B. Raider-Roth (Lebanon, NH: Brandeis University Press, 2002), 57. Brenner was the sister of the Hebrew writer Yosef Haim Brenner.

61. The quotation is cited by the philosopher Franz Rosenzweig in his introduction to Cohen's *Jüdische Schriften*, I: lx, and is reproduced in Lawrence Kaplan, "Suffering and Joy in the Thought of Hermann Cohen," *Modern Judaism* 21, no. 1 (2001): 16.

62. On the source of the melody, the dating of its transcription by Abraham Zvi Idelsohn, and disputes over whether Idelsohn or Moshe Nathanson wrote the lyrics, see Edwin Seroussi and James Loeffler, "The Secret History of 'Hava Nagila,'" *Tablet*, September 19, 2019, https://www.tabletmag.com/sections/arts-letters/articles/secret-history-hava-nagila.

63. For a broader historical and biographical context on Ha-Shomer Ha-Tsa'ir and Ya'ari, see Ofer Nur, *Eros and Tragedy: Jewish Male Fantasies and the Masculine Revolution of Zionism* (Boston: Academic Studies Press, 2014); and Aviva Halamsih,

Kibbutz: Utopia and Politics: The Life and Times of Meir Yaari, 1897–1987 (Boston: Academic Studies Press, 2017). Ha-Shomer Ha-Tsa'ir became a kibbutz movement and political party (later known as Mapam), of which Ya'ari was a longtime leader.

64. Many thanks to the journalist Dina Kraft, Pollak's great-niece, for sharing her family story, which is confirmed (though without mentioning Pollak by name) in Amos Elon, *The Israelis: Founders and Sons* (New York: Penguin, 1981), 144.

65. Kraft learned the shocking truth about the commune when she found her great-uncle's tombstone in the Kinneret cemetery. The Israeli journalist Yael Chen wrote up the story in "Ha-kever," *Maariv Sofshavua'*, July 10, 1992, 10–15.

66. Almog, *Sabra*, esp. 3, 6, 19–20, 61–72, 157–59. Matan Boord's ongoing research demonstrates that this vision of the sabra was very much an ideal type, not a reflection of lived reality. For a similar discussion of the myth of the British "stiff upper lip," see Thomas Dixon, *Weeping Britannia: Portrait of a Nation in Tears* (New York: Oxford University Press, 2015).

67. *Davar,* December 19, 1947.

68. Hizky Shoham, *Carnival in Tel Aviv: Purim and the Celebration of Urban Zionism* (Boston: Academic Studies Press, 2014).

69. Menachem Klein, *Lives in Common: Arabs and Jews in Jerusalem, Jaffa, and Hebron* (London: Hurst, 2014), 87–89.

70. Neumann, *Land and Desire*, 93.

71. On the 1929 riots as the key event leading to a hardening of and separation between Jewish and Arab identities in Mandate Palestine, see Hillel Cohen, *Year Zero of the Arab-Israeli Conflict: 1929* (Waltham, MA: Brandeis University Press, 2015).

72. Oz Almog, *The Sabra: The Creation of the New Jew* (Berkeley: University of California Press, 2000), 192–193, 196–197.

73. "Response to the Arab Riots," reproduced in Eran Kaplan and Derek Penslar, eds., *The Origins of Israel, 1882–1948: A Documentary History* (Madison: University of Wisconsin Press, 2011), 221. For a thorough treatment of Zionist–Arab labor relations during the period of the Yishuv and a thoughtful deconstruction of Zionist claims to have benefited Arab workers, see Zachary Lockman, *Comrades and Enemies: Arab and Jewish Workers in Palestine, 1906–1948* (Berkeley: University of California Press, 1996).

74. Shapira, *Land and Power.* The term still appears in the IDF Code of Ethics; see https://www.sefaria.org/sheets/361396.27?lang=bi&with=all&lang2=en (accessed August 19, 2022).

75. On the global history of Palestine during the early years of the war, see Dan Diner, *Ein Anderer Krieg: Das Jüdische Palästina und der Zweite Weltkrieg 1935–1942* (Munich: Deutsche Verlags-Anstalt, 2021).

76. Dina Porat, *The Blue and the Yellow Stars of David: The Zionist Leadership in Palestine and the Holocaust, 1939–1945* (Cambridge, MA: Harvard University Press, 1990).

77. Oz Almog, *The Sabra: The Creation of the New Jew.* Berkeley: University of California Press, 2000, 202–208. Almog goes so far as to claim that most Israeli soldiers in 1948 did not feel hatred or a lust for vengeance, but massacres of Palestinian civilians and looting of their property suggest otherwise. See Benny Morris, *The Birth of the Palestinian Refugee Problem Revisited* (New York: Cambridge University Press, 2004.) Moreover, Shay Hazkani has documented that depictions of Arabs in training materials for IDF soldiers were crafted to spark hatred and rage against Arabs; Hazkani, *Dear Palestine: A Social History of the 1948 War* (Stanford, CA: Stanford University Press, 2021). I deal with this subject in chapter 6.

78. In Israel there is a popular myth that the new arrivals were unfit to fight and died in droves as cannon fodder, particularly in the IDF's unsuccessful attempts to conquer the Latrun salient from Jordan. In fact the newcomers fought well, did not die at disproportionately high rates, and some had served in European armies before the war. Yaakov Markovitsky, *Gahelet lohemet: Giyus hutz la-aretz be-milhemet ha-atsma'ut* (Tel Aviv: Ministry of Defense, 1995). The book's arguments are nicely summarized in Markovitsky, "Ha-gahal: Giyus hutz la-aretz be-milhemet ha-atsma'ut," in *Milhemet ha-atsma'ut tasha"ch tasha"t: diyun mehudash*, ed. Alon Kadish (Tel Aviv: Ministry of Defense), 2004, 525–537.

79. According to a survey carried out by the Branch for Public Opinion Research of the Haganah (the Yishuv's primary militia) in Haifa in March 1948, "Two bank managers, who took a leave of absence for more than six months, went overseas claiming that they prefer being jobless than in constant danger. . . . The number of those willing to flee the country for the duration is increasing. The interviewer witnessed a young man falsifying documents in Yiddish for a friend who sought permission from the authorities to leave the country in order to visit his supposedly gravely ill mother." Haganah Archive, Tel Aviv, 80/54/2.

80. The surveys and supplementary materials are in the Haganah Archive, Tel Aviv, 80/54/2.

81. Moshe Naor, *Social Mobilization in the Arab/Israeli War of 1948: On the Israeli Home Front* (London: Routledge, 2013).

82. Nathan Alterman, "Leyl ha-matsor," in *Simhat ha-'aniyim* (Tel Aviv: Mahbarot le-sifrut, 1941, 87.

83. *Hatzofeh le-yeladim,* July 8, 1948, reproduced in "Itonut lohemet: Hishtakfut milhemet ha-atsma'ut be-itonei ha-yeladim," in *Am be-milhemah: kovitz mehkarim al ha-hevrah ha-ezrahit be-milhemet ha-atsma'ut,* ed. Mordechai Baron and Meir Chazan (Jerusalem: Yad Ben Zvi, 2007), 441–465.

84. Jeffrey Herf, *Nazi Propaganda for the Arab World* (New Haven, CT: Yale University Press, 2010).

85. Rona Yona, "A Kibbutz in the Diaspora: The Pioneer Movement in Poland and the Klosova Kibbutz," *Journal of Israeli History,* 31, no. 1 (2012): 9–43. As Kenneth Moss observed, however, during the 1930s many Polish Jews regarded Zionism through an opportunistic rather than idealistic lens; the increasingly bleak conditions of their lives and restrictive immigration laws in North America forced them to consider emigration to Palestine as a survival strategy, not a means of self- or collective fulfillment. See Kenneth Moss, *An Unchosen People: Jewish Political Reckoning in Interwar Poland* (Cambridge, MA: Harvard University Press, 2021).

86. Daniel Heller, "Obedient Children and Reckless Rebels: Jabotinsky's Youth Politics and the Case for Authoritarian Leadership, 1931–1933," *Journal of Israeli History* 34, no. 1 (2015): 45–68; and *Jabotinsky's Children: Polish Jews and the Rise of Right-Wing Zionism* (Princeton, NJ: Princeton University Press, 2017).

87. Erica Simmons, *Hadassah and the Zionist Project* (Lanham, MD: Rowman & Littlefield, 2006); Dvora Hacohen, *To Repair a Broken World: The Life of Henrietta Szold, Founder of Hadassah* (Cambridge, MA: Harvard University Press, 2021). For a list of Hadassah's initiatives, see Samuel Halperin, *The Political World of American Zionism* (Detroit: Wayne State University Press, 1961), appendix 5.

88. Naomi Cohen, *The Year after the Riots: American Jewish Responses to the Palestine Crisis of 1929–30* (Detroit: Wayne State University Press, 1988), 50, 63, 88, 91, 95.

89. From the Central Conference of American Rabbis' 1937 Columbus Platform, https://www.jewishvirtuallibrary.org/the-columbus-platform-1937 (accessed December 29, 2021).

90. Halperin, *Political World of American Zionism,* appendix 5. These figures combine membership in the Zionist Organization of America, Hadassah (the Women's Zionist Organization of America), the Labor Zionist organizations Poalei Tsion and Pioneer Women, and the Religious Zionist organizations Mizrahi and Mizrahi Women.

91. Menachem Kaufmann, *An Ambiguous Partnership: Non-Zionists and Zionists in America, 1939–1948* (Detroit: Wayne State University Press, 1991), 11–16. In 1944 the AJC undertook a reorganization that resulted in an increase in membership to eighteen thousand by 1949. But its executive remained the province of middle-aged, affluent professionals and businessmen, often of Central European origin. Until the early 1960s, the AJC as a whole remained, in the words of Naomi Cohen, an "exclusive club." Cohen, *Not Free to Desist: The American Jewish Committee, 1906–1966* (Philadelphia: Jewish Publication Society, 1972), 338.

92. Jonathan Sarna, *American Judaism* (New Haven, CT: Yale University Press, 2004), 263.

93. Dan Lainer-Vos, *Sinews of the Nation: Constructing Irish and Zionist Bonds in the United States* (New York: Polity, 2013), 46–47.

94. *The Sentinel* [Chicago], May 27, 1948, 31.

95. *The Sentinel*, April 22, 1948, 14.

96. Merle Curti, *American Philanthropy Abroad* (New Brunswick, NJ: Rutgers University Press, 1963), 524. I explore the 1948 UJA campaign in depth in "Solidarity as an Emotion: American Jews and Israel in 1948," *Modern American History* 5, no. 1 (2022): 27–51.

97. Deborah Dash Moore, *To the Golden Cities: Pursuing the American Jewish Dream in Miami and L.A.* (Cambridge, MA: Harvard University Press, 1996), 237–238.

98. Digital copy provided by the United States Holocaust Memorial Museum, https://collections.ushmm.org/search/catalog/bib241078.

99. Marc Lee Raphael, *A History of the United Jewish Appeal, 1939–1982* (Providence: Scholars Press, 1982), 37.

100. *UJA Report from Israel*, United States Holocaust Memorial Museum, RG-60.1348, Film ID: 2924.

101. I first learned of the song from my colleague Harold Troper of the Ontario Institute for Studies in Education. The Mudcat Café, an online discussion group devoted largely to folk music, has a discussion on this subject with thirty-five contributions, submitted between 2005 and 2014. It begins with John Mehlberg's transcription of the song, sung by a man in his early sixties, recorded at Indiana University, Bloomington, IN, on April 2, 2005, https://mudcat.org/thread.cfm?threadid=81174.

102. Submission by John Mehlberg, The Mudcat Café, May 19, 2005, https://mudcat.org/thread.cfm?threadid=81174.

103. Marshall Sklare and Benjamin B. Ringer, "A Study of Jewish Attitudes toward the State of Israel," in *The Jews: Social Patterns of an American Group* (Glencoe, IL: Free Press, 1958), 441.

104. Sklare and Ringer, "A Study of Jewish Attitudes," 444.

105. Sklare and Ringer, "A Study of Jewish Attitudes," 449. For more examples of this kind of language in UJA fundraising, see Rachel B. Deblinger, "In a World Still Trembling: American Jewish Philanthropy and the Shaping of Holocaust Survivor Narratives in Postwar America (1945–1953)," (PhD diss., University of California at Los Angeles, 2014), 101, 107–108.

106. "And it Came to Pass," December 7, 1947, *The Eternal Light* (as of November 2019, accessible at www.oldtimerradiodownloads.com/drama/eternal-light but no longer operative).

CHAPTER 4 — ZIONISM SINCE 1948

1. This process is usually attributed to the 1967 Arab–Israeli war, but as Emily Alice Katz has argued, it began earlier. See *Bringing Zion Home: Israel in American Jewish Culture, 1948–1967* (Albany: SUNY Press, 2015). On the impact of Uris's *Exodus* on American Jewry, see Michael Silver, *Our Exodus: Leon Uris and the Americanization of Israel's Founding Story* (Detroit: Wayne State University Press, 2010). On the ubiquity of invocations of love in American Jewish debates about Israel since 1967, see Levin, "Another Nation: Israel American Jews, and Palestinian Rights, 1948–1977" (PhD diss., New York University, 2019) and Sarah Anne Minkin, "Fear, Fantasy, and Family: Israel's Significance to American Jews" (PhD diss., University of California at Berkeley, 2014).

2. Shlomo Avineri, *The Making of Modern Zionism: The Intellectual Origins of the Jewish State*, rev. ed. (New York: Basic Books, 2017), 230–231.

3. Reproduced in Gil Troy, ed., *The Zionist Ideas: Visions for the Jewish Homeland: Then, Now, Tomorrow* (Philadelphia: Jewish Publication Society, 2018), 295–296.

4. Avineri, *Making of Modern Zionism*, 233–336.

5. My argument on this point agrees with Dov Waxman, *Trouble in the Tribe: The American Jewish Conflict over Israel* (Princeton, NJ: Princeton University Press, 2016).

6. Paula Kabalo, "Pioneering Discourse and the Shaping of an Israeli Citizen in the 1950s," *Jewish Social Studies* 15, no. 2 (2009): 82–110.

7. Reproduced in Troy, *Zionist Ideas*, 453.

8. On the phenomenon of what Rogers Brubaker calls "homeland nationalism," see his book *Nationalism Reframed: Nationhood and the National Question in the New Europe* (Cambridge: Cambridge University Press, 1996), esp. 107–147.

9. On contempt and disgust for the survivors, see Idith Zertal, *From Catastrophe to Power: The Holocaust Survivors and the Emergence of Israel* (Berkeley: University of California Press, 1998). On disgust as an emotion originating from gustatory, olfactory, visual, and tactile reactions to organic material, see the pioneering work of Aurel Kolnai, *On Disgust* (Chicago: Open Court, 1929; English trans. 2004).

10. Orit Rozin, *The Rise of the Individual in 1950s Israel: A Challenge to Collectivism* (Waltham, MA: Brandeis University Press, 2011), 139–161.

11. Nir Kedar, *David Ben-Gurion and the Foundations of Israeli Democracy* (Bloomington: Indiana University Press, 2021).

12. Noam Sheizaf, "The 52 Words that Foretold the Future of Israel's Occupation in 1967," *Haaretz,* May 26, 2017, https://www.haaretz.com/israel-news/.premium-52-words-foretold-the-future-of-israel-s-occupation-in-1967-1.5476758.

13. "200,000 at Western Wall in First Pilgrimage since Dispersion," *Jerusalem Post,* June 15, 1967, 4.

14. "Jerusalem of Gold" (in Hebrew and English), https://israelforever.org/interact/multimedia/yerushalayim_shel_zahav/ (accessed July 29, 2021).

15. Reproduced in Troy, *Zionist Ideas,* xx.

16. Donniel Hartmann, "Israel and World Jewry: The Need for a New Paradigm" (2011), in Troy, *Zionist Ideas,* 486–488.

17. As Yaacov Yadgar has observed in *Israel's Jewish Identity Crisis: State and Politics in the Middle East* (Cambridge: Cambridge University Press, 2020), Israel is committed to being a Jewish state, but because of a lack of consensus as to what Jewishness consists of, the state is limited to defining itself in demographic terms.

18. "A Tribe of Brothers and Sisters" (in Hebrew and English), https://lyricstranslate.com/en/-אחים-ואחיותתשבת-shevet-achim-ve-achayot-tribe-brothers-and-sisters.html (accessed July 29, 2021).,.

19. Archives of the American Jewish Historical Society (AAJHS), UJA I412.

20. *My Brother's Keeper: A Picture Story of the United Jewish Appeal 1939–1958,* Archives of the American Jewish Historical Society (AAJHS), UJA I412.

21. Charles Liebman, "Diaspora Influences on Israel: The Ben-Gurion–Blaustein 'Exchange' and Its Aftermath," *Jewish Social Studies 36,* no. 3–4 (1974): 271–280; Arieh Feldenstein, *Ben-Gurion, Zionism, and American Jewry, 1948–1963* (London: Routledge, 1979), 19–23; Zvi Ganin, *An Uneasy Relationship: American*

Jewish Leadership and Israel, 1948–1957 (Syracuse, NY: University of Syracuse Press, 2006), 26–47. See also the special issue of *Israel Studies* on "Marking 70 Years of the 1950 Ben-Gurion–Blaustein 'Understanding,'" 25, no. 3 (2020).

22. Julius Rosenwald to Jacob Blaustein, November 24, 1951, AAJHS, Boris Smolar papers, Box 3, Folder 4.

23. Boris Smolar, "Between You and Me," October 4, 1968, AAJHS, Boris Smolar papers, Box 6, Folder 1.

24. The itinerary is in AAJHS, Boris Smolar Papers, Box 6, Folder 1.

25. Raphael Levy (UJA Director of Publicity) to Boris Smolar, March 7, 1955, AAJHS, Boris Smolar Papers, Box 6, Folder 1.

26. Dan Lainer-Vos, *Sinews of the Nation: Constructing Irish and Zionist Bonds in the United States* (New York: Polity, 2013). For a broader discussion of financial instruments as a means of forging attachments between diasporas and homelands, see Anupam Chander, "Diaspora Bonds," *New York University Law Review* 76, no. 4 (2001): 1005–1099.

27. Lainer-Vos, *Sinews of the Nation*, 95.

28. Lainer-Vos, *Sinews of the Nation*, 124.

29. Katz, *Bringing Zion Home.*

30. Alexander Kaye, "'Or la-goyim': From Diaspora Theology to Zionist Dogma," *Journal of Israeli History* 38, no. 1 (2020): 191–211.

31. Silver, *Our Exodus.*

32. Michael Barnett, *The Star and the Stripes: A History of the Foreign Policies of American Jews* (Princeton, NJ: Princeton University Press, 2016).

33. Sikata Banerjee, *Muscular Nationalism: Gender, Violence, and Empire in India and Ireland, 1914–2004* (New York: New York University Press, 2012).

34. See, for example, Beth Baron's account of elite female nationalist activists in early twentieth-century Egypt in *Egypt as a Woman* (Berkeley: University of California Press, 2005).

35. "That's My Wife!" (1956), Spielberg Jewish Film Archive, 10:20, https://www.youtube.com/watch?v=vLDuoI9OIaE (accessed July 5, 2022).

36. Nathan Abrams, *Norman Podhoretz and Commentary Magazine: The Rise and Fall of the Neocons* (New York: Continuum, 2010), 91, n.45.

37. Naomi Cohen, *American Jews and the Zionist Idea* (New York: Ktav, 1975), 139; Mark Lee Raphael, *A History of the United Jewish Appeal, 1939–1982* (Providence: Brown Judaic Studies, 2020), 77–79.

38. For details on the fundraising drives, see Boris Smolar, "Between You and Me," June 16, 23, and 30, 1967, aAAJHS, Boris Smolar papers, Box 6, Folder 1.

39. Smolar, "Between You and Me," June 30, 1967.

40. Smolar, "Between You and Me," July 7, 1967.

41. The 1966 and 1967 study mission itineraries, which list the names of the participants, are in AAJHS, Boris Smolar papers, Box 6, Folder 1.

42. Selections from the interview, carried out by Aliza Becker, are reproduced in Geoffrey Levin, "Emotions and a Genre of Jewish Politics: American Jewish Advocacy for Israeli-Palestinian Peace, 1967–1977," unpublished manuscript, 8–10.

43. For a brief overview of the centrality of Zionism and Israel in American Jewish summer camps, see the pamphlet by David Friedman and David Zisenwine, *Israel in Jewish Summer Camps* (Jerusalem: CRB Foundation, 1998). On the summer camps creating a deliberately incomplete simulacrum of Israel, see Dan Lainer-Vos, "Israel in the Poconos: Simulating the Nation in a Zionist Summer Camp," *Theory and Society* 43, no. 1 (2014): 91–116. On the use of Hebrew in the camps, see Sarah Bunin Benor, Jonathan Krasner, and Sharon Avni, *Hebrew Infusion. Language and Community at American Jewish Summer Camps* (New Brunswick, NJ: Rutgers University Press, 2020).

44. Bill Adler, *Jewish Wit & Wisdom* (New York: Dell, 1969), 94–95.

45. Production information is available at https://www.discogs.com/Bob -Booker-And-George-Foster-The-Yiddish-Are-Coming-The-Yiddish-Are-Coming /release/4473540 (accessed July 22, 2021). In a telephone interview on August 13, 2022, Booker told me about his and Foster's backgrounds, motivations for creating the record, and the album's success in non-Jewish markets (e.g., Utah), as well as Jewish ones. Unlike the team's previous albums, however, which approached or reached the top of the *Billboard* sales charts, this one made it only to no.165. JB [*sic*], "The Yiddish Are Coming" (October 14, 2020), https://thjkoc .net/2020/10/14/the-yiddish-are-coming (accessed August 19, 2022).

46. On American Jewish veneration of Dayan, see Mark Raider, "Moshe Dayan: 'Israel's No. 1 Hero' (in America)," *Journal of Israeli History* 37, no. 2 (2018), 2–60.

47. Gamal Abdel Nasser, the Egyptian president and a former colonel in the Egyptian army.

48. The song is available at https://www.youtube.com/watch?v=Lo33G4Ge E5E (accessed July 18, 2022).

49. Smolar, "Between You and Me," October 26, 1973 (see also October 19, 1973), AAJHS, Boris Smolar papers, Box 14.

50. Boris Smolar, "Between You and Me," October 26, 1973.

51. Boris Smolar, "Between You and Me," November 9, 1973, AAJHS, Boris Smolar papers, Box 15.

52. Matthew Berkman, "Transforming Jewish Philanthropy: Finance and Institutional Evolution at the Jewish Federation of New York, 1917–1986," *Jewish Social Studies: History, Culture, Society* 22, no. 2 (Winter 2017): 184.

53. Berkman, "Transforming Jewish Philanthropy," 182.

54. Gal Beckerman, *When They Come for Us, We'll Be Gone: The Epic Struggle to Save Soviet Jewry* (New York: Mariner, 2011). Many thanks to Denis Kozlov for letting me read his research in progress on this topic.

55. Berkman, "Transforming Jewish Philanthropy," 185.

56. Steven M. Cohen and Charles S. Liebman, "Israel and American Jewry in the Twenty-First Century: A Search for New Relationships," in *Beyond Survival and Philanthropy: American Jewry and Israel,* ed. Allon Gal and Alfred Gottschalk (Cincinnati: Hebrew Union College Press, 2000), 8.

57. Cohen and Liebman, "Israel and American Jewry," 20.

58. John Judis, "Hillel's Crackdown on Open Debate Is Bad News for American Jews," *New Republic,* January 6, 2014, reproduced at https://carnegieendowment.org/2014/01/06/hillel-s-crackdown-on-open-debate-is-bad-news-for-american-jews-pub-54112.

59. See the essays by Samuel Norich and Shoshana Cardin, in Gal and Gottschalk, *Beyond Survival and Philanthropy,* 187–203; "United Jewish Communities History," http://www.fundinguniverse.com/company-histories/united-jewish-communities-history/ (accessed July 23, 2021).

60. See Howard Weisband's response to Norich and Cardin, in Gal and Gottschalk, *Beyond Survival and Philanthropy,* 204–209.

61. Pew Research Center, "A Portrait of Jewish Americans," October 1, 2013, https://www.pewforum.org/2013/10/01/jewish-american-beliefs-attitudes-culture-survey/.

62. Pew Research Center, "U.S. Jews' Connections with and Attitudes toward Israel," May 11, 2021, https://www.pewforum.org/2021/05/11/u-s-jews-connections-with-and-attitudes-toward-israel/.

63. Peter Beinart, *The Crisis of Zionism* (New York: Picador, 2012); Theodore Sasson, *The New American Zionism* (New York: New York University Press, 2014).

64. Shaul Kelner, *Tours that Bind: Diaspora, Pilgrimage, and Israeli Birthright Tourism* (New York: NYU Press, 2010), 105; emphasis in original.

65. Kelner, *Tours that Bind*, 135–140.

66. Pew Research Center, "U.S. Jews' Connections with and Attitudes toward Israel."

67. American Zionist Movement, "The Jerusalem Program," https://azm.org /wzo/jerusalem-program (accessed July 30, 2021). Eretz Hakodesh's platform is available at https://azm.org/wp-content/uploads/2020-Eretz-Hakodesh-Platform -and-Slate.pdf (accessed July 30, 2021). The party also promised to "strive to bol- ster Israeli society by creating economic opportunity for all, in particular those with limited skills and living below the poverty line." This was a euphemistic reference to moving ultra-Orthodox males from a lifetime of yeshiva study into gainful employment.

68. Sasson, *New American Zionism*, 123.

69. Norman Lamm, *Our Dependence upon Israel's Independence* (New York: Israel Aliyah Center, Teveth 5726 [January 1966)]; Bergman's sermon of April 29, 2020, is available at http://www.yutorah.org/sidebar/lecture.cfm/955507/rabbi -sammy-bergman/reishit-tzmichat-geulateinu/ (accessed July 30, 2021).

70. Sara Yael Hirschhorn, *City on a Hilltop: American Jews and the Israeli Settler Movement* (Cambridge, MA: Harvard University Press, 2017).

71. BT Berakhot 34b:20, Maimonides, *Mishneh Torah: The Laws of Kings and their Wars* 12:1–2.

72. Boris Smolar to the Joint Distribution Committee, May 20, 1970, AAJHS, Boris Smolar papers, Box 5, Folder 6.

73. AAJHS, Boris Smolar papers, Box 4, Folder 5.

74. Levin, "Emotions and a Genre of Jewish Politics," 19–25.

75. See J Street's mission statement at https://jstreet.org/about-us/mission -principles/#.YQCXjC2cZj4 (accessed July 30, 2021).

76. Ari Shavit, *My Promised Land* (New York: Spiegel and Grau, 2013).

77. Judis, "Hillel's Crackdown on Open Debate."

78. Hillel International, "Hillel Israel Guidelines," https://www.hillel.org /jewish/hillel-israel/hillel-israel-guidelines (accessed July 28, 2021).

79. Minkin, "Fear, Fantasy, and Family," 3.

80. American Zionist Movement, "Jerusalem Program"; American Zionist Movement, "Mission," https://azm.org/mission (accessed July 30, 2021). In Israeli

Zionism, in contrast, the country's Arab citizens could not be ignored. In 2018 a new Basic Law (which had constitutional status) affirmed Jewish primacy in the state of Israel and demoted the status of the Arabic language. For analyses of the law, see Simon Rabinovitch, ed., *Defining Israel: The Jewish State, Democracy and the Law* (Cincinnati: Hebrew Union College Press, 2018).

81. Susie Linfield, *The Lion's Den: Zionism and the Left from Hannah Arendt to Noam Chomsky* (New Haven, CT: Yale University Press, 2020), 229–261.

82. Hannah Arendt, "To Save the Jewish Homeland," in Arendt, *The Jewish Writings,* ed. Jerome Kohn and Ron H. Feldman (New York: Shocken, 2008), 388–401.

83. "Eichmann in Jerusalem: An Exchange of Letters between Gershom Scholem and Hannah Arendt," in Hannah Arendt, *The Jew as Pariah* (New York: Grove, 1978), 241–242.

84. Jewish Voice for Peace, "Our Approach to Zionism," https://jewishvoice forpeace.org/zionism/ (accessed July 29, 2021).

85. Anti-Defamation League, "Jewish Voice for Peace," July 19, 2013, https:// www.adl.org/resources/backgrounders/jewish-voice-for-peace.

86. Howard Jacobson, *The Finkler Question* (London: Bloomsbury, 2010).

87. Paul Reiter, *On the Origins of Jewish Self-Hatred* (Princeton, NJ: Princeton University Press, 2012). The phenomenon predates the term's invention, as one sees from the cases of such tortured fin de siècle German Jews as the writer Otto Weininger, whose disgust for his own Jewishness led him to suicide at the age of twenty-three, and the industrialist Walther Rathenau, whose 1896 screed "Hear O Israel!" demanded radical alterations in Jewish comportment and carriage. See selections from their writings in *The Jew in the Modern World: A Documentary History,* ed. Paul Mendes-Flohr and Jehuda Reinharz, 3rd ed. (New York: Oxford University Press, 2011), 814–820.

88. See, e.g., Jarrod Tanny, "Are Anti-Zionists the New Self-Hating Jews?" *Times of Israel,* April 12, 2021, https://blogs.timesofisrael.com/are-anti-zionists -the-new-self-hating-jews/.

89. This theme is raised in both Sasson, *New American Zionism,* and Waxman, *Trouble in the Tribe.*

CHAPTER 5 — ZIONISM AND THE INTERNATIONAL COMMUNITY

1. Daniel Gordis, "When Balance Becomes Betrayal," *Times of Israel,* November 18, 2012. https://blogs.timesofisrael.com/when-balance-becomes-betrayel/ [*sic*]).

2. Nachman Ben-Yehuda, *Betrayal and Treason: Violations of Trust and Loyalty* (Boulder, CO: Westview, 2001), 11, 14, 27.

3. Theodor Herzl, *The Jewish State* (New York: American Zionist Emergency Council, 1946/Dover Press, 1988), 113.

4. Herzl, *Jewish State*, 148.

5. Herzl, *Jewish State*, 96.

6. Herzl, *Jewish State*, 96.

7. Raphael Patai, ed., *The Complete Diaries of Theodor Herzl* (New York: Herzl Press, 1960), 687 (entry for October 7, 1898).

8. Todd Hall, *Emotional Diplomacy: Official Emotion on the International Stage* (Ithaca, NY: Cornell University Press, 2015). Whereas Hall limits his focus to relations between states, in this chapter I focus on relations between a state-seeking actor and established states. The power imbalance between them plays a determinative role in the crafting of the emotional narrative by the weaker party.

9. Isaiah Berlin, *Personal Impressions* (New York: Viking, 1980), 39.

10. The definitive biographical studies of Weizmann are Jehuda Reinharz, *Chaim Weizmann: The Making of a Zionist Leader* (New York: Oxford University Press, 1985) and *Chaim Weizmann: The Making of a Zionist Statesman* (New York: Oxford University Press, 1993); and Moti Golani and Jehuda Reinharz, *Ha-av Ha-meyased: Hayim Vaitsman, biografiyah, 1922–1952* (Tel Aviv: Am Oved, 2020).

11. Chaim Weizmann to Ahad Ha-am, December 14–15, 1914, *The Letters and Papers of Chaim Weizmann, Series B: Papers, Volume Seven*, ed. Leonard Stein (London: Oxford University Press, 1975), 82; emphasis in original.

12. Mayir Vereté, "The Balfour Declaration and Its Makers," *Middle Eastern Studies* 6, no. 1 (1970): 48–76; Jonathan Schneer, *The Balfour Declaration: The Origins of the Arab-Israeli Conflict* (New York: Random House, 2010); Reinharz, *Chaim Weizmann: The Making of a Zionist Statesman*; Daniel Guttwein, "The Politics of the Balfour Declaration: Nationalism, Imperialism, and the Limits of Zionist-British Cooperation," *Journal of Israeli History* 35, no. 2 (2016): 117–152.

13. Hall, *Emotional Diplomacy*.

14. Quoted in the *American Jewish News*, March 7, 1919.

15. For an elaboration of this concept see Yosef Hayim Yerushalmi, *Servants of Kings and Not Servants of Servants: Some Aspects of the Political History of the Jews* (Atlanta: Tam Institute for Jewish Studies, Emory University, 2005).

16. See Weizmann's remarks at a meeting of American Jewish leaders, May 25, 1941, in *The Letters and Papers of Chaim Weizmann: Series B: Papers, Volume Two: December 1941–April 1952*, ed. Bartnett Litvinoff (New Brunswick, NJ: Transaction Books, 1984), paper 52, 419.

17. "British Cabinet Endorses Jewish State in Palestine," *The Sentinel*, November 16, 1917, 3.

18. Daniel Jütte, *The Age of Secrecy: Jews, Christians, and the Economy of Secrets, 1400–1800* (New Haven, CT: Yale University Press, 2015).

19. "An Historic Declaration: Great Britain Thanked for Palestine Mandate," *Philadelphia Jewish Exponent*, August 6, 1920, 32.

20. Reproduced in Nicole Eustace, *Passion Is the Gale: Emotion, Power, and the Coming of the American Revolution* (Chapel Hill: University of North Carolina Press), 413.

21. "Boston Zionists Will Celebrate First Passover of Liberation," *Jewish Advocate*, March 28, 1918, 44.

22. *The Jewish Chronicle*, December 7, 1917, 8.

23. "By [Jerusalem's] vivid light we can see great new hopes arising for mankind, old systems disestablished, and still older polities recalled to power. In its illumination war-torn Europe can perhaps discern the finger of destiny beckoning the nations to look for the hope of a brighter future to the ancient land in which so many of the regenerative impulses of the world have been born." "Jerusalem" (lead editorial), *Jewish Chronicle*, December 14, 1917, 5.

24. *Canadian Jewish Chronicle*, November 16, 1917, 1.

25. *Canadian Jewish Chronicle*, November 16, 1917, 10.

26. Freiman's opening address to the Canadian Zionist Federation's annual convention, cited in Gerald Tulchinsky, *Canada's Jews: A People's History* (Toronto: University of Toronto Press, 2008), 330.

27. Thanks to archivist Michael Friesen of the Ontario Jewish Archives for his email communication to me of June 21, 2017, on this subject. In another act of commemorative naming, during World War II, at a time when restrictive covenants prevented Jews from purchasing desirable lakeshore cottage properties north of Toronto, the Zionist activist Rose Dunkelman arranged through a third party to purchase lakeshore land for the establishment of a Jewish cottage community. The community, which opened in 1942, was named Balfour Beach.

28. "The Jews at International Diplomatic Meetings," *Jewish Advocate*, January 23, 1919, 27.

29. Even before the issuing of the Balfour Declaration, the Russian provisional government under Alexander Kerensky recognized the Jewish claim to Palestine. Armenian nationalists and Camille Huysmans, secretary of the Socialist International, quickly followed suit. By September 1918, France, Italy, Greece, and Serbia had recognized the declaration—in some cases, due to extensive lobbying and pressure by Britain, which was not reported in the Jewish press. By the end of the year, recognition had also come from Siam, Hungary, and Cuba.

30. "Declaration of the Common Aims of the Independent Mid-European Nations, Adopted by Their Representatives, Independence Hall, Philadelphia, Pennsylvania, United States of America, October Twenty-Sixth One Thousand Nine Hundred and Eighteen," https://www.pitt.edu/~votruba/qsonhist/assets/1918 -Philadelphia_Declaration_of_the_Mid-European_Nations.pdf (accessed December 31, 2021). The document was signed by representatives of the "Czecho-Slovaks, Poles, Jugoslavs, Ukrainians, Uhro-Rusins, Lithuanians, Roumanians and Italian Irredentists, Unredeemed Greeks, Albanians, Zionists and Armenians."

31. *Jewish Advocate*, January 10, 1918, 7.

32. *American Jewish Weekly News*, December 27, 1918, 714.

33. Cited in Arthur Daniel Hart, *The Jew in Canada: A Complete Record of Canadian Jewry from the Years of the French Régime to the Present Time* (Toronto: Jewish Publications, 1926), 305.

34. *B'nai B'rith Messenger*, October 28, 1927, 1.

35. *American Jewish Weekly News*, December 27, 1918, 714.

36. *American Jewish Weekly News*, January 3, 1919, 727.

37. *American Jewish Weekly News*, February 14, 1919, 823.

38. *American Jewish Weekly News*, March 7, 1919, 871.

39. Stephen S. Wise, *Challenging Years* (New York: Putnam's, 1949), 123.

40. *Jewish Chronicle*, December 7, 1918, 8.

41. *The Sentinel*, November 17, 1922, 32.

42. Chaim Weizmann, *The Jewish People and Palestine: Statement Made before the Palestine Royal Commission in Jerusalem, on November 25th, 1936* (Jerusalem: Zionist Organization and Keren Hayesod, 1937), 18. For Sokolow's comment, see Martin Levin, *The Story of Hadassah* (Jerusalem: Geffen, 2002), 63.

43. *Jewish Advocate*, June 6, 1918, 26.

44. Amanda Behm, "Settler Historicism and Anticolonial Rebuttal in the British World, 1880–1920," *Journal of World History* 26, no. 4 (2015): 785–813. See also

Arie Dubnov, "Notes on the Zionist Passage to India, or: The Analogical Imagination and Its Boundaries," *Journal of Israeli History* 35, no. 2 (2016): 177–214.

45. For an exploration of parallels and distinctions between Zionists and the British Empire's subject peoples in terms of both British policy and the peoples' self-perceptions, see Maryanne Rhett, *The Global History of the Balfour Declaration: Declared Nation* (London: Routledge, 2016).

46. Arye Naor, "The Purifying Effect of Truth: Jabotinsky's Interpretation of the Balfour Declaration," *Israel Studies* 22, no. 3 (2017): 37, 39.

47. Norman Rose, "The Seventh Dominion," *Historical Journal* 14 (1971): 397–416, and *The Gentile Zionists* (London: Frank Cass, 1973), 71–80; Colin Shindler, *The Rise of the Israeli Right* (Cambridge: Cambridge University Press, 2015), 137; Naor, "Purifying Effect of Truth," 31–47.

48. Cited in Naomi Cohen, *The Year after the Riots: American Responses to the Palestinian Crisis of 1929–30* (Detroit: Wayne State University Press, 2004), 63.

49. Cohen, *Year after the Riots*, 87.

50. For a different genealogy of Zionist accusations of British betrayal, rooted in the Yishuv rather than the diaspora and originating in a later period, see Arie Dubnov, "On Vertical Alliances, 'Perfidious Albion' and the Security Paradigm." *European Judaism* 52, no. 1 (2019): 67–100.

51. Cohen, *Year after the Riots*, 150.

52. *Jewish Chronicle*, April 4, 1930, 11 (editor's leader), 42 (from "our Jerusalem correspondent").

53. *Jewish Chronicle*, October 24, 1930, 27.

54. *Jewish Chronicle*, October 31, 1930, 24–25.

55. *Jewish Chronicle*, February 20, 1931, 7.

56. *Jewish Chronicle*, February 27, 1931, 7–8.

57. *Jewish Examiner*, August 21, 1936, 27.

58. See, for example,, *Philadelphia Jewish Exponent*, April 9, 1937, 4–5.

59. *Philadelphia Jewish Exponent*, August 13, 1935, 35.

60. *Jewish Advocate*, June 9, 1937, 38.

61. *Jewish Exponent*, July 23, 1937, 21–22.

62. *Jewish Advocate*, May 26, 1939, 20.

63. *Jewish Advocate*, May 19, 1939, 20.

64. *Detroit Jewish Chronicle* May 19, 1939, 13.

65. *Philadelphia Jewish Exponent,* May 19, 1939, 9.

66. *Canadian Jewish Chronicle,* March 3, 1939, 3

67. *Canadian Jewish Chronicle,* March 3, 1939, 3

68. *Canadian Jewish Chronicle,* April 14, 1939, 3.

69. Aaron Berman, *Nazism, the Jews, and American Zionism 1933–1948* (Detroit: Wayne State University Press, 1990); Zohar Segev, *Mi-politika'im ethniyim le-manhigim le'umiyim: ha-hanhagah ha-tsionit-amerikanit, ha-sho'ah, ve-hakamat medinat yisra'el* (Sede Boker: Ben-Gurion Institute, 2007).

70. Reproduced in Natan Aridan, "Anglo-Jewry and the State of Israel: Defining the Relationship, 1948–1956," *Israel Studies* 10 (2005): 127.

71. "Lifeline to a Promised Land" (January 5, 1947) and "The Undeterred" (September 21, 1947), *The Eternal Light,* http://www.oldtimerradiodownloads.com/drama/eternal-light (accessed December 20, 2019); the link is now broken).

72. *Jewish Chronicle* (Detroit), December 23, 1947, 12.

73. *The Sentinel,* April 22, 1948, 5.

74. *Jewish Advocate,* February 12, 1948, 6.

75. *Jewish Chronicle* (Detroit), March 25, 1948, 12.

76. *The Sentinel,* October 28, 1948, 8.

77. Derek Penslar, "Declarations of (In)dependence: Tensions within Zionist Statecraft, 1896–1948," *Journal of Levantine Studies* 8, no. 1 (2018): 29–30.

78. Elad Ben-Dror, *UNSCOP and the Arab-Israeli Conflict: The Road to Partition* (London: Routledge, 2023). See also Avinoam Patt, *Home and Homeland: Jewish Youth and Zionism in the Aftermath of the Holocaust* (Detroit: Wayne State University Press, 2009).

79. Idith Zertal, *From Catastrophe to Power: The Holocaust Survivors and the Emergence of Israel* (Berkeley: University of California Press, 1998).

80. Jeffrey Herf, *Israel's Moment: International Support for and Opposition to Establishing the Jewish State, 1945–1949* (New York: Cambridge University Press, 2021); Ben-Dror, *UNSCOP and the Arab-Israeli Conflict.*

81. Uri Bialer, *Between East and West: Israel's Foreign Policy Orientation 1948–1956* (New York: Cambridge University Press, 1990); James Loeffler, *Rooted Cosmopolitans: Jews and Human Rights in the Twentieth Century* (New Haven, CT: Yale University Press, 2018), 184–201.

82. Gadi Heimann, *Franco-Israeli Relations, 1958–1967* (London: Routledge, 2017); Carol Fink, *West Germany and Israel: Foreign Relations, Domestic Politics, and the Cold War* (Cambridge: Cambridge University Press, 2019).

83. Warren Bass, *Support Any Friend: Kennedy's Middle East and the Making of the U.S.-Israel Alliance* (New York: Oxford University Press, 2004); Noam Kokhavi, *Nixon and Israel: Forging a Conservative Partnership* (Albany: SUNY Press, 2009); Dennis Ross, *Doomed to Succeed: The U.S.-Israel Relationship from Truman to Obama* (New York: Farrar, Straus, and Giroux, 2016).

84. Shaul Mitelpunkt, *Israel in the American Mind: The Cultural Politics of U.S.-Israeli Relations, 1958–1988* (New York: Cambridge University Press, 2018); Amy Kaplan, *Our American Israel: The Story of an Entangled Alliance* (Cambridge, MA: Harvard University Press, 2018).

85. "100,000 Jews May Become Refugees," *B'nai B'rith Messenger*, January 18, 1957, 1; "Knowland Slaps down Dulles over Sanctions Controversy," *B'nai B'rith Messenger*, February 8, 1957, 1; "Opposition to Dulles Policy Is Very Vocal," *B'nai B'rith Messenger*, March 1, 1957.

86. *B'nai B'rith Messenger*, February 22, 1957, 1.

87. "We All Know the Answer" (editorial), *The Sentinel*, January 17, 1957, 7.

88. Moshe Sharett, *Yoman ishi* (Jerusalem: Sifriat Maariv, 1978), 874; Neil Caplan, "Israel v. Oom-Shmoom, Sharett v. Ben-Gurion," *Israel Studies* 25, no. 1 (2020): 28.

89. Quoted in "Stand by Israel" (editorial), *The Sentinel*, February 14, 1957, 7.

90. *Kansas City Jewish Chronicle*, June 2, 1967, 8. References to Vietnam appeared elsewhere in the Jewish press at this time.

91. *Jewish Advocate*, June 1, 1967, 24; June 8, 1967, 31.

92. *Jewish Advocate*, October 18, 1973, 7, 14.

93. *Jewish Advocate*, October 26, 1973, 23; November 1, 1973, 32.

94. "The seeds of the Jewish National Homeland were germinated by Great Britain in the Balfour Declaration, Jewish statehood became an embryo under the League of Nations and was finally born out in the United Nations. . . . Now only the United States is committed to its survival." *Jewish Advocate*, November 8, 1973, 40, 45.

95. Jewish Telegraphic Agency, *Daily News Bulletin*, October 18, 1973, See also the bulletin for October 16, 1973.

96. Jewish Telegraphic Agency, *Daily News Bulletin*, October 17, 1973.

97. *Jewish Advocate*, November 15, 1973, 47, 51.

98. Mitelpunkt, *Israel in the American Mind*, 186–87.

99. Loeffler, *Rooted Cosmopolitans*, 231–246; Gil Troy, *Moynihan's Moment: America's Fight against Zionism as Racism* (New York: Oxford University Press, 2013).

100. Troy, *Moynihan's Moment*, 140.

101. Troy, *Moynihan's Moment*, 144–145, 159.

102. Troy, *Moynihan's Moment*, 167.

103. Troy, *Moynihan's Moment*, 159, 173–174, 177. See also Boris Smolar's upbeat assessment of the UN vote in "Between You and Me," November 28, 1975, in AAJHS, Box 15.

104. Kaplan, *Our American Israel*, 118–132.

105. Tal Elmaliach, "The 'Revival' of Abram Leon: The 'Jewish Question' and the American New Left," *Left History* 21, no. 2 (2017): 77–85.

106. Letty Cottin Pogrebin, *Deborah, Golda, and Me: Being Female and Jewish in America* (New York: Crown, 1991), 154.

107. Reproduced in Marjorie N. Feld, *Nations Divided: American Jews and the Struggle over Apartheid* (New York: Palgrave Macmillan, 2014), 92–93.

108. Troy, *Moynihan's Moment*, 179–181.

109. Jewish Telegraphic Agency, *Daily News Bulletin*, March 27, 1979; *The Jewish Floridian*, April 13, 1979, 2a.

110. *The Jewish Press*, September 22, 1978, 42. The newspaper's former editor and longtime columnist, Meir Kahane, had previously expressed harsh criticism of both Begin and Sadat. See *The Jewish Press*, November 25, 1977, 24.

111. *The Jewish Floridian*, June 30, 1978, 3a.

112. *The Jewish Floridian*, July 7, 1978, 4a; October 6, 1978, 4a; October 13, 1978, 1a.

113. *The Jewish Floridian*, April 7, 1978, 1a, 7a; May 12, 1978, 1a; December 22, 1978, 4a.

114. *The Jewish Floridian*, March 16, 1979, 4a.

115. *The Jewish Floridian*, February 2, 1979, 1a, 2a.

116. *The Jewish Floridian*, September 21, 1978, 1; September 27, 1978, 3.

117. *The Jewish Press*, September 22, 1978, 42.

118. *The Jewish Press*, March 30, 1979, 1.

119. *The Jewish Press*, March 30, 1979, 1.

120. Jewish Telegraphic Agency, *Daily News Bulletin*, December 4, 1991.

121. Jewish Telegraphic Agency, *Daily News Bulletin*, December 4, 1991.

122. Jewish Telegraphic Agency, *Daily News Bulletin*, December 13, 1991.

123. Jewish Telegraphic Agency, *Daily News Bulletin*, December 17, 1991.

124. For example, Deborah Kalb, writing for the JTA, credited Palestinian and Israeli negotiators in Oslo with taking first steps without any U.S. intervention. The successful completion of the negotiations, however, "would not have been possible without prodding from the United States. . . . Both the Bush and Clinton administrations deserve credit for fostering the climate that led to the accord," *Daily News Bulletin,* September 2, 1993.

125. Israel's claim of Jerusalem as its capital has been controversial since the country was created. According to the UN partition proposal of 1947, Jerusalem and its environs were to be under international administration. During the 1948 war, however, Israel and Jordan took control of the western and eastern parts of the city, respectively, and in 1967 Israel conquered the Jordanian-held part. Palestinians want the city, at least its eastern part, to be the capital of their envisioned state. Contending that Jerusalem's final status is still disputed, and not wanting to imply recognition of Israel's annexation of the city and its environs, virtually all countries that recognize Israel have placed their embassies in Tel Aviv. After 1948 about a dozen countries—all Latin American except for Haiti and The Netherlands—had embassies in Jerusalem, but they moved them to Tel Aviv after Israel's formal annexation of eastern Jerusalem in 1980. As of the time of writing, only the United States, Guatamala, Honduras, and Kosovo have their embassies in Jerusalem.

126. Republican Jewish Coalition, "RJC Applauds Trump for Recognizing Jerusalem as Israel's Capital, Releases NY Times Ad Thanking Him," December 5, 2017, https://www.rjchq.org/rjc_applauds_trump_for_recognizing_jeru salem_as_israel_s_capital_releases_ny_times_ad_thanking_him.

127. "Israeli Organization Reveals Trump Coin in Expression of 'Gratitude' over Embassy Move," Fox News, May 20, 2018, https://www.foxnews.com/world/israeli -organization-reveals-trump-coin-in-expression-of-gratitude-over-embassy-move.

128. National Public Radio, December 6, 2017, https://www.npr.org/sections /thetwo-way/2017/12/06/568748383/how-is-the-world-reacting-to-u-s-plan-to -recognize-jerusalem-as-israeli-capital. See also Netanyahu's expression of gratitude in comments to journalists at https://www.youtube.com/watch?v=3_Vobl UHqjQ.

129. "Israel's Netanyahu Wants to Name Golan Settlement after Trump," *Al-Jazeera*, April 23, 2019, https://www.aljazeera.com/news/2019/4/23/israels-netanyahu-wants-to-name-golan-settlement-after-trump.

130. Oliver Holmes, "Jerusalem Gives Thanks to Trump by Naming a Roundabout in His Honour," *The Guardian*, May 8, 2018, https://www.theguardian.com/world/2018/may/08/israel-trump-jerusalem-embassy-roundabout-thanks-mayor.

131. Joseph Frager, "Gratitude & Appreciation to President Trump and Administration before the High Holy Days," Israel National News/Arutz 7, September 4, 2020, https://www.israelnationalnews.com/news/286603; Tzvi Allen Fishman, "Meeting Trump and Our Hakarat Hatov Gratitude," *Jewish Journal*, October 30, 2020, https://jewishjournal.com/commentary/323974/meeting-trump-and-our-hakarat-hatov-gratitude/.

132. Miriam Adelson, "Thank You, Mr. President. Thank You, Dear Friend!," *Israel Hayom*, January 20, 2021, https://www.israelhayom.com/opinions/thank-you-mr-president-thank-you-dear-friend/.

133. Anshel Pfeffer, "Donald Trump Thinks the Jews Aren't Grateful Enough," *Haaretz*, September 22, 2018, https://www.haaretz.com/israel-news/2018-09-22/ty-article-opinion/.premium/donald-trump-thinks-the-jews-arent-grateful-enough/0000017f-f614-d044-adff-f7fdd7560000).

134. Colleagues in departments of Jewish Studies have shared with me social media postings comparing them to kapos, and I have received menacing emails using similar language.

CHAPTER 6 — HATING ZIONISM

1. Sianne Ngai, *Ugly Feelings* (Cambridge, MA: Harvard University Press, 2007).

2. Eran Halperin, "Group-Based Hatred in Intractable Conflict in Israel," *Journal of Conflict Resolution* 52, no. 5 (2008): 715–736.

3. Daniel Lord Smail, "Hatred as a Social Institution in Late-Medieval Society," *Speculum* 76, no. 1 (2001): 90–126.

4. Thomas Brudholm, "Hatred as an Attitude," *Philosophical Papers* 30, no. 3 (2010): 289–313; Andreas Dorschel, "Is Love Intertwined with Hatred?" in *Exploring the World of Human Practice: Readings in the Philosophy of Aurei Kolnai*, ed. Zoltan Balazs (Budapest: Central European University Press, 2015), 299–311.

5. Nahum Sokolow, *Hibbat Zion* (Jerusalem: Reuven Mass, 1941), 179.

6. Derek Penslar, "Antisemites on Zionism: From Indifference to Obsession," in *Israel in History: The Jewish State in Comparative Perspective* (London: Routledge, 2006), 114–116.

7. Quoted in Moshe Zimmerman, *Wilhelm Marr: The Patriarch of Antisemitism* (New York: Oxford University Press, 1986), 88.

8. Eugen Dühring, *Die Judenfrage als Frage der Rassenschädlichkeit für Existenz, Sitte, und Cultur der Völker*, 4th ed. (Berlin: H. Reuther, 1892), 122–123.

9. The quotation comes from the sixth edition of Dühring's book (Leipzig: O. R. Reisland, 1930), 127–128.

10. André Lavagne, the chief of Marshal Philippe Pétain's civilian staff, quoted in Michael Marrus and Robert O. Paxton, *Vichy France and the Jews* (New York: Basic Books, 1981), 315.

11. For Rosenberg's and Hitler's views on Zionism, see Francis Nicosia, *The Third Reich and the Palestine Question* (Austin: University of Texas Press, 1985), 20–28, and Robert Wistrich, *Hitler's Apocalypse: Jews and the Nazi Legacy* (London: Weidenfeld and Nicolson), 154–163. The quotation from *Mein Kampf* is reproduced in Wistrich, 155. On the centrality of concepts of Jewish criminality in Nazi antisemitism, see Michael Berkowitz, *The Crime of My Very Existence: Nazism and the Myth of Jewish Criminality* (Berkeley: University of California Press, 2007).

12. Neil Baldwin, *Henry Ford and the Jews: The Mass Production of Hate* (New York: Public Affairs, 2002), 73–78, 185–188, 261–265.

13. The essays written by Cameron, approved by Ford, and published in the *Dearborn Independent* were also published in four volumes under these titles: *The International Jew: The World's Foremost Problem* (1920), *Jewish Activities in the United States* (1921), *Jewish Influences in American Life* (1921), and *Aspects of Jewish Power in the United States* (1922).

Here I drew on "Did the Jews Foresee the World War" (August 1, 1920) in vol. I and "Will Jewish Zionism Bring Armageddon?" (May 28, 1921) in vol. III. All four volumes are available at https://en.wikisource.org/wiki/The_International _Jew (accessed August 3, 2021).

14. "Dr. Fosdick Sees Danger for Zionism; Objects to Political Feature," *JTA Daily Bulletin*, May 26, 1927, https://www.jta.org/1927/05/26/archive/dr-fosdick-sees -danger-for-zionism-objects-to-political-feature (accessed August 3, 2021).

15. *Boston Jewish Advocate*, September 30, 1948, 15a–17a.

16. Yehoshua Porat, "Anti-Zionist and Anti-Jewish Ideology in the Arab Nationalist Movement in Palestine," in *Antisemitism through the Ages*, ed. Shmuel Almog (Oxford: Pergamon, 1988), 217–226.

17. Eliezer Be'eri, "The Jewish Arab-Conflict during the Herzl Years," *Jerusalem Quarterly* 41 (1987): 13.

18. Muhammad Muslih, *The Origins of Palestinian Nationalism* (New York: Columbia University Press, 1988), 75–78. The quotation is on 78.

19. On the origins of the Palestinian nationalist claim that Jews comprise a religious, not a national, community, see Jonathan Marc Gribetz, *Defining Neighbors: Religion, Race, and the Early Zionist-Arab Encounter* (Princeton, NJ: Princeton University Press, 2016), 53–71.

20. Elyakim Rubinstein, "'Ha-protokolim shel ziknei tziyon' ba-sikhsukh ha-'aravi-yehudi," *Ha-mizrah he-Hadash* 25 (1985): 37–42.

21. *Daily Bulletin*, August 20, 1964, https://www.jta.org/1964/08/20/archive/john-birch-society-lists-israel-as-50-75-under-communist-control (accessed August 4, 2021)..

22. "Behind the Balfour Declaration: Britain's Great War Pledge to Lord Rothschild: The Meaning for Us," *Journal of Historical Review* 6, no. 4 (1985), https://www.historiography-project.com/jhrchives/v06/v06p389_John.php (accessed August 4, 2021), quotation is between N47 and N48.

23. See https://www.haaretz.com/us-news/.premium-how-chicago-s-dyke-march-adopted-an-anti-semitic-slur-dear-to-far-rightists-1.5494579; .https://mosaicmagazine.com/observation/2016/03/whore-you-calling-a-zio/ (accessed May 28, 2018).

24. *Your Ward News*, November 2015, 10; see also April 2015, 13.

25. *Your Ward News*, December 2015, 10.

26. *Your Ward News*, July 2015, 2; September 2015, 3.

27. Zeev Sternhell, "Why Benjamin Netanyahu Loves the European Far-Right," *Foreign Policy*, February 24, 2018, https://foreignpolicy.com/2019/02/24/why-benjamin-netanyahu-loves-the-european-far-right-orban-kaczynski-pis-fidesz-visegrad-likud-antisemitism-hungary-poland-illiberalism/ (accessed August 4, 2021).

28. *Haaretz,* July 22, 2018, https://www.haaretz.com/israel-news/israeli-nation-state-law-backed-by-white-nationalist-richard-spencer-1.6295314 (accessed August 4, 2021).

29. Joshua Shanes, "'Pro-Israel' Evangelicals Furious at Netanyahu's Fall Turn to Sickening Antisemitism," *Haaretz,* June 6, 2021, https://www.haaretz.com

/israel-news/.premium.HIGHLIGHT-pro-israel-evangelicals-furious-at-netanyahu
-s-fall-turn-to-sickening-antisemitism-1.9878749 (accessed August 4, 2021).

30. David Hirsch, *Contemporary Left Antisemitism* (London: Routledge, 2017); Cary Nelson, *Israel Denial: Anti-Zionism, Anti-Semitism, and the Faculty Campaign against the Jewish State* (Bloomington: Indiana University Press, 2019).

31. For example, "Palestine and Praxis: Open Letter and Call for Action," Scholars for Palestinian Freedom, https://palestineandpraxis.weebly.com (accessed August 4, 2021).

32. See https://bdsmovement.net/what-is-bds (accessed August 4, 2021).

33. Ravid Hecht, "Ben & Jerry's and 'Terrorism'? Lapid and Herzog Are Embarrassing Israel," *Haaretz*, July 23, 2021, https://www.haaretz.com/opinion/.premium -ben-jerry-s-and-terrorism-lapid-and-herzog-are-embarrassing-israel-1.10023414 (accessed August 4, 2021).

34. Anti-Defamation League, tweet of July 19, 2021, https://twitter.com/ADL /status/1417236021457084417 (accessed August 4, 2021).

35. Max Weber, *Politik als Beruf* (Munich: Dunker & Humblot, 1926), 8.

36. Mitch Ginsburg, "When Moshe Dayan Delivered the Defining Speech of Zionism," *Times of Israel*, April 28, 2016, https://www.timesofisrael.com/when -moshe-dayan-delivered-the-defining-speech-of-zionism/ (accessed August 5, 2021). These sentences were deleted in a later studio recording of the eulogy, and they are missing from a number of versions of the text circulating on the internet. Compare the original and expurgated versions at https://tarbutil.cet.ac.il/anthology /על-הספד-רועי-רוטברג-של-משה-דיין/ (accessed November 20, 2022).

37. Compare Google Ngram curves for the two terms over the period 1900–2020 with the historical and literary examples of the usage of the term *Existenzrecht* at https://www.linguee.com/german-english/translation/existenzrecht.html (accessed August 5, 2021).

38. Derek Penslar, "What if a Christian State Had Been Established in Modern Palestine?" in *What Ifs? Of Jewish History from Abraham to Zionism*, ed. Gavriel Rosenfeld (Cambridge: Cambridge University Press, 2016), 142–164.

39. Jennifer Mitzen, "Ontological Security in World Politics: State Identity and the Security Dilemma," *European Journal of International Relations* 12, no. 3 (2006): 341–370.

40. Elliott Horowitz, *Reckless Rites: Purim and the Legacy of Jewish Violence* (Princeton, NJ: Princeton University Press, 2006); Yisrael Yuval, *Two Nations in*

Your Womb: Perceptions of Jews and Christians in Late Antiquity and the Middle Ages (Berkeley: University of California Press, 2006).

41. "And cursed be he who cries out: Revenge!/Vengeance like this, for the blood of a child/ Satan has yet to devise." From "On the Slaughter," trans. Peter Cole, https://www.theparisreview.org/blog/2014/07/31/on-the-slaughter/ (accessed August 9, 2021).

42. Uri Tzvi Greenberg, "We Were Not Likened to Dogs among the Gentiles," in *Modern Hebrew Poetry: A Bilingual Anthology*, ed. Ruth Finer-Mintz (Berkeley: University of California Press, 1986), 126.

43. Tom Segev, *The Seventh Million* (New York: Hill and Wang, 1993), 140–152.

44. Shay Hazkani, *Dear Palestine: A Social History of the 1948 War* (Stanford: Stanford University Press, 2020), 80–91.

45. Many thanks to Yael Berda for her conversations with me on this topic.

46. Arieh Saposnik, *Becoming Hebrew: The Creation of a Jewish National Culture Babel in Zion* (New York: Oxford University Press, 2008) 183–192; Liora Halperin, "A Murder in the Grove: Conceptions of Justice in an Early Zionist Colony," *Journal of Social History* 49, no. 2 (2015): 427–451.

47. Vladimir Jabotinsky, "On the Iron Wall," in *The Origins of the State of Israel, 1882–1948: A Documentary History*, ed. Eran Kaplan and Derek J. Penslar (Madison: University of Wisconsin Press, 2011), 257–263.

48. Michael Brenner, "Jabotinsky and the Jewish State," *Times of Israel*, November 27, 2014, https://blogs.timesofisrael.com/jabotinsky-weighs-in-on-the-jewish -state-proposal/ (accessed August 9, 2021). See also Yosef Gorny, *From Binational Society to Jewish State: Federal Concepts in Zionist Political Thought, 1920–1990, and the Jewish People* (Boston: Brill, 2006), 97–103.

49. Menachem Begin, *The Revolt* (New York: Tolmitch E-Books, 2013), Loc 282.

50. Begin, *The Revolt*, Loc 312.

51. Eran Kaplan, *The Jewish Radical Right: Revisionist Zionism and Its Ideological Legacy* (Madison: University of Wisconsin Press, 1995); Peter Bergamin, *The Making of the Israeli Far-Right: Abba Ahimeir and Zionist Ideology* (London: I. B. Tauris, 2021).

52. Hillel Cohen, *Year Zero of the Israeli-Palestinian Conflict: 1929* (Waltham, MA: Brandeis University Press, 2015).

53. Roger Petersen, *Understanding Ethnic Violence: Fear, Hatred, and Resentment in Twentieth-Century Eastern Europe* (Cambridge: Cambridge University Press, 2001), 30–32.

54. Stephen D. White, "The Politics of Anger," in *Anger's Past: The Social Uses of an Emotion in the Middle Ages*, ed. Barbara Rosenwein (Ithaca, NY: Cornell University Press, 1998), 127–152.

55. Hazkani, *Dear Palestine*, 88.

56. Max Bergholz, *Violence as a Generative Force: Identity, Nationalism, and Memory in a Balkan Community* (Ithaca, NY: Cornell University Press, 2018), 278.

57. Fatma Müge Göçek, *Denial of Violence: Ottoman Past, Turkish Present and Collective Violence against the Armenians, 1789–2009* (New York: Oxford University Press, 2015).

58. For example, Efraim Karsh, *Palestine Betrayed* (New Haven, CT: Yale University Press, 2010).

59. Benny Morris, *Israel's Border Wars, 1949–1956: Arab Infiltration, Israeli Retaliation, and the Countdown to the Suez War* (Oxford: Clarendon Press, 1993).

60. Eli Podeh, "History and Memory in the Israeli Educational System: The Portrayal of the Arab-Israeli Conflict in History Textbooks (1948–2000)," *History and Memory* 12, no. 1 (2000): 65–100.

61. Shira Robinson, *Citizen Strangers: Palestinians and the Birth of Israel's Liberal Settler State* (Stanford, CA: Stanford University Press, 2013).

62. Janice J. Terry, "Zionist Attitudes towards Arabs," *Journal of Palestine Studies* 6, no. 1 (1976): 67–78.

63. Sara Ahmed, *The Cultural Politics of Emotion* (Edinburgh: University of Edinburgh Press, 2004), 42–61.

64. *The Jewish Defense League: Principles and Philosophies* (New York: Jewish Defense League, n.d.), https://www.nli.org.il/en/books/NNL_ALEPH002585345/NLI (accessed December 7, 2021).

65. Shaul Magid, *Meir Kahane: The Public Life and Political Thought of an American Jewish Radical* (Princeton, NJ: Princeton University Press, 2021).

66. Meir Kahane, *They Must Go!* (New York: Grosset & Dunlap, 1981), 202.

67. Kahane, *They Must Go!* 221.

68. Kahane, *They Must Go!* 275.

69. Ehud Sprinzak, *The Ascent of Israel's Radical Right* (New York: Oxford University Press, 1991); Robert Friedman, *Zealots for Zion: Inside the West Bank Settlement Movement* (New Brunswick, NJ: Rutgers University Press, 1994); Ami Pedahzur, *The Triumph of Israel's Radical Right* (New York: Oxford University Press, 2012).

70. Reproduced in Anshel Pfeffer, *Bibi: The Turbulent Life and Times of Benjamin Netanyahu* (Toronto: Signal/McClelland & Stewart, 2018), 358.

71. The name of both a Palestinian neighborhood and refugee camp in East Jerusalem.

72. The chanting may be heard on a video of a match on January 25, 2017, between Beitar Jerusalem and Bnei Sakhnin at https://www.youtube.com/watch ?v=otxRkFwp824 (accessed July 18, 2022). It was also reported following a January 2018 match; https://www.timesofisrael.com/israeli-soccer-club-vows-crack down-on-racist-fans-after-anti-arab-chants/ (accessed July 18, 2022). For background to these incidents see Ephraim Lavie, Meir Elran, and Muhammed Abu Nasry, "Hatred and Racism between Jews and the Arab Palestinian Minority in Israel: Characteristics, Consequences, and Coping Strategies," in *Strategic Survey for Israel 2016–2017*, ed. Anat Kurz and Shlomo Brom (Tel Aviv: Institute for National Security Studies, 2017), 225–234. For a general survey of Israeli Jewish perceptions of Arabs, see Daniel Bar-Tal and Yona Teichman, *Stereotypes and Prejudice in Conflict: Representations of Arabs in Israeli Society* (Cambridge: Cambridge University Press, 2005).

73. "Most Israelis Support Soldier Accused of Shooting Palestinian, Says Poll," *The Guardian*, March 29, 2016, https://www.theguardian.com/world/2016/mar /29/most-israelis-support-soldier-accused-of-shooting-palestinian (accessed July 8, 2022).

74. Ami Pedazhur and Yael Yishai, "Hatred by Hated People: Xenophobia in Israel," *Studies in Conflict and Terrorism* 22, no. 2 (1999): 101–117. Quotations from 112.

75. Sammy Smooha, *Arab-Jewish Relations in Israel: Alienation and Rapprochement* (Washington, DC: United States Institute for Peace, 2010), 21–22.

76. Pew Research Center, *Views of the Jewish State and the Diaspora*, March 8, 2016, https://www.pewforum.org/2016/03/08/views-of-the-jewish-state-and-the -diaspora/ (accessed December 7, 2021).

77. Tamar Pileggi, "New Poll Shows Strong Anti-Arab Sentiment among Israeli Jews," *Times of Israel*, December 10, 2018, https://www.timesofisrael.com /new-poll-shows-strong-anti-arab-sentiment-among-israeli-jews/ (accessed December 7, 2021).

78. Or Kashti, "'Map of Hatred': Half of Israeli Religious Teens Would Strip Arab Right to Vote, Poll Finds," *Haaretz*, February 19, 2021, https://www.haaretz .com/israel-news/.premium-israeli-religious-teens-would-rescind-arab-vote-poll -1.9551732 (accessed December 7, 2021).

79. Dahlia Moore and Salem Aweiss, "Hatred of 'Others' among Jewish, Arab, and Palestinian Students in Israel," *Analyses of Social Issues and Public Policy* 2, no. 1 (2002): 151–172.

80. Kashti, "'Map of Hatred.'"

81. "After Lod Synagogues Torched, Rivlin Accuses 'Bloodthirsty Arab Mob' of 'Pogrom,'" *Times of Israel*, May 12, 2021, https://www.timesofisrael.com/after-lod-synagogues-torched-rivlin-accuses-bloodthirsty-arab-mob-of-pogrom/ (accessed August 13, 2021); B. Bar-Peleg, "Minister Backs Calls for Armed Jews to Come Defend Mixed City of Lod," *Haaretz*, June 1, 2021, https://www.haaretz.com/israel-news/.premium-minister-says-calls-for-armed-jews-to-come-defend-mixed-city-are-legitimate-1.9863621 (accessed August 13, 2021).

82. See https://www.pewforum.org/2021/05/11/u-s-jews-connections-with-and-attitudes-toward-israel/ (accessed August 13, 2021).

83. For ostensibly liberal views of Palestinians by American West Bank settlers, see Sara Yael Hirschhorn, *City on a Hilltop: American Jews and the Israeli Settler Movement* (Cambridge, MA: Harvard University Press, 2017). On the "settler rabbi" Menachem Froman's conciliatory approach to his Palestinian neighbors, see Shaul Magid, "West Bank Rabbi Menachem Froman's Zionist Post-Zionism, and What it Can Teach American Jews," *Tablet,* August 4, 2015, https://www.tabletmag.com/sections/israel-middle-east/articles/froman-zionist-post-zionism (accessed September 16, 2021).

CONCLUSION

1. Hannah Arendt, *Men in Dark Times* (New York, Mariner, 1968), 6. This quotation and the quotations in the next two notes are reproduced in Tsiona Lida, "Between Silence and Sentiment: The Role of Emotions in Hannah Arendt's Writing on Jewish Politics" (master's thesis, University of Edinburgh, 2018). I am grateful to Ms. Lida for allowing me to quote from her thesis and for our conversations about these texts.

2. Hannah Arendt, "Days of Change" (1944), in *Hannah Arendt: The Jewish Writings*, ed. Jerome Kohn and Ron H. Feldman (New York: Schocken, 2007), 215.

3. Hannah Arendt, "With Our Backs to the Wall" (1942), in *Hannah Arendt: The Jewish Writings*, ed. Jerome Kohn and Ron H. Feldman (New York: Schocken, 2007), 165.

4. Gefen has in recent years adopted hawkish political views and embraced the settler movement. Carolina Landsmann, "Be Strong Up There," *Haaretz*, August 6, 2022, https://www.haaretz.com/opinion/2022-08-26/ty-article-opinion/.premium/be-strong-up-there/00000182-d656-d972-a7d6-dfdeb2820000.

Index

Figures indicated by page numbers in italics

Foster, George: *The Yiddish Are Coming!*
The Yiddish Are Coming! (with Booker),
154–155, *155*, 289n45
France, 22, 50, 51, 73–74, 75, 197–198, 216
Frankel, Zecharias, 31–32
Frederickson, George, 82, 88
Freiman, Archie, 184
Freud, Sigmund, 7
Frevert, Ute, 10
Frishman, David, 106–107
Froman, Menachem, 63
frontier societies, 92
Fulbright, J. William, 156

Gans, Chaim, 42
Garcia Granados, Jorge, 197
Gat, Azar, 20
Gay, Peter, 5, 260n6
Gaza Strip, 14, 92–93, 160, 175, 199, 223,
224, 236. *See also* Occupied Palestinian
Territories; West Bank
Gefen, Aviv, 308n4; "Song of Hope,"
245
General Jewish Labor Bund, 2, 35–36, 99
General Zionism, 40
German Jews, 21, 31, 130
Germany, 21, 179, 198, 215–217
Gildersleeve, Virginia, 218
Giliomee, Hermann, 70–71
Ginzberg, Asher (Ahad Ha-Am), 38–39,
45, 72, 115–116
Göçek, Fatma Müge, 232
Golan Heights, 75, 156, 201, 209
Goldberg, Isaac, 184–185
Goldstein, Baruch, 235
Gordis, Daniel, 175, 176
Gordon, Judah Leib, 47
Goren, Shlomo, 60
Gottheil, Richard, 114
grace, 182–183
Graetz, Heinrich, 28, 33–35, 36, 103–104,
264n30
gratitude: about, 176–177, 210–211, 243;
vs. assertions of right and indepen-
dence, 185–187; for Balfour Declara-
tion, 181, 182, 183, 184, 185, 186, 187–188;
for Begin, 206–207; for Carter, 205;
dependence and, 181, 182, 183, 187–189;
diplomacy of, 181–182, 185–186, 190;
end of, 202–203; grace and, 182–183;

for League of Nations, 184–185; for
Trump, 209–210
Great Britain. *See* United Kingdom
Great Powers. *See* international
community
Greenberg, Leopold, 190
Greenberg, Uri Tzvi: "We Were Not
Likened to Dogs among the
Gentiles," 228
Grossman, David, 91
Guedella, Hayim, 106
Gurevitch, Zali, 84, 95, 165, 276n70
Gur-Horon, Adya, 61
Gush Emunim, 59

Haas, Jacob de, 192
Ha-Asif (journal), 106
Hadassah (Women's Zionist Organi-
zation of America), 45, 73, 130, 151
Haganah, 127, 128, 283n79
halakhic Zionism, 58–59
Halevi, Yehuda, 34
Hall, Todd, 179, 181, 293n8
Halperin, Eran, 213
Halperin, Liora, 79
Hamas, 63, 175, 223, 236, 238
Ha-Po'el Ha-Tsa'ir (The Young
Worker), 73
happiness, 122–123, 125
Harper, Stephen, 221
Hartman, Donniel, 144
Ha-Shomer Ha-Tsa'ir (The Young
Guard), 73, 123
Hasidim, 270n84. *See also* ultra-
Orthodox Jews
Haskalah, 29–30, 52
"Hatikvah" (The Hope), 110, 130, 279n30
hatred: about, 213–215, 227, 239–240; vs.
anger, 213, 225–226; denial of, 232–233;
within Jewish civilization, 227–228;
Jewish self-hatred, 172, 292n87; of
Jews by Palestinians, 237–238; in
Judaic Zionism, 243; love and, 213–214,
222–223, 230–231, 233–234; of Palestinian
Arabs, 228–229, 233, 234–237, 238–239,
243; political value of, 231–232. *See also*
anger; antisemitism; anxiety; fear;
rage
"Hava Nagila" (Come, Let Us Rejoice),
122–123, 281n62

About the Author

DEREK J. PENSLAR is the William Lee Frost Professor of Jewish History at Harvard University in Cambridge, Massachusetts. He previously taught at Indiana University, the University of Toronto, and Oxford University. Penslar takes a comparative and transnational approach to Jewish history, which he studies within the contexts of modern capitalism, nationalism, and colonialism. He is a fellow of the Royal Society of Canada and an honorary fellow of St. Anne's College, Oxford.